Victorian Scandals on Trial

AF813531

ABOUT THE AUTHOR

Roger Ede has spent a lifetime in law. He is a former District Judge and Family Court Judge. Previously he was a criminal law solicitor, criminal policy advisor and lecturer in law. He has trained criminal defence solicitors in England and Wales; and presented and taken part in programmes for lawyers and judges in countries in Europe, Asia and Africa. He is a published author of books on criminal defence practice.

BOOKS BY THE SAME AUTHOR

Criminal Defence
Good Practice in the Criminal Courts
With Anthony Edwards
Active Defence
A Solicitor's Guide to Police and Defence Investigation
With Eric Shepherd
Forensic Practice in Criminal Cases
With Lynn Townley
Poisonous
A novel

THANKS

All the source publications for these trials are available for comprehensive study, thanks to the generosity of Harvard University Law School. These works, along with numerous others, can be accessed in their collection *Studies in Scarlet – Marriage and Sexuality in the US-UK 1815–1914.*

Victorian Scandals on Trial

Murder, Mischief, Mayhem and Morality in the Nineteenth Century

26 Trials of libel, gross indecency, divorce, adultery, murder, perjury, abduction, breach of promise, bastardy, custody, rape, and brothel keeping in England, Ireland and the United States 1814–1911

ROGER EDE

Adapted by Roger Ede from books, pamphlets, newspaper, and court reports written at the time; with his contemporary commentary

PEN & SWORD
TRUE CRIME

First published in Great Britain in 2026 by
PEN AND SWORD TRUE CRIME
An imprint of
Pen & Sword Books Limited
Yorkshire – Philadelphia

Copyright © Roger Ede, 2026

Print ISBN 978 1 03618 512 1
ePUB ISBN 978 1 03618 513 8
ePDF ISBN 978 1 03618 514 5

The right of Roger Ede to be identified as Author of this work has been asserted by him in accordance with the Copyright, Designs and Patents Act 1988.

A CIP catalogue record for this book is available from the British Library.

All rights reserved. No part of this book may be reproduced, transmitted, downloaded, decompiled or reverse engineered in any form or by any means, electronic or mechanical including photocopying, recording or by any information storage and retrieval system, without permission from the Publisher in writing. NO AI TRAINING: Without in any way limiting the Author's and Publisher's exclusive rights under copyright, any use of this publication to 'train' generative artificial intelligence (AI) technologies to generate text is expressly prohibited. The Author and Publisher reserve all rights to license uses of this work for generative AI training and development of machine learning language models.

Typeset in Times New Roman 11/14 by SJmagic DESIGN SERVICES, India.
Printed and bound in the UK by CPI Group (UK) Ltd.

The Publisher's authorised representative in the EU for product safety is Authorised Rep Compliance Ltd., Ground Floor, 71 Lower Baggot Street, Dublin D02 P593, Ireland.
www.arccompliance.com

For a complete list of Pen & Sword titles please contact
PEN & SWORD BOOKS LIMITED
George House, Units 12 & 13, Beevor Street, Off Pontefract Road,
Barnsley, South Yorkshire, S71 1HN, England
E-mail: enquiries@pen-and-sword.co.uk
Website: www.pen-and-sword.co.uk

or

PEN AND SWORD BOOKS
1950 Lawrence Rd, Havertown, PA 19083, USA
E-mail: uspen-and-sword@casematepublishers.com
Website: www.penandswordbooks.com

MIX
Paper | Supporting responsible forestry
FSC www.fsc.org
FSC® C013604

Contents

Introduction

The detailed records written in the nineteenth century of the trials of serious crimes and broken relationships open a fascinating window on how society functioned then. The published accounts in pamphlets, books and newspaper reports, often over-long and in florid and overblown language, have been adapted and rewritten in this book for a contemporary audience, with commentaries to make them accessible and show how the law and society's attitudes have developed over time.

In these pages some parties are well known, such as Oscar Wilde. Two plays of Wilde's, *An Ideal Husband* and *The Importance of Being Earnest*, were on the West End stage at the time when he was charged with gross indecency. Queen Caroline, the wife of George IV, was tried in the House of Lords for 'a most unbecoming and degrading intimacy' with her servant Bartolom Bergami. There are prominent American citizens. Stanford White, the famous American architect who designed Madison Square Garden, was shot by the very rich Harry Kendall Thaw, the son of an American coal and railroad baron. Mortimer Smith, the editor of the *Albany Castigator* newspaper, wrote about the immorality of a well-known married Wall Street banker, David Groesbeck, whose wife looked on in disgust as he frolicked in the hay with her friend Emma. The state of Albany prosecuted Mortimer Smith for libel.

There are femme fatales. Evelyn Nesbit was a young artist's model seduced by Stanford White and later married to Harry Kendall Thaw. Beulah Binford, the 'other woman' in the Beattie murder case, was the subject of the silent film *Beulah Binford's own Story*, banned by the American National Board of Censorship.

There are members of the nobility. The 6th Duke of Marlborough, whose first and third marriages were to a first cousin, was in a 'state of decrepitude' and wheelchair-bound when he married his third wife, Jane. The Duchess was twenty-four years his junior and a near relative of his first wife. Colonel Berkeley, who later became the 1st Earl Fitzhardinge, fathered two children with his secret mistress, the actress Maria Foote, whilst seducing a Mrs Waterhouse, whose husband Donald sued the colonel for adultery.

There are politicians and dignitaries. The Lord Viscount Glerawley was contesting an election in Ireland when Lady Glerawley, fourteen years his junior, was having an affair with an army captain ten years her junior. Sir Charles Wentworth Dilke, MP for Chelsea, was named as co-respondent in the divorce of Donald Crawford MP from his wife Virginia. Dilke was reputed to have been the lover of Virginia's mother.

The trials include the abduction of women, particularly heiresses, after it became an offence. Edward Gibbon Wakefield, accused of abducting Ellen Turner, an heiress and daughter of the MP for Blackburn and High Sheriff of Cheshire, was later celebrated for his work on the colonisation of South Australia and New Zealand. The trials include actions for breach of promise of marriage. Miss Sydney Scrope-Ferrers sued Major Dudley Apthorp, whose defence was that she was a gold digger, already married to another man.

There are claims for compensation for 'criminal conversation' (another term for adultery) by wronged husbands. Mr Gill paid people to spy on his wife and tried to bore a hole through a wall in an abandoned house to watch her with Mr Aubrey next door. The remedy of a Decree of Restitution of Conjugal Rights was available to a deserted husband, enforceable by imprisonment if his wife refused to return home. It was difficult to obtain a divorce, particularly for a wife, who was required to establish incest, bigamy, cruelty, or two years desertion in addition to adultery. Following a separation or divorce, the father had the right to custody, even of an infant child who was still being breastfed. It was thought that the mother's knowledge of the loss of her children would stop her from leaving her husband and that if she was not well treated by her husband it was better for the children that the couple stayed together than the children know that their parents could not bear to live with each other. Poor unmarried mothers were housed and their children schooled in workhouses, in exchange for work.

There are the inevitable murders by poisoning. Adelaide Bartlett was accused of poisoning her husband Edwin, ten years her senior, with chloroform and the post-mortem was conducted in their first-floor bedroom. Edith Carew was accused of poisoning her husband Walter with Fowler's Solution of Arsenic in their home in the ex-pat quarter of Yokohama, Japan. Edith's father was the Mayor of Glastonbury. There are gruesome murders. The body of Miss Alice Bowlsby was found having been forced into a trunk in Chicago. The parts of the dismembered body of Hannah Brown were located in Stepney, Camberwell, and the Edgware Road. Harriet Gaskell was shot in Portugal in a suicide pact gone wrong and William Sawyer was tried for her murder in England.

The evidential and procedural rules were vastly different. A defendant in a criminal case or a plaintiff in a perjury trial was not allowed to give evidence on their own behalf. It was argued that their evidence was bound to be biased because of their interest in the outcome of the case and that would cause them to perjure themselves. Henry Stanton, the main witness when suing his wife Louisa for perjury for making false accusations about his cruelty towards her, was excluded from the witness box. Roman Weinzoeptlein, a Roman Catholic priest accused of raping a parishioner after pulling her from the confessional box, was prevented from giving his account to the court of what had happened. For some offences, instead of having to attend a secular court, a clergyman was allowed to choose trial by an ecclesiastical court under canon law where the court was likely to be more lenient towards him.

Only Quakers were allowed to affirm, everyone else had to take the oath on the Bible. A jury's verdict had to be unanimous and just one disagreeable juror could upset the outcome of a trial. In America, jurors were allowed to disclose what had happened in the privacy of the jury room. Wildes Walker's adultery took place whilst he was a serving prisoner in New York, and in the subsequent divorce and custody trial eleven jurors posted a public notice complaining that the one dissenting juror was very wrong. That lone juror then defended himself with a public counter-notice against this 'malicious and uncalled for attack'. The jurors could only be men.

Chapter 1

Oscar Wilde

Libel and Gross Indecency Trials

1895

'The pleasure to me was being with those who are young, bright, happy, careless and free. I do not like the sensible and I do not like the old'

In 1892, Oscar Wilde completed writing *Salome*, in French. The one-act play was published in France the following year. Aubrey Beardsley drew the illustrations and the cover for the English edition of the play in 1894. On 14 February 1895, Oscar Wilde's play *The Importance of Being Earnest* opened at St James's Theatre. Information was received by the theatre's management that John Sholto Douglas, the 9th Marquess of Queensberry, was intending to cause a disturbance on the play's first night and make a public statement against Wilde. Wilde was a close acquaintance of the Marquess's son Lord Alfred Douglas ('Bosie'), and the Marquess did not approve. Wilde wrote to a friend: 'Bosie's father is going to make a scene tonight. I am going to stop him.' The Marquess arrived at the theatre with a bouquet of vegetables. Although he had paid for his seat, he was turned away by the police, and his money was refunded.

Oscar Wilde was the son of Sir William Wilde, a distinguished Irish eye surgeon. He had married Miss Lloyd in 1884, and in 1895 they lived in a red brick terrace house, number 16 (later renumbered 34) Tite Street, Chelsea, with their two sons, aged 8 and 9. Wilde was a member of the Albemarle Club and so was the Marquess. On 18 February 1895, the Marquess wrote out a card in the presence of the club's hall porter and told him to give it to Mr Wilde: 'Oscar Wilde, posing as a sodomite'. The hall porter put the card in an envelope and passed it to Wilde on 28 February.

Wilde was offended by the card and complained to the police. On 2 March 1895, the Marquess attended Marlborough Street Police Court and was charged with publishing a libel against Wilde. On 9 March, at the same court, the committal proceedings took place. Wilde arrived accompanied by the Marquess's two sons, Lord Alfred Douglas and Lord Douglas of Harwick. The Marquess had letters that Wilde had written to Bosie. Mr Carson QC, for the defence, claimed that the Marquess had written the card to bring matters to a head and had acted to save his son Lord Alfred Douglas from Wilde. The Marquess was committed to stand trial at the Old Bailey.

The Libel Trial

On 3 April 1895, the libel trial began before Mr Justice Collins. Sir Edward Clarke prosecuted. Wilde was called to give evidence and was cross-examined by the defence. Wilde claimed that the Marquess had come to his house and accused him and Lord Alfred Douglas of improper conduct. The Marquess had claimed, 'I don't say that you are at it, but you look it, and you pose as it, which is just as bad. If I catch you and my son together again in any public restaurant, I will thrash you … it is a disgusting scandal.' Wilde replied, 'If it be so, you are the author of the scandal.' Wilde admitted that he was aged 40 whilst Lord Alfred Douglas was 24.

Alfred Wood received clothing from Lord Alfred Douglas and discovered letters from Wilde to Douglas in the pocket of a coat. Wilde explained how Wood told him that he needed money and in exchange for £15 or £20 Wood handed over four letters to him. They were not the most salacious letters Wilde had written. Wilde was preparing his play *A Woman of no Importance* for production when he was approached on the first night by a Mr Allen, claiming that he had the originals of Wilde's letters to Lord Alfred Douglas. Allan referred to the most controversial of the letters and remarked menacingly that 'a very curious construction can be put on that letter'. 'Art is rarely intelligible to the criminal classes,' Wilde replied. Allan then offered the letter to Wilde for £10. '£10,' protested Wilde 'you have no appreciation of literature. If you had asked me for £50, I might have given it to you.' 'A man has offered me £60 for it,' Allan replied. Wilde told him that he should take the £60 and added that he was glad that someone had considered a letter of his worth that amount. The letter was later returned to Wilde and published as a sonnet in *The*

Spirit Lamp, a magazine edited by Lord Alfred Douglas. A line of it read: 'It is a marvel that those red rose-leaf lips of yours should be made no less for music and song than for madness of kisses.'

The defence referred to Wilde's book *The Picture of Dorian Gray* and a poem *In Praise of Shame*, which he had contributed to a magazine *The Chameleon.* The poem concluded with the words: 'Of all sweet passions shame is the loveliest.' The defence claimed that it was immoral and obscene. Wilde was accused of not being concerned about whether writing was moral or immoral. He replied, 'I am not doing good or evil but trying to make a thing that will have some quality of beauty.' He had written: 'There is no such thing as a moral or immoral book. Books are well written or badly written.' He was asked if he had ever known the feelings he described in *Dorian Gray*. 'No, it's a work of fiction,' he replied. A phrase that he had written, 'I quite admit that I adored you madly,' was put to him. 'Have you ever adored a man madly?' he was asked. 'I have never given adoration to anybody except myself,' Wilde replied.

The defence painted a picture of Wilde going about with young men who were not coequal with him in position or age; and associating with some of the most immoral characters in London, such as a Mr Taylor, whom they described as a most notorious character who occupied rooms that were a shameful den. They alleged that Taylor was Wilde's right-hand man and had introduced young men to him. 'His books were written by an artist for artists, he tells us,' the defence reported, 'but look at the young men to whom he was introduced. They were all aged 18 to 20. Look at the manner of their introduction. They were all treated to money and presents,' leading to the conclusion that there was something unnatural in the relations between Wilde and the young men.

Names of young men were put to him: Edward Shelley, Alphonse Conway, Frederick Atkins, Charles and William Parker, Scarfe and Sidney Mavor. Wilde admitted dining with them, giving them presents of silver cigarette cases, money and clothes and putting them up in hotels with him, but claimed, 'I received nothing in return except the pleasure of their company.' 'The pleasure to me was being with those who are young, bright, happy, careless and free. I do not like the sensible and I do not like the old.'

The defence had a list of witnesses whom they intended to call to give evidence about Wilde's relationships with these young men. It was clear to Wilde that the Marquess had found these men with the help of private investigators, and that they were likely to make serious allegations against him if they gave evidence. Since 1885 it was a criminal offence for a man of any age to commit gross indecency with another man.

Sir Edward Clarke accepted that based upon Wilde's letters and literature (the publications *Dorian Gray* and *The Chameleon*) which the jury had considered, they could conclude that there was sufficient justification for the Marquess to use the word 'posing' about Wilde and he could not resist a verdict of not guilty with reference to that word. Wilde followed his advice and withdrew from the trial. He later tried to explain his actions in a letter to the *Evening News*. He wrote that it would have been impossible for him to have proved his case without putting Lord Alfred Douglas in the witness box against the Lord's father. He would not let the Lord do that and so he had decided to retire from the case and bear on his own shoulders what ignominy and shame might result from his having prosecuted the Marquess.

The jury, on the judge's instructions, found the plea of justification that the 'libel' was published for the public benefit, proved, and returned a verdict of not guilty. The Marquess was discharged. The trial finished on 5 April 1895, and Wilde was driven to the Holborn Viaduct Hotel, where he was joined by Lord Alfred Douglas and Lord Douglas of Harwick. They went later to the Cadogan Hotel, Sloane Street.

The Marquess's lawyers sent the witness statements they had collected, intending to use them against Wilde in the libel trial, to the Director of Public Prosecutions, together with the shorthand notes of the trial. A representative of the Director met with the Home Secretary, Mr Asquith, the Attorney General, and the Solicitor General. They agreed that a warrant for Wilde's arrest should be applied for. The Chief Magistrate, Sir John Bridge, examined the statements and issued the warrant. Police officers were sent to the Cadogan Hotel, and Wilde went with them to Scotland Yard and then to Bow Street Police Station, where he was placed in a cell overnight. Meanwhile, two plays of Wilde's were on the stage: *An Ideal Husband* and *The Importance of Being Earnest.* Wilde was charged that being a male person, he did on 20 March 1893, and diverse other dates, unlawfully commit diverse acts of gross indecency with Charles Parker.

The Marquess sent a message to Wilde that it would be best if he left the country, but that if he took Lord Alfred Douglas with him, the Marquess would follow them and shoot Wilde.

The Committal Proceedings

On 19 April 1895, the committal proceedings took place at Bow Street Police Court before the Chief Magistrate. Wilde was brought by van from Holloway Prison. Wilde was charged with committing acts of gross indecency with men; and conspiring with Taylor to procure the commission of acts of gross indecency by Wilde: contrary to the Criminal Law Amendment Act 1885. During the proceedings, Taylor was arrested on similar charges and placed in the dock with Wilde. A string of witnesses were called, some of whom gave damning evidence against Wilde and Taylor. Charles Parker spoke of misconduct between him and Wilde at the Savoy Hotel; Alfred Wood alleged acts of impropriety between him and Wilde at Wilde's house in Tite Street; Antonio Migge, a masseuse, said that he saw a young man in Wilde's bed at the Savoy Hotel; Jane Cotter, a chambermaid, discovered a boy occupying Wilde's bed; Frederick Atkins found a man named Schwabe in bed with Wilde in a hotel in Paris and saw Wilde kiss a waiter and put his arms around the waiter's neck.

Wilde and Taylor were committed for trial at the Old Bailey. Wilde was granted bail, with sureties.

The First Trial

The Old Bailey trial began on 26 April 1895, before Mr Justice Charles. Sir Edward Clarke QC MP defended Wilde. There were twenty-five counts on the indictment referring to acts of gross indecency alleged to have been committed by Wilde and the procuring of those acts by Taylor; conspiracy by Wilde and Taylor to procure the commission of acts of gross indecency by Wilde; acts of gross indecency by Taylor; and acts of gross indecency by Wilde with persons unknown. Both men pleaded not guilty to all counts.

There was legal argument as to the fact that the defendants were entitled to give evidence on their own behalf in respect of the charges under the Criminal Law Amendment Act 1885, but not the three counts alleging conspiracy. This led to the withdrawal of those three counts, the prosecution branding them 'unnecessary'.

The prosecution's first and principal witness was Charles Parker. He was said to be a reformed person living a respectable life and reluctant to give evidence. He had given evidence at the committal hearing in the magistrates' court. He was described as slim, clean-shaven, aged 21, with a fair, girlish face. He said that in 1893 he and his brother William were out of work when Taylor approached them. Taylor told him that there was a lot of money to be made if he met with men and that Oscar Wilde was a very good man for giving money to boys whom he liked. Taylor asked Charles and his brother William to meet him at his lodgings, 13 Little College Street, Westminster.

Taylor arranged for the Parker brothers to meet Wilde, who took them to the Solferino, a restaurant in Rupert Street. They were shown to a private room upstairs where a dinner table was laid for four. They were given champagne and brandy, and Wilde addressed Charles, saying, 'This is the boy for me. Will you go to the Savoy Hotel with me?' Charles agreed and they took a cab to the hotel. Wilde led Charles to a sitting room on the second floor, where he was given whisky and soda. Wilde then took him into a bedroom where they committed acts of indecency. Wilde gave Charles £2 and told him to call at the Savoy a week later. Charles returned as instructed and had supper and champagne with Wilde followed by further indecent acts. He stayed with Wilde for two hours and Wilde gave him £3.

Parker described how he visited Wilde in rooms at St James's Place, where Wilde had a sitting room and bedroom, and on one occasion committed an indecent act with him there and also in a room in the Albemarle Hotel, Picadilly. Wilde gave him a silver cigarette case and a gold ring, which Parker pawned.

Taylor had been paying rent of £3 per month for the upper rooms of a baker's shop in Westminster. Witnesses described how the rooms had heavily draped windows; incense candles burning all day and were filled with the heavy scent of perfume. Parker told how he and William stayed with Taylor in his rooms for about a fortnight. He said that he last saw Wilde about nine months previously in Trafalgar Square. Wilde had stopped his cab and told Parker he was looking as pretty as ever.

Alfred Wood gave evidence. He had received a telegram from Lord Alfred Douglas and in response went to the Café Royal, where he was introduced to Wilde. Wilde bought him a drink and then took him for dinner at the Florence in Rupert Street. They dined in a private room and Wilde gave him £3. They went to Wilde's house in Tite Street, Chelsea, and Wood stayed there for about one hour. Two or three days later, he met Wilde by invitation on the corner of Tite Street. They went to the bedroom in Wilde's house. Wood said, 'I don't remember committing any act of indecency that night.'

Wilde visited Wood in his room in Langham Street. He gave Wood £2 or £3 and bought him half a dozen shirts, some collars and handkerchiefs, and a silver watch and chain. Wood explained how he found letters from Wilde to Lord Alfred Douglas in clothes the Lord had given him.

Frederick Atkins, aged 20, a music hall comedian performing as 'Fred Denny', who had been a witness at the committal, gave evidence. He had been introduced to Taylor by a young man named Schwabe and by Taylor to Lord Alfred Douglas and Wilde at a dinner at the Florence restaurant, where he saw Wilde kiss a waiter and put his arms around the waiter's neck. Wilde had put his arms around Atkins and said that he liked him. He travelled to Paris as Wilde's private secretary and stayed at 29 Boulevard des Caprines, where they had an inter-connected bed-sitting room and bedroom. He went on his own to the Moulin Rouge in the evening, despite Wilde cautioning him that women were the ruin of young fellows. When he returned late to their hotel, he found Schwabe in bed with Wilde. Wilde had a hairdresser in Paris curl Atkins's hair. Wilde gave him a silver cigarette case and money. He denied having 'criminal relations' with Wilde.

Sidney Mavor, who had given evidence at the committal, followed Atkins into the witness box. He was introduced to Wilde at a dinner in Kettner's restaurant. He stayed with Wilde overnight in the Albemarle Hotel and met Wilde several times in Taylor's rooms but denied committing any indecent acts with him. Wilde gave him a silver cigarette case.

Edward Shelley, also a witness at the committal, was next in the witness box. He worked as a clerk at Bodley Head, Wilde's publishers. He dined, drank champagne, whisky and soda and smoked cigarettes with Wilde first in a public room in the Albemarle Hotel and after in Wilde's sitting room there. 'We talked about books and me,' he said. 'Wilde asked, "Will you come into my bedroom?" I didn't know what he meant. As I went into the room he kissed me. I got into bed and Wilde did the same. He was in bed with me all night.' Shelley described certain acts of indecency with Wilde: 'I had been drinking a lot of wine.' Wilde saw him the next day, kissed him again and repeated the previous night's acts.

Antonio Migge, also a witness at the committal, explained how he was a masseur in the Savoy Hotel in March 1893 when he occasionally massaged Wilde. One morning, he went into Wilde's bedroom without knocking, and saw a young man in Wilde's bed whilst Wilde was getting dressed.

Wilde was called to give evidence in his defence. He denied all the accusations made against him of immoral conduct: 'it is entirely untrue …

you should not kiss a young man of 18 years … I don't care to travel alone … I like having company.'

The prosecutor read *In Praise of Shame* to the jury, the poem of Wilde's published in *The Chameleon*. Wilde described it as a beautiful poem. He explained that the word 'shame' was used in the sense of 'modesty' and in 'shame that turns cold lips to fire', 'to fire' means 'a quickened sense of modesty'.

The prosecutor asked Wilde whether words in a poem written by Lord Alfred Douglas referred to unnatural love: 'I am the love that dare not speak its name'. Wilde replied, 'No' and went on to explain that it referred to 'such a great affection of an elder for a younger man … that deep spiritual affection, that is as pure as it is perfect. It is so much misunderstood that it may be described as the "love that dare not speak its name." It is intellectual … when the elder man has intellect and the younger man has all the joy, hope and glamour of life before him … the world mocks it.' Wilde denied all the accusations made against him of immoral conduct.

When Mr Justice Charles summed up, he spoke of an evidential issue: where acts of indecency were alleged to have been committed with the consent of the witnesses, those persons were accomplices in the crimes and as such their evidence must be corroborated by other evidence before it could be considered. If there was no corroboration, he would direct an acquittal. But there had been corroboration. Not the eyewitness kind, which you would not expect. The corroboration lay in the fact of Wilde's acquaintance with these young men and his dealings with them.

'Judge him not by the works he has published,' Mr Justice Charles continued, 'especially the book *Dorian Gray*. You may criticise the work but because a novelist puts into the mouth of his villain the most abominable sentiments it must not be supposed that he shares them.' The judge referred to Wilde's letter to Lord Alfred Douglas: 'those red rose-leaf lips'. 'Is this letter of a horrible and indecent character?'

The jury retired but were unable to reach a unanimous verdict on all counts. Of the original twenty-five counts, three were abandoned by the prosecution, two were struck out by the judge, and the jury found Wilde and Taylor not guilty on three counts (alleging attempts to procure Sidney Mavor and Frederick Atkins for acts of gross indecency). It was agreed that a fresh trial would take place at the next sessions. The trial judge refused to consider bail and said that Wilde must apply to a judge in chambers. A judge granted bail on 3 May and Wilde was released from custody on

9 May after the sureties had been taken. He was refused admission to more than one hotel that night and eventually took refuge at his brother's rooms in Chelsea, having been harassed by a mob who followed him about.

The Second Trial

The new trial began on 22 May 1895, before Mr Justice Alfred Wills, who lived in Wilde's street at 42 Tite Street. The defence advocates argued for separate trials for Taylor and Wilde. The judge agreed and Taylor was tried first. He was convicted of committing acts of gross indecency with William and Charles Parker and remanded for sentence at the conclusion of Wilde's trial.

Wilde was accused of committing acts of gross indecency with Edward Shelley, Alfred Wood, Charles Parker and persons unknown. Wilde was represented by Sir Edward Clarke, as before, and prosecuted by Mr C.F. Gill. Edward Shelley, Charles Parker, William Parker and Antonio Migge gave evidence for the third time within the space of four weeks (committal hearing in Bow Street Police Court, original trial and this new trial). Alfred Wood gave evidence for the second time. Jane Cotter and Alice Saunders, chambermaids, and Anne Perkins, housekeeper, told how they were all concerned about the staining on Wilde's bed in the Savoy Hotel. Jane Cotter said that she saw a boy, aged 18 or 19, in Wilde's bed. Mr Vogel, the owner of the Albemarle Hotel, spoke of how the youthfulness of Wilde's visitors attracted unwanted attention.

Oscar Wilde gave evidence in his defence. He was asked again about his letter to Lord Alfred Douglas: 'those red rose-leaf lips of yours'. He replied that it was 'a beautiful way for an artist to address a young man of culture and charm'. Another letter to the Lord was read by the prosecutor: 'I cannot listen to your curved lips saying hideous things to me … don't do it; you break my heart. I must see you soon. You are the divine thing I want, the thing of grace and beauty.'

He was asked about the presents he gave. 'I have a great fancy for giving cigarette cases. I might have given seven or eight.' He was asked what pleasure he got from the society of boys; what he did with them. 'I read to them. I read one of my plays to them … I like to be liked; I like their society simply because I like to be lionised … praise from anyone is very delightful … I like bright boys … they enjoyed it as schoolboys would enjoy a treat.

It was something they didn't get every day. I give young men money with pleasure.'

The judge withdrew the count against Edward Shelley from the jury, telling them that he was an accomplice, and his evidence was not corroborated. He then summed up. He said that he would rather have tried the most shocking murder case than be engaged in a case with the horrible nature of these charges. He would not comment on whether the letters to Lord Alfred Douglas showed actual criminal conduct or not. On the one hand, the Marquess of Queensberry had drawn from those letters the conclusion that most fathers would. On the other, Wilde claimed to be an exceptional person. How much allowance must you give to that when considering the letters? He befriended Wood and Charles Parker. The jury must ask themselves, were those the kind of young men with whom you would care to sit down to dine? Were they the sort of people you would expect to find in the company of men of education? Charles Parker was a valet, and his brother, William, was a groom. They were both unemployed. Alfred Wood was a clerk, also out of work. It was remarkable, the judge said, for Wilde even to foregather with a man of the social position of Wood. It was important in Wood's case to consider the character of his first introduction to Wilde. He warned the jury against assuming that if two men shared a bed it inevitably meant that they were committing a criminal act. Poverty often compelled the sharing of a bed.

The jury retired and when they returned, announced their findings: Wilde was guilty of acts of gross indecency with Charles Parker at the Savoy Hotel on the night that they met and again one week later, and at St James's Place and then at the Albemarle Hotel; an act of gross indecency with Alfred Wood at Tite Street; and acts of gross indecency with persons unknown in bedrooms at the Savoy Hotel.

The judge sentenced Wilde. 'The crime of which you have been convicted is so bad … that I must refrain myself from using the language that would instantly occur to every man or woman who heard the details of these two terrible trials. People who can do these things must be dead to all sense of shame … it is the worst case I have ever tried … that you, Wilde, have been the centre of a circle of extensive corruption of the most hideous kind among young men, it is impossible to doubt. I shall pass the severest sentence that the law allows. In my judgement it is totally inadequate for a case like this.' Wilde was sentenced to imprisonment for two years with hard labour.

Wilde was taken to Pentonville Prison, then to Wandsworth Prison. On 13 November he was moved to Reading Prison, where he served his sentence. His play *Salome* premiered at the Comedie-Parisienne in Paris in 1896, whilst he was in prison.

Constance, Wilde's wife, changed her name to Holland to avoid the embarrassment of being associated with him. At her instigation, Wilde signed a deed of separation shortly before his release from prison, giving her sole custody of their children. He was released in 1897 and crossed to the Continent. Constance died in 1898 following surgery, aged 40. Wilde died in Paris in 1900 of cerebral meningitis, aged 46.

COMMENT

Christopher Millard published *Oscar Wilde Three Times Tried* (432 pages, limited to 999 copies) in Paris in 1912. The title quotes Wilde: 'Three times I have been tried. The first time I left the (witness) box to be arrested, the second time to be led back to the House of detention, the third time to pass into prison for two years.' In the preface, Millard explained the reason for the book:

> 'Once in every six or seven years', wrote Macaulay, 'our virtue becomes outrageous.' It was never more outrageous than in its ecstatic horror over Oscar Wilde. Unfortunately, no accurate record of Oscar Wilde's trial exists … so far there has been no attempt to give a fair picture of the trial. Such picture is now necessary … for the sake of Wilde's literary work. The increasing interest in Wilde, both in England and America, makes such a task urgent … as an aid to that task this book has been published.

Christopher Sclater Millard (1872–1927) was the author of several important books on Wilde, including an acclaimed bibliography of his works. *Oscar Wilde Three Times Tried* was the first complete account of the trials and it later became the basis for the 1960 film, *The Trials of Oscar Wilde*, starring Peter Finch as Wilde. Millard was sentenced to three months with hard labour in 1906 for gross indecency and again in 1918 to twelve months for the same offence.

Sir John Betjeman immortalised Wilde's arrest in his 1937 poem *The Arrest of Oscar Wilde at the Cadogan Hotel:*

> Mr Woilde, we'ave come for tew take yew
> Where felons and criminals dwell:
> We must ask yew tew leave with us quoietly
> For this is the Cadogan Hotel.

The Marquess of Queensbury was tried for the libel of Oscar Wilde at the Old Bailey. Libel ceased to be a criminal offence in England and Wales with the 2009 Coroners and Justice Act, which abolished the offences relating to the publication of defamatory material: seditious libel, defamatory libel, and obscene libel. Defamation remains a civil wrong.

Wilde was prosecuted under section 9 of the Criminal Law Amendment Act 1885: any male person who in public, or private, commits or is party to the commission of or who procures or attempts to procure the commission by any male person of an act of gross indecency with another male person, shall be guilty of a misdemeanour and, being convicted thereof shall be liable at the discretion of the court to be imprisoned for any term not exceeding two years with or without hard labour. Previously, the crime of gross indecency was limited to an act with a male of under 13 years old. The Criminal Law Amendment Act 1885 came into force on 1 January 1886.

In Wilde's first gross indecency trial the jury could not reach a unanimous verdict. In England and Wales, it was not until the 1967 Criminal Justice Act that a majority verdict of ten to twelve jurors was acceptable. Justification for the change to a majority verdict was that tampering with the jury to 'nobble' just one juror could upset the outcome of a trial.

The jurors were always men until the passage of the Sex Disqualification (Removal) Act 1919.

In Oscar Wilde's second gross indecency trial, the judge withdrew the count accusing him of gross indecency with Edward Shelley. The judge told the jury that because Shelley was an accomplice, his evidence would need to be corroborated, which it was not. By the end of the eighteenth century a general practice of discouraging a conviction founded solely upon the testimony of an accomplice had grown up, as the accomplice may elect to save himself from punishment by procuring the conviction of others. In time, the law changed and a case in the Court of Criminal Appeal, R v Baskerville [1916] 2 KB 658, laid down the rule that the judge should warn the jury of the danger of convicting a prisoner on the uncorroborated testimony of an accomplice, but they may still convict upon such evidence. Failure to give such a warning would result in the conviction being quashed.

Sir Edward George Clarke KC, MP (1841–1931) was solicitor general in the Conservative government 1886–1892. He was a leading advocate in the late Victorian era. He represented Oscar Wilde in his prosecution of the Marquess of Queensbury for libel and defended him in both jury trials. He defended Adelaide Bartlett in the Pimlico poisoning case in 1886 (below). He is also known for defending Patrick Staunton in the Penge murder of 1877 and securing the acquittal of Chief Inspector Clarke, the head of the detective department at Scotland Yard in the trial of the detectives, 1877.

It would appear that the principle of judicial independence was not enforced rigorously in the nineteenth century. As previously mentioned, the judge in Oscar Wilde's second trial, Mr Justice Alfred Wills, lived at 42 Tite Street, Chelsea. Wilde and his wife Constance lived at 16 (now 34) Tite Street with their two children from 1884 to 1895. In contemporary times, a judge who was a close neighbour of the defendant in an important trial would recuse themself in similar circumstances. A Nevada Supreme Court Justice recused herself in 2025 from a pending appeal in which a respondent was her neighbour.

A petition to the Queen was prepared in November 1895 to obtain Wilde's early release from prison. It was signed by Frederick York Powell, Professor of Modern History, Oxford University. A second petition was printed but not presented as a letter from the Home Secretary recommended that no grounds existed which would justify him in advising the Queen to mitigate Wilde's sentence.

It is surprising how speedily criminal justice moved in the nineteenth century. Oscar Wilde received the offensive card he regarded as libellous on 28 February 1895. He complained to the police and the Marquess was committed for trial on 9 March. The libel trial took place at the Old Bailey on 3–5 April. After he withdrew from the proceedings and the Marquess handed the damning witness statements his detectives had taken to the DPP, Wilde was examined and committed for trial on 19 April. His first trial at the Old Bailey took place between 26 April and 1 May. The second trial at the Old Bailey was from 22 to 25 May. In 2026, those proceedings would have stretched over several years.

The Picture of Dorian Gray is about a young man of good birth, great wealth and great personal beauty, whose friend paints a picture of him.

Dorian Gray wishes to remain like the picture and not age. His wish is granted and the picture ages with the years, but he doesn't. In the end, he stabs the picture and falls dead. The picture is restored to its pristine beauty while his friends find the body of a hideous old man on the floor.

In 1895 on 6 April, at the time of Wilde's arrest, his play *An Ideal Husband* staged its 111th performance at the Haymarket Theatre, and on 8 May *The Importance of Being Earnest* staged its 86th performance at St James's Theatre. After his death, *Salome* was performed on New York's Broadway in 1917. It was banned in England and Wales until 1931. In *Salome*, Jokanaan (John the Baptist) resists Salome's advances and refuses to let her kiss him, calling her a 'daughter of Sodom'. She dances the dance of seven veils for her stepfather Herod and in exchange demands the head of Jokanaan. She kisses the lips of the severed head.

'Ah! I have kissed thy mouth Jokanaan. There was a bitter taste on my lips. Was it the taste of blood? … But perchance it is the taste of love … They say that love hath a bitter taste … But what of that? I have kissed thy mouth Jokanaan.'

Whilst in Reading Prison, Wilde wrote *De Profundis*, a forty-four-page letter to Lord Alfred Douglas. It was published in 1905, after his death:

> Suffering is one very long moment. We cannot divide it by seasons. We can only record its moods and chronicle their return. With us time itself does not progress. It revolves. It seems to circle round one centre of pain. The paralysing immobility of a life every circumstance of which is regulated after an unchangeable pattern, so that we eat and drink and lie down and pray, or kneel at least for prayer, according to the inflexible laws of an iron formula: this immobile quality, that makes each dreadful day in the very minutest detail like its brother.

Relative values: Wilde gave Charles Parker £2 and Parker and Alfred Wood £3 after the indecent acts. The equivalent value in 2026 would be £228 and £342 respectively.

Chapter 2

The Shrigley Abduction

The Trial of Edward Gibbon Wakefield, William Wakefield and Frances Wakefield

1827

Taken from boarding school and married for her inheritance

Ellen Turner was the daughter and only child of William Turner, the High Sheriff of Cheshire, who lived in Shrigley Hall, near Macclesfield. He was the owner of a considerable amount of land and property in Chester. Ellen turned 15 on 12 February 1826.

Edward Gibbon Wakefield, aged 30, had been admitted to the Bar at Gray's Inn in 1813, but he never practised law. He worked as a King's Messenger in Europe and then in a diplomatic capacity. He had eloped to Scotland at the age of 20 with a 17-year-old heiress, Eliza Pattle. Her mother had accepted the marriage and settled £70,000 on the young couple. Eliza died four years later in 1820, giving birth to their third child. Wakefield needed money to acquire an estate and enter Parliament.

Frances Davies, the daughter of Dr Davies, lived near Shrigley Hall and knew of the Turner family. She later secretly married Mr Wakefield senior. Edward was living in Paris with his brother William when Frances joined them in January 1826. She told Edward about the wealthy Turner family and their young daughter who was heiress to a large fortune. Frances returned home at the beginning of February and Edward and William travelled from Paris to Macclesfield to join her at the doctor's house.

Frances called upon an acquaintance of hers and the Turners, Anne Brocklehurst, and obtained an introduction to the Turner family. She went with Anne to Shrigley Hall, where she met Mr Turner and his sister, Miss Critchley. She enquired about Ellen, who had gone back the day before to the Misses Daulbys' school in Liverpool, where she had boarded for five years. Frances did some scouting, meeting Mr Grimsditch, the Turners' solicitor, on Saturday 4 March, telling him about her visit to Shrigley Hall and how she had not seen Mrs Turner. Mr Grimsditch told her that Mrs Turner was unwell, and he thought she had a 'paralytic affection'. He added that Mr Turner was going to London on the Monday evening.

Frances sent for Robert Bagshaw, a banker, on 5 March and borrowed £160. She was at home with Edward and William when she met him. She told the banker that she needed the money to release her cousin from prison, where he was detained for an unpaid debt. The Wakefield brothers later used £40 of the money to buy a second-hand carriage. Edward said it was to be delivered to Captain Wilson (an alias) at the Albion Hotel, Manchester. On Monday, 6 March, the Wakefield brothers arrived at the Albion Hotel in the morning. Edward Wakefield called himself Captain Wilson. They bought the carriage and left with it.

On Tuesday, 7 March, Mr Turner arrived in London and met Mr Grimsditch. Meanwhile, Edward, William and Edward Thevenot, a Frenchman whom they employed as their servant, went in the carriage towards Liverpool. They had a letter which they had forged, addressed to Miss Daulby, the principal of Ellen's school, and signed by John Ainsworth M.D., a fictitious doctor:

> Shrigley, Monday night
> 6th March
> Half past 12
>
> Madam,
> I write to you by the desire of Mrs Turner of Shrigley, who has been seized with a sudden and dangerous attack of paralysis. Mr Turner is unfortunately from home, but has been sent for, and Mrs Turner wishes to see her daughter immediately. A steady servant will take this letter and my carriage to you to fetch Miss Turner, and I beg you that no time may be lost in her departure … it is probable that she may soon become incapable of recognising anyone. Mrs Turner particularly wishes that her daughter should not be informed of the extent of the danger, as without this precaution, Miss Turner may be very anxious on the journey, and this house is so crowded,

> and in such confusion and alarm, that Mrs Turner doesn't wish anyone to accompany her daughter.
>
> The servant is instructed not to let the boys drive too fast, as Miss Turner is rather fearful in a carriage.
>
> I am madam,
> Your obedient servant

William was dropped off at Warrington, and the carriage was driven by a post-boy from an inn at Prescott. Edward got out near the school. Mr Thevenot spoke to Miss Elizabeth Daulby and presented the letter. He said that he was the Turners' only servant, recently hired, and that the carriage belonged to Dr Ainsworth, which is why Miss Daulby was not suspicious when Ellen did not recognise Mr Thevenot or the carriage. He told Miss Daulby that Mrs Turner was ill the night before, dropping her knife and fork at dinner. They would pick up another physician, Dr Hull, in Manchester on the return journey. Miss Daulby read the letter and within fifteen minutes of his arrival, Mr Thevenot left with Ellen.

Mr Thevenot and Ellen travelled to the Albion Hotel in Manchester on 7 March. Mr Thevenot told Ellen that her mother was ill, and they were to wait for her father: 'I expect him here any minute.' He said that they would go on to Shrigley afterwards. The landlord said that Ellen looked a little confused. Her uncle, Robert Turner, lived in the same street as the hotel, about 300 yards away, and it was later noted that she could have got a message to him. Edward Wakefield then presented himself to Ellen. Ellen was aware of the current volatility in the world of commerce, so she was not surprised when Edward told her, 'Your father sent me to tell you that it is the embarrassed state of his affairs which occasioned you being sent for from school,' and that he was to take her to him at a place in Yorkshire. She believed and trusted him. Mr Thevenot gave instructions that if she rang the bell from her room, a hotel servant was not to answer it as he would go himself. Edward asked for a bedroom and adjoining sitting room on their return in six weeks' time.

At the later trial in Lancaster Castle, the defence called a stream of witnesses to show that Ellen was not being restrained and appeared to be at ease with Edward. They left for Delph, where the post-boy at the inn was asked by defence counsel, 'Was she in good spirits?' The witness was tipsy. 'Ask *him* whether *he* is in good spirits,' the prosecuting counsel said to much laughter. They travelled to Huddersfield, where the driver said that

Ellen and Edward were laughing and talking as they walked up the hills behind the carriage, and how at one point she took his arm. In Huddersfield, a waiter said that they appeared to be 'as agreeable as man and wife'. The chambermaid at the George Inn, Huddersfield, said that Ellen came downstairs on Edward's arm. The post-boy and the waiter at the George both said that Ellen and Edward were talking and laughing as they got into and sat in the carriage.

The post-boy at the White Lion, Halifax, drove them to Keighley. He said that he heard them laughing. The landlady of the Devonshire Arms, Skipton, heard them laughing and said that she was in good spirits. They travelled to Settle, and Kirby Lonsdale, where Ellen was said to laugh loudly from the carriage when the landlady fell in the doorway. She told how Ellen declared, 'What a beautiful morning it has turned out to be. We are quite favoured with the morning.' She appeared in very good spirits. The post-boy at Kirby Lonsdale drove them to Kendal and described how Ellen smiled at Edward as they talked. They breakfasted at The Kings Arms, Kendal where the chambermaid said they were agreeable together. The post-boy drove them to Shap. He described Ellen as happy, rather fatigued and pale.

They had arrived in Kendal at 6am in the morning of 8 March and Edward pretended to obtain a letter at the Post Office. Between Kendal and Carlisle, he told her, 'Your father is not here … here is a rich banker of the name of Wakefield. He is our uncle. The Ryle and Daintry's Bank in Macclesfield, where your father has his accounts, has failed. This has plunged your father into ruin. I am your father's dearest and nearest friend, and I have persuaded my uncle to lend your father £60,000 which has relieved him for the present.'

Later he told her, 'The Blackburn Bank, where your father also has accounts, has also failed. Your father's affairs are in a worse condition than before. My uncle now demands security for the sum he has lent your father, the security being the estate at Shrigley. Your father might be turned out of doors any day.' He said that he had a letter from Mr Grimsditch, who suggested that the property becomes hers and she marry Edward as security for the loan. 'It would be in your power to decide whether to turn your father out or not.' Ellen replied, 'I must see my papa first, before I can answer such a matter as that.' Edward said that she would see her father in Carlisle, and they continued towards there.

On Wednesday, 8 March, they arrived at the Crown Inn, Penrith. They left the next morning, after breakfast. The chambermaid said that they had three beds in three separate bedrooms, each bed looked to have been slept in by one person and Ellen and Edward appeared 'very loving on both their sides'. Edward Baxter, the post-boy at the Crown Inn, Penrith, drove them to Carlisle. On 9 March, they arrived at the Bush Inn, Carlisle. The landlady invited Ellen, who looked very dispirited, to get out of the carriage, but Edward put his hand across the door and said 'no'. Ellen was described by another woman there as looking 'the picture of despair'.

Edward asked for horses to Gretna and William Graham, the postilion at the Bush Inn, drove them. After leaving Carlisle, Edward told her that her father was attempting to cross the border to Scotland as the Sheriff's officers were in pursuit of him, and he and Ellen should meet him in Scotland. He then told Ellen that the people she'd seen around the carriage in Carlisle were actually Sheriff's officers looking for her father and that her father was with Mr Grimsditch, hiding in a back room at the inn in Carlisle. He said that her father had requested that if ever she loved him, she wouldn't hesitate to accept Edward as her husband.

She believed Edward and consented. At the trial, she was asked what had induced her to consent and she replied, 'The fear, that if I did not, my papa would be ruined.'

The post-boy at Penrith said that they were in very good spirits, laughing and talking. The head waiter at Carlisle said how they played draughts together.

William Graham knew to take them to the Gretna Hall inn, where he called David Laing, the 'parson', who arrived shortly after. Laing performed a ceremony, which was witnessed by the landlord and William Graham. Laing placed a ring on her finger, and she and Edward embraced. Laing produced a certificate of marriage and he, the two witnesses, and the married couple signed it. They dined at the Gretna Hall afterwards. The landlord said that they behaved very affectionately towards each other at the dinner. His daughter told how before the wedding ceremony, she saw Ellen sitting on Edward's lap on a sofa. After the ceremony, she had hold of his hand.

They returned from Gretna to the Bush Inn, Carlisle. Ellen thought that she would see her father there, but they told her that he was now 'at liberty' and they would find him in London, where he had gone on business. They took her to a hotel in Hanover Square, then said that her father had gone on urgent business to Calais and she must follow. Edward introduced Ellen as his wife to the owner of the Quillac Hotel, Calais, and they stayed there for five days. Ellen used the name Madame Wakefield and believed that she was his wife. Edward rented two inter-connecting bedrooms with a sitting room.

Mr Turner, Mr Grimsditch and the family at Shrigley learnt about the marriage from a notice in a London newspaper on 11 March. Miss Daulby found out on 12 March and went to Shrigley the next day. Mr Grimsditch had discovered the circumstances surrounding the marriage by 14 March. He approached the Foreign Secretary and obtained warrants for the arrest of Edward and William from Bow Street Police Court. He travelled to Calais accompanied by Mr Critchley and Robert Turner, Ellen's uncles, and Ellis, a Bow Street Officer. They confronted Edward in the Quillac Hotel. Mr Critchley said that Edward told him how Miss Turner was a very fine girl, and the heiress to one of the largest fortunes in the county, and that he was determined to possess her for himself. Mr Critchley told Ellen that he had every reason to believe that the marriage was illegal and she exclaimed, 'Thank God for it! It is the happiest intelligence that could be conveyed to me.'

Mr Grimsditch told Edward that they'd come at the request of Mr Turner to take back his daughter. He said that Edward had stolen her, and they would prosecute him. Edward asked: 'But is the marriage legal? If it is I must keep her. If it is not, I can have no claim on her.' Mr Grimsditch refused to discuss the legality of the marriage, said that he had a warrant in his pocket, they were authorised to take her back and 'take her we will'. He added angrily, 'You have got possession of Miss Turner, a mere child whom you'd never seen, by means of a forged letter and you deserve to be shot. It will be the death of Mrs Turner, if she isn't dead already and we have left Mr Turner in London, broken hearted.' Edward replied, 'I have a daughter, and if a man were to take her off in the same manner, I believe I would send a bullet through his head. I dare say she will fly to you, and from me when she sees you.'

Edward confirmed that, 'Miss Turner is the same Miss Turner as she was when I took her away; there has been no consummation of the marriage.' Ellen was fetched from her room, where she had been with her uncles. In front of the pair, Mr Grimsditch said, 'We find that you have practised upon this poor child the most extraordinary deception and fraud ever heard of. It is a cruel case; we will take her from you and put you in the custody of the Bow Street Officer.' Edward asked: 'Have you taken any legal opinion on the validity of the marriage? I claim her as my wife.' Ellen said, 'I am not your wife. I will never go near you again. You have deceived me.' She clung to her uncle Mr Critchley. Edward said, 'You must acknowledge that I have behaved towards you as a gentleman.' Ellen replied, 'Yes'.

Mr Grimsditch said angrily, 'I am surprised that you can for a moment suppose this is a legal marriage! A marriage obtained by fraud cannot be legal. She is under 16, it is clearly illegal. The marriage is void.' Edward replied, 'I haven't used force. But I don't intend to justify my conduct.' He agreed that Ellen should go with her uncles.

Edward wrote to his brother:

> My dear William … she has been told all; and was very anxious to leave me when she knew all. I expected as much … and let her go. I made and gave a solemn declaration that she and I have been brother and sister. How this may affect the validity of the marriage I know not … I was bound, and it was wise, to give some comfort to Mr Turner … there can be no doubt that the law can punish us. For myself, I will meet it come what may; but if you are able, get away as soon as possible … the grand question now is, is the marriage legal? They all said 'no'.

The Trial

William was arrested in Dover and granted bail. Edward Thevenot fled to France. The three defendants, Edward, William and Frances Wakefield, stood trial in Lancaster Castle on 23 March 1827 before Judge Baron Hullock and a jury. Four counsel appeared for the prosecution: Serjeant Cross, John Williams, Mr Brougham and Mr Starkie. And four for the defence: Mr Scarlett, Mr Coltman, Mr Park and Mr Pattison.

The 'ceremony' of marriage had taken place in Scotland, part of the same kingdom but a different state for the purposes of the law. This meant that the taking and marrying were not completed in England, and the offenders could not be indicted for a felony under the statute of Henry VII:

> That whereas women having substances, or being heirs apparent, for the lucre of such substances, have been oftentimes

> taken by misdoers, contrary to their will, and after married to such misdoers or to others, by their assent, or defiled – what person or persons, from henceforth, that taketh any woman so against her will unlawfully, such taking, procuring or abetting to the same, and also receiving wittingly, the same woman taken against her will, knowing the same, shall be felony.

Instead, they were charged with four counts of conspiracy: to carry away a female under the age of 16 and marry her (conspiracy to commit a felony); and take away an heiress against her will and marry her (conspiracy to commit a capital felony); all high misdemeanours, punishable by five years' imprisonment. Only one charge claimed they used force to conspire to marry her without her consent.

The prosecutor wished to call Ellen to give evidence. The defence argued that she was not a competent witness because she was married to the defendant Edward Wakefield. The law of England did not allow a wife to be a witness against her husband, 'lest it should provoke implacable animosity between them', unless he had assaulted her or committed some other crime against her that could only be proved with her evidence.

The judge questioned the legality of the marriage. Was the ceremony conducted according to Scottish law? Did the circumstances of the marriage invalidate it? Only Miss Turner could speak to the circumstances.

The defence argued that in Miss Turner's case, the marriage took place without the least use of force. Whatever persuasion was employed, she was at liberty to act as she pleased. A deception on the part of a man, by which he obtains a young lady's free consent to marry, for example that he will make a handsome settlement on her when he has no means, would not invalidate a marriage. There would have to be a menace or threat, force, or terror.

The prosecutor argued that she was a competent witness to prove that her consent to the marriage was obtained by intimidation: that if she refused, her father would be seized by the sheriff's officers, taken to prison and his reputation ruined for ever. And such intimidation was tantamount to force.

The judge decided to allow Ellen to give her evidence. He would decide later whether it was admissible.

The defence called David Laing, the 'pastor', about the marriage ceremony in Scotland. He said that he had married them 'in old ordinary form of the Church of Scotland. That is the way it has been done for centuries.' He used to be a pedlar and had been issuing marriage certificates for forty-eight years. He was not a Scottish clergyman, and a prayer book had not been produced. 'Some go before a clergyman,' he said, 'but if you go before a person and own yourself to be man and wife, that is the way for many in Scotland. I have been in the courts in Edinburgh, and my marriages have always been held good.'

The defence called Duncan McNeil, a Scottish barrister. He said that he was well acquainted with the Scottish law relating to contracts of marriage and had heard nothing from Miss Turner or Mr Laing to invalidate the marriage. He admitted that he had never heard of a case in Scotland with facts similar to those.

The prosecutor told the jury, 'This was a marriage by a drunken pedlar at an alehouse before the landlord and a post-boy. Is that a marriage according to the service of the Church of Scotland?' The judge decided that Ellen's evidence was admissible as proof against the Wakefield brothers and added, 'I am doubtful if the marriage was good.'

The defence addressed the jury. Mr Scarlett accepted that what the Wakefield brothers had done in taking Ellen could not be 'justified'. But he referred to the evidence of many of the witnesses about how pleased and happy she was to be in Edward's company and how they appeared to everyone as a loving couple. At perfect liberty to go home to her father, she chose instead to remain with Edward and gave her full and free consent to the marriage. He spoke at length about the lack of proof against Frances Wakefield.

The prosecutor, in his closing speech, said that the conspiracy was complete when the forged letter was delivered to Miss Daulby in Liverpool and Ellen was taken away in the carriage, so that the crime was completed in England. The only reason that Miss Turner may have been cheerful was that she had gone through the marriage ceremony to 'accomplish the preservation of her family'. The Wakefield brothers had admitted that they did what was alleged and Frances Wakefield was the suggester and contriver.

The judge asked the jury: 'What could their object have been, in taking away a young girl under the age of 16, an heiress, other than that with which they are charged?' She consented to the marriage out of fear that otherwise her father would be ruined.

The prosecutor withdrew the conspiracy alleging force, on the judge's indication that there was no evidence on that count. The jury retired for forty-five minutes and found all three defendants guilty of the three remaining counts.

The next morning, there was reference to a second indictment that charged only Edward Wakefield and William Wakefield with the abduction of Ellen Turner under the age of 16. At first it seemed as if the prosecution were proceeding on that as well as the remaining three counts of conspiracy on the first indictment. There was then an 'arrangement' whereby the Wakefield brothers 'submitted' to a verdict of guilty on the second indictment and the prosecution didn't ask for a verdict on the first indictment. The jury returned a verdict on the second indictment of guilty for both Wakefield brothers. Frances Wakefield walked free as the brothers were committed to be sentenced. On 14 May 1827, the Wakefield brothers appeared in the Court of the King's Bench in Westminster Hall and were each sentenced to three years imprisonment.

COMMENT

The report of the trial (303 pages) claimed to contain 'the only authentic and correct report of this interesting trial'. The author gave the reasons for the 'intense interest: the extraordinary circumstances of forgery, fraud and deception; the cunning and depravity displayed in the formation of the plot; the artful wickedness developed in its execution.' He described how 'At the early hours of seven in the morning all the avenues to the court were crowded to excess by persons anxious to gain admittance.'

The Abduction of Women Act 1487 was passed in the second Parliament of King Henry VII: *An Act against the taking away women against their wills*. Three conditions had to be satisfied for it to be a felony crime: she must have land, tenements, moveable goods or be an heir; she must be taken against her will; she must then be married to the mis-doer or someone else by his consent or be carnally known.

The Abduction Act 1557 section 3 criminalised the taking away any unmarried woman under the age of 16 years from the possession, custody, or governance of her father or guardian. An unlawful taking was punished by two years' imprisonment and a taking with marriage by up to five years' imprisonment.

In the Shrigley abduction it was argued that the charge could not be proved because the marriage was in Scotland, taking the crime outside the jurisdiction of England and Wales. The prosecution secured a conviction by relying on the 1557 Act, the crime being completed when Ellen was taken from the custody of the headmistress at her school. The Offences

Against the Person Act 1828 expanded the crime of abduction to cover females with no property interest. The 1828 Act also made the forcible abduction of a woman with intent to marry, as opposed to actual marriage, a felony punishable by transportation or imprisonment with hard labour not exceeding four years.

Henry Peter Brougham (1778–1868) was the barrister who led the prosecution of the Wakefields. He was an MP from 1810 until 1830, when he became First Baron Brougham and Vaux. He was appointed Lord Chancellor in 1830 and became an advocate for liberal causes, including the abolition of the slave trade, free trade, and Parliamentary reform. He established the Central Criminal Court and is credited with helping to defeat the 1820 Pains and Penalties Bill (a Bill to divorce George IV and Queen Caroline, see Chapter 3). He also defended Captain Burn against Viscount Glerawley (see Chapter 26).

James Scarlett (1769–1844), 1st Baron Abinger, was the most successful lawyer at the bar in his time. He defended the Wakefields, Joseph Haynes in the action brought by Maria Foote (see Chapter 4), prosecuted Mr Gill in his action against Mr Aubrey (see Chapter 15) and prosecuted Viscount Glerawley in his action against Captain Burn.

After serving his sentence, his hopes of a political career in England and Wales dashed, Edward Wakefield looked to the colonies for his future. He never reached Australia but still managed to publish a *Sketch on a Proposal for Colonising Australia* in 1829. He was also a key player in the formation of the South Australia Association. The New Zealand Company was created to colonise New Zealand and he persuaded them to appoint his brother William as leader of their expedition to New Zealand. In 1853, Edward finally travelled to New Zealand and served in the first New Zealand General Assembly. He died in New Zealand in 1862. His obituary in the *Daily Telegraph* said that 'administrative and constructive reform in the British Empire can scarcely be traced to the single hand of any other man.'

William Turner was elected MP for Blackburn from 1832 until 1841.

At the age of 17, Ellen's disputed 'marriage' to Edward was annulled by Ellen's petition to Parliament, despite a counter-petition from Edward. She married a wealthy neighbour and died giving birth at the age of 19.

Shrigley Hall is in the village of Pott Shrigley, Cheshire. It was built in about 1825 for William Turner. It is now a hotel and country club.

The legality of the Bow Street officer's arrest of Edward in France is uncertain. There was no extradition treaty between the two countries. As the

British Foreign Secretary was involved, there most likely was informal co-operation between the two governments to facilitate it.

The abduction of women was made a felony in 1487 only because there had been petitions to Parliament in the fifteenth century to address the problem of men who abducted women of means and forced a marriage.

In 1437 Isabel Boteler was the wife of Sir John Le Boteler (Butler). Five years after he died, she was at home in the manor house in Bewsey when William Poole and other men broke in. Poole raped her and took her almost naked to Wales, where he imprisoned her and forced her to marry him. When a King's writ was issued, she was found but Poole fled to a remote part of Wales where the writ did not run.

In 1438 Margaret Malefant was the wife of Thomas Malefant, knight. After the death of her husband, she was sent counterfeit letters from him (of whose death she was unaware) asking her to hasten to London to comfort him. Lewis Leyson, a servant, took her to Wales instead on the pretext of keeping her safe. He starved her, imprisoned her, threatened her and forced her to marry him. He then raped her.

In 1452 Jane Heronville (Lady Beaumont) was married to Sir Henry Beaumont. Jane was abducted after her husband's death by Edward Lancaster. She was about to marry Charles Nowell when she was abducted whilst hearing mass, placed on horseback and taken to an unknown church where a priest performed a marriage ceremony against her protests. The coerced marriage was later voided, and she married Nowell.

In 1485 Jane Statham was heiress to the manor of Morley in Derbyshire. Soon after the death of her first husband, John Sacheverell, at the Battle of Bosworth Field in 1485, Jane was betrothed to William Zouche of Castle Eton, a near neighbour. She was ambushed by a party of one hundred men led by Henry Willoughby of Wollaton. She was then raped by his younger brother Richard and forced to marry him. Her forced marriage was later annulled after she petitioned Parliament for assistance.

Relative values: The £70,000 settled on Eliza Pattle by her mother in 1816 would be the equivalent of £5,934,842 in 2026. The £160 that Frances borrowed to finance their abduction plan would be the equivalent of £13,515 in 2026. And the £40 that the Wakefields paid for a second-hand coach to carry Ellen away would be the equivalent of £3,391 in 2026.

In an 1835 register of Liverpool teachers, Miss Elizabeth Daulby is listed against 'ladies' seminary, 21 Chatham Street'.

Chapter 3

Queen Caroline of Brunswick

A Trial Before the House of Lords to Deprive Her of Her Title of Queen Consort and Dissolve Her Marriage to George IV

1820

The giddy antics of Queen Caroline and her paramour, the servant Bergami

Caroline, the daughter of the Duke of Brunswick, was engaged in 1794 to her first cousin George, Prince of Wales, although she had never met him. He was already illegally married to Maria Fitzherbert, a marriage that violated the Royal Marriages Act 1772. Lord Malmesbury questioned Caroline's suitability as a bride for the Prince: she lacked judgement, decorum, and tact, spoke her mind too readily, acted indiscreetly and often neglected to wash or change her dirty clothes. George and Caroline married in 1795 whilst George was drunk. She became Princess of Wales. He regarded Caroline as unattractive, unhygienic, and suspected that she was not a virgin. He was in debt and hoped that parliament would increase his allowance if he married an eligible princess. She had said to Lord Malmesbury, 'The Prince is very fat and he's nothing like as handsome as his portrait.'

Their marriage was troubled from the start. Popular with the public for her common touch, she was regarded as a wronged wife. They separated shortly after the birth of their only child Princess Charlotte in 1796. Charlotte lived separately from her parents and was cared for by a governess. Whilst Caroline lived an independent life, apart from George, allegations were made about her infidelity and claims that a young boy, William Austin, was her illegitimate son. A secret commission made up of the Prime Minister, the Lord Chief Justice, the Lord Chancellor, the Home Secretary and three senior members of the Lords, was set up in 1806 to investigate these claims.

Meanwhile, Caroline was not allowed to see her daughter. They found that the claims were without substance.

By 1811, King George III was insane. The Prince of Wales was made Regent and restricted Caroline's access to Charlotte even more. Feeling alienated from society by George and gossip mongers, Caroline agreed to leave England in 1814, in return for receiving an annual allowance to pay for her travels.

In 1816, Princess Charlotte married Prince Leopold of Saxe-Coburg-Saalfeld. Caroline was not informed about the wedding by George, nor invited to attend. In November 1817, Charlotte died whilst giving birth to a stillborn son. Caroline only heard the news of Charlotte's death from a letter that George had written to the Pope.

Caroline travelled abroad until 1820. Meanwhile, in 1817 the Government established the Milan Commission, which took three years to collect evidence about Caroline's alleged adultery and immoral behaviour whilst on her travels. Under the direction of the Foreign Office and control of Colonel Brown, the Commission was said to have unlimited resources and funding. It was later accused in the House of Lords of preparing a one-sided case against Caroline: selecting only witnesses who had bad things to say about her; coaching them; and paying them compensation to give evidence against her.

On 29 January 1820, George III died. Caroline's husband became George IV and Caroline became Queen of England. She made plans to return to England. The King didn't want her back and they could not divorce because Caroline would not admit to adultery. The Government offered Caroline £50,000 per year to stay abroad. She turned down the offer.

The Milan Commission's work was presented to a committee of fifteen members of the House of Lords. They approved the introduction of the Pains and Penalties Bill 1820: 'A Bill to deprive Her Majesty Caroline, Amelia, Elizabeth of the Title, Prerogatives, Rights, Privileges and Pretensions of Queen Consort of this Realm, and to dissolve the Marriage between His Majesty and the said Queen.' The preamble to the Bill set out the charges against her. Caroline returned to England in June 1820 to protest against it. She had public support, and it was feared that her presence would cause trouble for the unpopular King.

The Lords sat for fifty-one days hearing the case for and against the passage of the Bill. Lord Eldon was the Lord Chancellor. Advocates for the Government included the Attorney General Sir Robert Gifford and the Solicitor General Sir John Copley. Advocates for the Queen included Mr Henry Brougham, Mr Thomas Denman, and Mr John Williams.

On 19 August 1820, the Attorney General introduced the Bill by describing the allegations against the Queen as 'one of the most serious offences both against the laws of God and man – that an adulterous intercourse carried on'. Before he could open his case, a motion was moved in parliament that declared the Bill 'unnecessary for the public safety or the security of the country'. The motion was defeated.

The Case for the Bill

The Attorney General opened his case for the Bill by setting out the evidence he would call about the Princess's travels. In 1814, the Princess (as she then was) went to her first home, Brunswick in Germany. Then she travelled to Milan, where she lived for three months. During her time there, she received Bartolomeo Bergami into her service as a *valet do place*. She travelled on to Rome and Naples.

Travelling with her was the young William Austin, now 13 years old, who used to share her bedroom and attend to her domestic comfort. On 9 November 1814, it was decided that he was getting too grown up to sleep in her room and he was placed in the servants' quarters. Bergami replaced him, sleeping in a room next to Caroline's that communicated directly with hers. Intercourse was assumed to have commenced with Bergami then and continued until he left her service several years later. It was on that first night that Caroline dismissed her servant and headed towards Bergami's bedroom. The next morning, when she and Bergami both happened to get up late, her bed was found to have not been slept in, whilst his bed bore the impressions of two bodies.

A few days later, Caroline gave a masked ball at the house of the King of Naples. Whilst she dressed, Bergami was sent for and retired into the room with her, and she changed for the ball in his presence. The dress that she wore as the Genius of History was ridiculed as 'indecent and disgusting'. She changed again into the dress of a Turkish peasant character with Bergami, her companion, also dressed as a Turkish peasant.

Bergami was kicked by a horse and bedridden. Caroline organised a servant to look after him. That servant described how he often saw Caroline go to Bergami's room and remain there for some time, and he heard them kissing. Caroline remained in Naples until March 1815. There was a public Masquerade at the Theatre St Charles in Naples, and Caroline chose Bergami as her companion. Her party wore dresses selected by her that were again called 'gross and indecent' and met with insults and disapproval from others attending. She went to Civitavecchia and Genoa, where she stayed until May. Bergami was seen walking and riding with Caroline, and her bed was said to be scarcely occupied at night whilst Bergami's looked as if it had been occupied by them both.

Bergami was a married man with a 3-year-old daughter, Victorina. Caroline took Victorina and Bergami's sister Faustina, brother Louis, and mother into her household. She excluded Victorina's mother, telling all that Bergami was unmarried. Louis served as a courier, but Faustina and their mother had no duties. On 15 May Caroline travelled to Milan. There she took in Bergami's second sister, who called herself the Countess of Oldi. Described as an uneducated woman with vulgar manners, she became Caroline's lady of honour. Caroline moved on to Venice. She was seen to toy with Bergami: she placed a gold chain around his neck, then he placed it around her neck, then she put it around his neck again. She gave him a blue silk morning gown, which he wore. They travelled on to Vaunes, where Caroline was seen to retire to Bergami's room for a long time. Then she continued to the Borromean Islands, Balazoni and Lugano. Their rooms were always close to each other, and he would sit at her dinner table.

From 15 to 26 November, Caroline's party sailed aboard the vessel *Leviathan*. She appointed Bergami Her Majesty's Chamberlain. They visited Elba, Palermo, and Messina, where they stayed until 6 January 1816. She was seen walking on the deck, arm in arm with Bergami, whom she called 'her dear' and 'her love'. They sailed on His Majesty's frigate *Clorinde* where, contrary to protocol, she dined with Bergami instead of the captain. They went to Syracuse and Catania. She was spotted coming out of Bergami's bedroom, undressed and carrying her sleeping pillow under her arm. She procured Bergami a Knighthood of Malta and designated him 'His Excellency'. She addressed him as *chevalier* (a mounted knight). In Augusta, she procured the title of Baron de la Fracina for Bergami and addressed him as Baron. Formal pictures were taken of Caroline and Bergami, which they exchanged with each other.

Her party sailed on the vessel *Polacca* to Tunis, Malta, Utica, Athens, the Greek Islands, Constantinople, and Ephesus. At Atum in Syria Caroline slept in a tent. It was reported that she was seen in bed undressed, with

Bergami, who was almost undressed, sitting on the edge of the bed. In Jerusalem, Caroline made Bergami a Knight of St Sepulchre, a Catholic Order. She created the Order of St Caroline and made Bergami the Grand Master. She boarded the *Polacca* again in Jaffa, sailing to Italy. It was hot and she had a tent placed on deck with a sofa and a bed for her and Bergami. They slept in the tent at night and also stayed in the tent for much of the daytime. On the vessel she was seen sitting on Bergami's knee, embracing and toying with him. A witness told how a bath would be placed in her cabin and prepared for her by Bergami and that he remained with her whilst she bathed. Caroline and her party celebrated the feast of St Bartholomew on 24 August, Bergami's saint's day, with drinking, rejoicing and festivities. She was even seen to mend his clothes.

They travelled to Lake Como, where a cousin of Bergamo's joined her service. A theatre was built so that Caroline could perform a play, with Bergami as her lover. She bought a house, Villa d'Este, on the shores of Lake Como, where Bergami was reportedly seen coming out of her bedroom wearing only a shirt and *robe-de-chambre*. A palace was built for Bergami at Barona, at Caroline's expense and costing several thousand pounds. It was called appropriately Villa Bergami. A carnival was staged at Caroline's house with scenes described as resembling a brothel.

On 18 February 1817, Caroline headed towards Germany. At Charente, Bergami was sent on ahead to obtain passes for the journey. Caroline ordered a female servant to sleep in her bedroom. Bergami returned in the middle of the night, sent the servant away and remained in Caroline's bedroom. In a hotel in Carlsruhe, Bergami was seen in his bedroom, naked, with his arms around Caroline's neck. Her cloak was also found on Bergami's bed. They travelled together in a separate coach from the others in her party. At short stops to change horses, she and Bergami would retire to a room together and lay on the same bed. They travelled to Milan and the Villa d'Este and Rome, where they resided at Rupinella Palace. Bergami was seen going into Caroline's bedroom in the early hours of the morning. He would also go into her room as she was dressing. In 1817, Caroline sold Villa d'Este and moved to the smaller Villa Caprile near Pesaro. By August 1817 she was in Milan. Bergami remained in her service until 1820.

The Attorney General was about to call a lengthy list of witnesses against the Queen. The defence complained that they didn't have a witness list, were not informed about the evidence that these witnesses were expected to give and didn't even know the names of the witnesses. All they had to rely on was the Attorney General's opening speech and the generalised preamble to the Bill that listed the charges against the Queen:

> Whereas in 1814 being in Milan, Italy, engaged into her service in a menial situation, Bartolom Bergami, a foreigner of low station who had before served in a similar situation.
>
> And whereas a most unbecoming and degrading intimacy commenced between Her Royal Highness and the said Bartolom Bergami.
>
> And whereas Her Majesty not only advanced the said Bartolom Bergami to a high situation in Her Royal Highness's household, and received into her service many of his near relatives, some of them inferior, and others in high and confidential situations about Her Royal Highness's person, but bestowed on him other great and extraordinary marks of favour and distinction, obtained for him orders of knighthood, and titles of honour, and conferred on him a pretended order of knighthood, which Her Royal Highness had taken upon herself to institute without any just lawful authority.
>
> And conducted herself towards the said Bartolom Bergami both in public and private, in the various places and countries which Her Royal Highness visited, with indecent familiarity and freedom, and carried on a licentious, disgraceful and adulterous intercourse with the said Bartolom Bergami, which continued for a long period of time causing great scandal and dishonour upon your majesty's family and her kingdom.
>
> To manifest our deep sense of such scandalous, disgraceful and vicious conduct on the part of Her Majesty, by which she has violated the duty she owed to Your Majesty, and has rendered herself unworthy of the exalted rank and station of Queen Consort of this realm, and to evince our just regard for the dignity of the Crown and honour of this situation, we Your Majesty's most dutiful and loyal subjects, the Lords Spiritual and Temporal and Commons in Parliament assembled, do hereby entreat Your Majesty, that it may be enacted that after the passing of this Act shall be deprived of the title of Queen and that the marriage between His Majesty and Caroline Amelia Elizabeth be dissolved, annulled and made void.

The Attorney General, leading the prosecution team, examined his witnesses over two weeks. The evidence about the Queens's travels, her sleeping arrangements and the favouritism displayed by her to Bergami included many titbits. 'I saw her Royal Highness pass from the corridor into Bergami's room twice, at midnight. She walked very softly and stooped, as she passed my bed to see if I was asleep. I had my eyes closed, pretending to be asleep. I heard them kissing.' 'She walked arm-in-arm with Bergami, at night.' 'He took her hand and kissed her lips as they parted.' 'He kissed her when he took her leave.' 'They shared a carriage and a bottle for Bergami to urinate into was found inside it.' 'I saw her more than once sitting on his knees, kissing her.' 'They both slept in the inner tent. Bergami would put his hand out from between the tent flaps to pass me the light they were using. Then he would close the tent from the inside.' 'He had an arm around her neck and was making love to her and kissing her. In the kitchen, he took a piece of polenta and put half in her mouth. Later, he did the same with a piece of sweetmeat. I saw them kiss about four times and lock themselves in his bedroom.' 'Mahomet danced and made a roll with his pantaloons to represent a "thing" and held it and gesticulated with it. The Princess laughed.'

Mr Brougham's cross-examination for the Queen of the former manservant Theodore Majocchi and Mr Williams' cross-examination of the former maid Louise Demont were described as masterpieces of forensic skills. Majocchi replied '*non mi recordo*' (I don't recall) to many straightforward questions that he should have been able to answer. For this he became the butt of many jokes and cartoons and the title of a humorous pamphlet. Demont was exposed as having been dismissed from Caroline's household for lying and was living in England under the Government's protection as Countess Columbier. Under scrutiny, the 'kissing' inside Bergami's bedroom at night became 'whispering' and the bath, accompanied by Bergami, would not have fitted in Caroline's cabin.

Mr Brougham was told that he could take as long as he chose to prepare the Queen's case and the Lords' adjourned from 9 September to 3 October. A publication warned the Lords that a verdict either way was fraught with danger:

> If her innocence, according to the prayers and vows of millions of her subjects be made manifest, the public indignation will be deep and, we fear, resentful. If, upon the evidence, which

> up to this day has been a description upon which a magistrate will hesitate to reprimand a common constable for neglect of duty, the legislature should ever be induced (and we solemnly protest that we cannot believe it ever will) to consider Her Majesty guilty of the charges, public opinion will refuse to ratify the sentence.

The Case Against the Bill

The defence called an equal number of witnesses and raised many issues: the Attorney General had made claims in his opening that were not covered or backed up by the witnesses that he called; prosecution witnesses had been bribed, coached and able to discuss their evidence with each other before the trial; she was the victim of a conspiracy between witnesses who perjured themselves in return for rewards; the Milan Commission had not presented the whole picture but was selective in its choice of witnesses and only interested in people who would say something bad about the Queen; the domestic 'spies' were disgruntled, discarded servants out for revenge; the defence would have difficulty procuring reliable evidence of events which had happened up to six years before; the prosecution had benefited unfairly from unlimited time, resources and lavish expenditure to assist them.

Mr Denham suggested that Caroline's housekeeper, not Caroline, had been responsible for arranging their rooms to be next to each other. He described Bergami as nothing more than a humble, kind and respectful servant who never lost sight of Caroline's dignity. Regarding intimacy between her and Bergami, he claimed that although there was evidence of opportunity, there was no evidence of the commission of adultery. They did not try to hide their actions together, which were innocent and pure. It was necessary for Caroline's safety that a male servant (Bergami) should attend near her at all times.

Mr Denham warned about the possible consequences of finding against her: the punishment would be 'the heaviest that could be inflicted on a Queen'. He stressed the unfairness if the Lords found the charges proved: 'She was separated from her husband for twenty-four years, not by any desire on her part, but his caprice, his act and his choice – not in consequence of any misconduct of his wife.' The King should not have permitted 'the most disgraceful facts that ever polluted the lips of man to be given in evidence against his wife'. 'The more depraved he showed his wife to be, the more he established his own cruelty and profligacy; and the more imputations he cast on her, the more he was to be despised for having deserted and abandoned her.'

The Lord Chancellor summed up briefly before a vote was taken on the Lord's second reading. Caroline and Bergami had slept under the same tent for five weeks; they were familiar towards each other; she took in his family to her household and promoted him in an extraordinary way; they took measures to ensure the togetherness of their bed chambers. Can you infer adultery took place from all that? Having asked the question, the Lord Chancellor answered it for himself: 'I express my firm belief that adulterous intercourse has taken place. This conclusion is consistent with the facts proved and the case stated.' And he said that it was necessary for foreign witnesses to have been paid for their time, otherwise they wouldn't have come to court. The second reading was passed by a majority of 28 (123 'yes', 95 'no').

Queen Caroline protested to the Lords against the proceedings, stating that they were contrary to the constitution, the spirit of the law and the principles of common justice. Her protest was entered in writing, saving her the need to appear in person to present it. The third reading vote was taken and passed by a majority of only 9 (108 'yes', 99 'no').

The Earl of Liverpool told the Lords that if the third reading had been carried by as considerable a number of peers as the second, he and his colleagues would have felt it their duty to persevere with the Bill and send it the Commons for legislation. Because of the narrow majority they were determined not to proceed further with it. That motion was carried, and the Bill never reached the Commons for debate.

George barred Caroline from his coronation in July 1821. She died three weeks later.

COMMENT

There are at least three reports of the proceedings in the House of Lords. In 1820, a book (763 pages) was written about *the immense importance of the proceedings before the House of Lords* by Edward Barron, who also wrote *The Royal Wanderer or The Secret Memoirs of Caroline.* In 1821, a book was published (642 pages) titled *Trial of Queen Caroline*, edited by J. Nightingale. Some years later, in 1874, a book with the same title (564 pages) was published in New York claiming to be one of a series of trials of great value.

The Royal Marriages Act 1772 regulated marriages of descendants of King George II. It stipulated that any such descendant (excluding a princess marrying into a foreign family) wishing to marry needed the reigning monarch's consent and failure to obtain it would render the marriage null and void. The Act was primarily intended to prevent unsuitable or politically unfavourable marriages within the Royal family. It was repealed by the Succession to the Crown Act 2013.

Caroline's father was Charles William Ferdinand, Duke of Brunswick-Luneburg. He was mortally wounded during the Napoleonic wars by a musket ball at the Battle of Jena in 1806. Her mother was Augusta of Great Britain, granddaughter of George II and sister of George III.

Maria Fitzherbert was already twice widowed when she met the Prince of Wales, the future George IV. She was a staunch Catholic and refused his offer to be his mistress. They married in secret because George III had not given his consent. They lived in Brighton, where George amassed debts of £600,000. Parliament cleared his debt on his agreeing to marry Caroline, a Protestant.

A Pains and Penalties Bill could retrospectively criminalise conduct and inflict penalties. The conduct described in this case was 'unbecoming and degrading intimacy' and the punishment was to deprive the Queen of her title and privileges and dissolve her marriage with King George IV.

As the proceedings were those of the passage of a Bill in the Houses of Parliament, the Queen was not a party and could not give evidence, just protest. The second reading of the Bill in the House of Lords took the form of a 'trial' in which their Lordships were judge and jury.

During the trial of Queen Caroline in 1820 it was claimed, without success, that a witness should not be allowed to swear to God unless they could show that they had recently been to confession and taken Holy Communion. Otherwise, the witness would not regard the oath as binding on them. The Quakers Act 1695 permitted a member of the Society of Friends to make a solemn declaration (affirm) rather than swear on the Holy Bible. The Affirmation Bill 1838 was debated in Parliament. Its object was to extend affirmation to people other than Quakers to avoid judges having to punish, and courts being deprived of the evidence of, such people who consciously objected to taking the sacred oath. The Bill was not passed into law. The Oaths Act 1888 finally permitted an affirmation from any person.

Were prosecution witnesses being rewarded financially for giving evidence against the Queen or just compensated for their losses? Merchant ship owners or captains who were witnesses described the payments they received of $800 or $1,000 per month as inadequate. Majocchi was paid eighty golden Napoleons (he denied receiving 150), whilst others received money whilst travelling and 8 golden Napoleons or 40 or 50 Francs for their troubles, with free travel and accommodation. Demont was said to have been paid 'a great sum'. A witness was told that if he had something to say against the Queen, he would 'receive a great present and become a great man'. Another witness was told that if he had anything to say against the Princess he would be paid. Mr Brougham said that better-paid witnesses had never come to his knowledge. Mr Denman claimed that 'Agents of the Milan Commission were endeavouring to corrupt individuals to commit perjury.'

Prosecution witnesses were examined in Milan and again in London before giving evidence. Was this just thorough preparation or was it witness coaching?

Mr Williams, for the Queen, complained that money was no object for the Milan Commission and had been largely and lavishly spent to set up the prosecution. There was no doubt that the Milan Commission had government support, resources, money and time and there was not a level playing field with the Queen's defence.

Did Caroline's servants have a motive for giving evidence against her? The Lords were told that, 'These domestic spies had been discharged from the service of the Princess. Our beds and tables are surrounded by snares. Discarded servants had it in their power at all times to depose to facts on which they could not be contradicted.'

When the Solicitor General challenged the defence to call Bartolomeo and Lois Bergami to give evidence, Mr Williams for the Queen complained that the Attorney General and his team were behaving as if this was a dispute between adversaries and they were advocates for just one party. They were responsible for arriving at the truth and should have collected and presented evidence for the Queen as well as for the Government. Many competent and compellable witnesses had not been called.

The argument from Mr Denham for the Queen, asking for forgiveness for Caroline who had suffered at the hands of a cruel husband, sending her away and not caring what happened to her, was not a defence to the charges. Instead, it was similar to telling a jury in 2026 that they could vote against the weight of the evidence in order to follow their conscience.

Was there an innocent explanation for Caroline and Bergami's closeness, her promotion of him, the arrangement of their bedrooms next to each other, and sharing tents? Or was it just evidence of their planned and organised adultery? Was their brazen behaviour in front of so many witnesses a sign that they had nothing to hide or just reckless disregard for what others thought? Was it love and lust that brought her together with a man of lower rank? Or was it snobbery that believed his lower rank meant that it couldn't be for any other reason?

A medal was struck to commemorate the Bill's withdrawal. It shows Caroline with a laurel wreath and the legend: *I rise by my difficulties.* The inscription *Queen of England* is on the reverse.

Relative values: The golden Napoleon was a French 20 Franc coin introduced in 1803 that featured the image of Napoleon I. The 80 Francs that Majocchi admits being paid was the equivalent of £6,720 in 2026. If he had received 150 coins, as alleged, that would be the equivalent of £12,600 in 2026. George's debts of £600,000 were the equivalent of £50,435,292 today. The $1,000 per month paid to the ship owner for time spent attending as a witness would be the equivalent of $27,500 today.

Chapter 4

Breach of Promise Trial Between Maria Foote, the Celebrated Actress, and Joseph Hayne

1824

'If she could not make MATRIMONY, he joked, she was determined to make a MATTER OF MONEY'

Maria Foote was an actress, a woman of great beauty and considerable talents. Born in 1797, her father was a theatre manager and put her on the stage as Juliet in *Romeo and Juliet* in 1810. She was under contract to the Covent Garden Theatre from 1814 until 1825, and paid the generous salary of £1,000 per year.

Colonel Berkeley was the eldest son of the late Lord Berkeley. He made Maria an offer of marriage but insisted that it remain a secret as he was applying to the Crown for a peerage and if it were known that he was marrying an actress it would be an impediment. He promised to marry her in the future and for five years she lived as his mistress without an allowance from him. She resided with her parents, and he never spent the night with her at their home. Instead, she visited him at Berkeley Castle during breaks between her theatrical engagements.

In 1821, Maria gave birth to Emily and the colonel insisted that it remain a secret. He said that if the child became public knowledge, he couldn't marry her. When Emily was 12 months old, Maria took a house at 31 Henrietta Street, Covent Garden, and arranged for people to take care of her daughter there, visiting her occasionally. In 1823, Maria became pregnant with Rosalind and finally realised the misery of her situation and that of her child. She gave the colonel a deadline: marry her by their second child's birth or she would have nothing further to do with him.

Maria was five months pregnant with their second child and still engaged to the colonel when in January 1824, Joseph Hayne, the defendant, took an interest in her and asked for permission to approach her. Maria's mother told Joseph that Maria had been engaged for a considerable time to the colonel. Joseph replied that he doubted that the colonel would marry her and he still entertained hopes of being permitted to spend time in private with her. Maria's mother told Joseph that if Maria wasn't married to the colonel by the end of the Covent Garden season in June, Maria would no longer consider herself engaged. What he wasn't told was that she already had one child with the colonel and was expecting their second. Joseph was a young man, aged 23, of independent fortune, with large estates at his disposal. He had a country house, a London residence in Upper Brook Street, Grosvenor Square, and his principal residence was Long's Hotel in Bond Street.

In May, Joseph wrote to Maria saying it was time for her to decide about the colonel. On 28 June, Joseph came to London and asked for her hand in marriage. She needed time to consider his proposal, and they agreed to spend the next night at the opera. She decided to tell Joseph everything about her past. The colonel found out about their opera date through spies of his, and on 29 June sought out Joseph and arranged to meet him. The colonel told Joseph about the children, ridiculed the idea of Maria marrying Joseph and produced a declaration for Maria to sign indicating which of the two men she would marry.

Joseph immediately wrote to Maria saying that after what the colonel had told him, it was impossible for them to marry. The Lord Chief Justice later told the jury that had Joseph not proposed again, he would have been justified in breaking off his first proposal. Maria thought the colonel's behaviour treacherous whilst Joseph was considerate and gentlemanly. She asked Joseph to meet her, so that she could explain her conduct. They met at the Castle Inn, Marlborough. The colonel found out about their meeting and sent Lord William Lennox to prevent it taking place. The Lord was delayed; their meeting took place and Joseph accepted Maria's explanation. He no longer renounced his offer of marriage.

On 9 July, Joseph wrote telling the colonel that he had no right to interfere between him and Maria. On 10 July, Lord William Lennox wrote to Joseph: 'He conceives that his authority to interfere will cease to exist when his children shall be delivered to him'. On 13 July, Joseph wrote to Maria, 'it will be advisable on your part to resign the children, as it appears, from professional advice which I have had, that he can claim them as of right … my love and regard can never be abated for you … I cannot bear the idea of you again returning to the theatre; you will be miserable if you do.' Maria reluctantly agreed to the colonel having custody of the children, and he agreed to sever all contact with her.

On 19 July, Joseph wrote to Maria: 'You are the sole object of my affection and without your regard I should be the most miserable man in the universe.' On 26 July Maria stipulated in a Bond executed by her and the colonel that she was giving up Emily Forbes born on 9 April 1821 and Rosalind Forbes born on 2 May 1824. Forbes was a name that Maria used. On seeing the Bond, Joseph said that his feelings, attachment, and admiration were as ardent as ever and he was still determined to marry her. Joseph was in a hurry to wed, and 4 September was fixed for the ceremony.

On 30 July, Joseph wrote: 'Your friends should be acquainted with my proposal to you … you have kindly said that you never doubted me.' On 11 August he wrote: 'No power on earth shall alter my affection for you or in any manner change these feelings I now profess.'

On 30 August, Joseph wrote to Maria that he had drafted a financial settlement. The wedding had been arranged for 4 September, the same day that his sister was due to marry. Then it was changed to Monday, 6 September. On Saturday, 4 September Joseph took Maria a ring and an armlet that he placed on her arm. He said that he'd execute the financial settlement at 9am on the wedding day morning. He sent his carriage for her wardrobe, ready for their honeymoon in the country. Joseph was having a large party on the Saturday evening but still had time to visit a private box where Maria and her mother were seated in the Haymarket Theatre, escort them home and stay with them until 1am. He told them that he'd return in a few hours to spend as much as possible of the Sunday with Maria.

Joseph didn't return later that morning, as arranged. Instead, Mr Bebb, his solicitor, called and spoke to Maria's father and then to her mother telling them that Maria had seen the last of Joseph. Joseph came to see them in the evening and said that he hadn't instructed Mr Bebb to deliver that message to them. It was his friends who were to blame. He hadn't returned on the Sunday morning, as arranged, because the whole party had attacked Maria's character and made vile reports and insinuations about her, and his friends had got him drunk and locked him in a room. When he was awake, his friends continued with their onslaught, and a servant had physically tried to block him from leaving Long's Hotel. The Attorney

General, representing Maria, later referred to the resistance to her marriage, 'from that disgraceful Bacchanalian party'.

Joseph said that he was determined to marry Maria as arranged on 6 September and he would meet them at their house at 9am, when he would execute the settlement. He stayed with them until 2am on the Monday. Before leaving he said that because of his family's opposition to the marriage, he would tell his servant at Long's to wake him at 10am, too late to stop him leaving earlier.

Joseph didn't appear later on the Monday morning for the execution of the settlement or for the wedding. Everyone waited for Joseph, who didn't arrive. No reason was given. A bridesmaid had travelled 200 miles to be there. At 3pm Maria sent a note to Joseph at Long's Hotel but the servant carrying the note was tricked when he arrived at the hotel and locked in a room by Mr Carter, Joseph's solicitor.

Maria knew that Joseph was controlled by a number of people whom the Lord Chief Justice later told the jury, 'acted by the base and infamous motives of sharing his money'. She wrote to him after six days, urging him to come to her house and explain himself. Maria was insulted and ridiculed by Joseph's detestable behaviour, and she wrote about the injury he had caused her. Joseph called at her parents' house, and they fixed 27 September for the wedding. He purchased the marriage licence and delivered it to her.

On 13 September, Joseph wrote: 'my heart and thoughts are still with you … my own inclination will never allow me to be separated from you … I cannot, will not, lose you'.

On 23 September, he offered to write to any friends that she named, informing them that he had renewed their engagement. On 25 September he joined her at the Haymarket Theatre, and they agreed to get married on Tuesday, 28 September. Joseph agreed to execute the settlement on the morning of Monday, 27 September.

On Sunday, 26 September, Joseph wrote: 'The tide of family influence, strengthened by many unhappy circumstances, is so strong against my pursuing further our late treaty that I am compelled … to relinquish'. Then on Wednesday, 29 September, he wrote: 'My love for you is unabated'. On 30 September, Maria replied: 'Your conduct is as inconsistent as it is cruel and unjust. Good God! Is this your mode of proving your professed love and regard?' Joseph replied on 30 September: *Farewell, forever, farewell.* A Mr Manning called to tell Maria that the settlement would not be executed after all.

Joseph wrote a letter to the *Morning Post* newspaper in an attempt to justify his conduct. He said when he had proposed marriage to Maria, he was unaware of her association with Colonel Berkeley and their two children as she had held herself out to be a paragon of virtue. He had also lent Maria's father £1,105, which had not been repaid, to purchase the situation of paymaster in the army.

The Trial

The breach of promise trial took place on 21 December 1824 in the Court of the King's Bench, Westminster, before Lord Chief Justice Abbott and a special jury. The Attorney General acted for Maria and Mr Scarlett represented Joseph. The Attorney General told the jury that in anticipation of marriage, Maria had turned down a new contract at the Covent Garden Theatre and disposed of her theatrical wardrobe, which would be expensive to replace. But the real loss, that the jury should quantify, was the rank and status that she would have acquired on marriage; her participation in his wealth; and that he had promised to settle £40,000 on her.

Mr Scarlett asked the jury why Maria had not brought the breach of promise claim against the colonel, 'an experienced and heartless designing seducer, instead of a thoughtless, foolish, and inexperienced young man. She could have selected a much better victim.' He then suggested that the colonel had never promised to marry her.

Mr Scarlett described Joseph as a 'young man of violent passion'. And she was 'just an actress – tainted in her private character and tarnished in her reputation, endeavouring to make the best match she could with a man of money. Her object was merely pecuniary … her sole aim to extract from the pockets of a young man all she can obtain.'

Mr Scarlett said that Joseph should have been disgusted at the way in which Maria had abandoned her children, without any arrangement to see them again. If she could not make *matrimony*, he joked, she was determined to 'make a matter of money'. He was saved from misfortune by the energy and perseverance of his friends. Had he been allowed to pursue his passion, he would have heaped ruin and misery on himself and the family. Her father had received £1,150 and she had received £1,000 and a shawl. She ought to be content with that rather than demand damages from the jury.

The Attorney General ridiculed Mr Scarlett, saying that he must have departed from his brief, because he couldn't believe that Joseph would have instructed his counsel to represent him as an extraordinary driveller and idiot, a simpleton and easy dupe. He may be young, but he was educated at Eton, where a young man acquires more knowledge of the world than a grown-up man acquires elsewhere. He had spent three years in Paris and resided in a fashionable London hotel on his return.

He dealt with the suggestion that the colonel never promised marriage as the reason for not claiming from him for breach: her proceedings against the colonel were rendered impossible by the approaches of Joseph.

The Lord Chief Justice summed up for the jury and included a remark about Maria's character. He said that a woman who had the misfortune to be seduced and had lived with another man could never come into a court of justice to ask for the same compensation as a woman of unblemished reputation. Also, he said, after the first proposal of marriage from Joseph, she had gone to Berkeley Castle and continued to live with the colonel. He told the jury to take account of her profession as an actress, saying that it should have some weight on them.

The jury retired for ten minutes only and awarded Maria £3,000 damages. Her stage career ended in 1831 when she married Charles Stanhope, 4th Earl of Harrington, and became Countess of Harrington.

COMMENT

The report of the trial (thirty-seven pages) advertised 'The Whole of the Love Letters.' The author wrote: 'So intense was the interest excited by the action brought by Miss Foote, the actress, against Joseph Hayne Esq., that the doors and avenues of the court were crowded to excess at an early hour. The Earl of Sefton, The Earl of Mountford, Lord Howard of Effingham and Count Vaudreuil had seats on the bench.'

A man's promise to marry a woman at some time in the future, where the woman accepted his offer, was a legally binding contract. A breach of the contract could result in the woman suing for damages. In the eighteenth and nineteenth centuries it was thought that the woman was more likely to give up her virginity to a man to whom she was engaged, and that if he later refused to marry her it would harm her reputation, she would be considered unchaste and have difficulty finding a husband. As well as demanding compensation for injury to her health and emotional state, and loss of reputation, the jury would consider how the breach had affected her financial situation and future social standing. They would compare her current situation to the lifestyle she could have enjoyed had they married and compensate her for the loss of status and financial stability that marriage would have brought. Wedding and other expenses incurred in expectation of marriage would also be compensated.

The contract could be broken by the man without penalty upon the discovery of significant facts such as her bad character, her defrauding him, her physical or mental incapacity, or that she was married already, as in the case of Major Dudley Apthorp and Miss Sydney Scrope-Ferrers (see Chapter 9).

In England and Wales, breach of promise as an actionable matter was abolished by the Law Reform (Miscellaneous Provisions) Act 1970. Danish Eva Haraldsted brought the last-known case, in 1969 against the footballer George Best. She was 21 years old and Best, having signed his autograph for her, persuaded a Danish newspaper to track her down and they became engaged. He broke the engagement off ninety-one days later, saying, 'I'm not the marrying type.' Three days later, she played in a charity football match against him. Her all-women team was Blinkers United, named after a Manchester nightclub Best used to frequent. The next match against him was a writ for breach of promise. It was settled out of court, where she received the derisory sum of £500.

In America, about a half of states still allow breach of promise actions. In India, sex on false promise of marriage constitutes rape.

The famous barrister Sir Patrick Hastings (1880–1952) wrote in his book *Cases in Court* how he disliked breach of promise trials. Unless the young man was trying to trick the woman, he regarded the law as interfering in purely domestic relationships: 'In a moment of joyous enthusiasm a young man invites a girl to marry him; with equal enthusiasm she accepts; the next morning he thinks better of it.' He was also of the opinion that a woman, unable to sue a young man just for seducing her, may seek retribution by an action for breach of promise.

Colonel Berkeley was born illegitimately on 26 December 1786, to the 5th Earl Berkeley and Mary Cole. In 1810, on the 5th Earl's death, the colonel claimed the title of Earl Berkeley unsuccessfully. In 1831 he was created 1st Baron Segrave and in 1841 1st Earl Fitzhardinge. Berkeley Castle was described as most interesting, but an uncomfortable and draughty old place. The colonel is reputed to have spent much of his time there with numerous 'frail ladies' who found him irresistible.

In 1825, Mr Judge, the editor of the *Cheltenham Journal*, wrote 'scurrilous paragraphs' week after week about Colonel Berkeley. Writing about the colonel's treatment of Maria Foote *his victim,* he described the colonel as 'faithless, a man in whose society the virtue of their daughters would be placed in the utmost danger. The illegitimate son of a butcher's daughter who had unfortunately produced more heirs at love than at law to Lord Berkeley.' Judge mocked the annual Berkeley Hunt and wrote that respectable families and 'fashionable' people were no longer attending because of the colonel's reputation. Colonel Berkeley sought revenge on Mr Judge. With two accomplices, he tricked his way into Judge's home and horsewhipped him severely. Judge brought an action for assault against the colonel and his accomplices and was awarded £500 damages by the jury.

Relative values: In 2026, Maria's £3,000 damages in 1824 would be worth £283,698; her £1,000 per year salary from the Covent Garden Theatre would be the equivalent of £95,484; and the promised settlement of £40,000 would be worth £3.8 million.

The Attorney General acted as counsel for Maria. He was the chief legal adviser to the King and to government. After 1890, an Attorney General in England was no longer allowed to practice privately at the same time.

The lengthy openings by counsel would not be allowed now, as they risk feeding the jury 'facts' which are not later given in evidence. Instead of an 'opening', which now provides a flavour of the case that the jury can expect to hear and helps them to understand the issues they are to try, counsel in these nineteenth-century cases frequently recited the prosecution and defence cases in full.

There are a number of engravings and pen and ink drawings of the exterior architecture of Long's Hotel,16 Bond Street, before it was rebuilt at the end of the nineteenth century. Donald Shaw wrote that Long's was well known for having a room set aside for the 'fastest and best men' to relax, socialise and drink brandy and sodas at 3 or 4am after leaving London's clubs. It also had a renowned coffee room where men could spend the day lounging around, pipe smoking, drinking champagne and chatting about horse racing. Byron was noted to have dined there in 1815. In 1824 Isaac Robert Cruikshank, the English Spy, published a hand-coloured engraving titled 'Evening and in High Spirits, a Scene at Long's Hotel, Bond St.'

Chapter 5

The Trial of Waterhouse v Colonel Berkeley, for Criminal Conversation

1821

'It is not necessary in a case of this sort, where such letters are produced as I have read, and which have passed between a young man and a young married woman, actually to prove that they had been seen between the sheets together'

In 1810 on the Isle of Man, John Waterhouse, aged about 20, met Jane, the eldest daughter of Captain and Mrs Blake. She was younger than him. They married on the island on 15 September 1812. He was described as an affectionate husband, and she as a beautiful and accomplished wife. They had three children, two girls and a boy.

In 1817, for the sake of his wife's health, they moved to Charlton Kings, a little village about a mile from fashionable Cheltenham. Mrs Waterhouse's aunt, Lady Wraxhall (her mother's sister), lived a quarter of a mile away. In the winter of 1818, Mrs Probyn, an old friend of Mrs Waterhouse, came to live in Cheltenham also for the benefit of her health.

In March 1819, Mr and Mrs Waterhouse went to the Berkeley Hunt Ball. The next day, Mrs Waterhouse called on Mrs Probyn and asked her if Colonel Berkeley had admired her dress or said something about it. Colonel William Fitzhardininge Berkeley lodged next door, and Mrs Probyn introduced Mr and Mrs Waterhouse to him, although it appears that Mrs Waterhouse had been following the colonel for some time. As Mrs Waterhouse leant on her husband's shoulder, she watched the colonel dismounting from his horse. According to Mrs Probyn, Mrs Waterhouse said to her husband something like, 'If ever I make love to, or intrigue with any man, it will be with Colonel Berkeley.' Mrs Probyn described how this was said 'playfully, not wantonly', as the Waterhouses appeared to be happily married.

On 5 April 1819, Colonel Berkeley received an anonymous letter dated 20 March: 'The lost depraved wretch, who has unwillingly cherished in her bosom a guilty passion … now adds to her guilt by confessing it to you … if you knew half the struggles she has had during that time with an infatuation violent as unaccountable … what has occurred within this fortnight has increased her guilty passion to madness … how distracting the most tender of hearts beats for you … oh, should you discover her, too well does she know her fate!'

In April 1819, Mr Waterhouse went to London to visit his ill brother. Mrs Ann Lydiard, in service with Mrs Waterhouse, told how after Mr Waterhouse had left, Colonel Berkeley called and stayed for half an hour.

On 19 April, the colonel received a letter addressed to him at Berkeley House, Spring Gardens, London: (I have been) 'confessing an unfortunate passion … further than blue eyes and very white teeth, there's nothing to admire in me … because my heart has chosen to bestow itself without your wish, or my consent, on you (*these*) letters I have written under the influence of an unfortunate and misguided passion.'

On 1 May 1819, Colonel Berkeley wrote to Mrs Waterhouse: 'Tonight, at nine, I will be in the appointed spot. If you love me, do not fail me.'

On 4 May 1819, Colonel Berkeley wrote to Mrs Waterhouse: 'You seem to have obtained an influence over me, that I deemed it impossible any woman could have arrived at. You appear to have persuaded the inmost recesses of my heart … you have established a sway over me, that I did not believe any woman in England but yourself could have done … you seemed to recoil from those caresses which my soul and my lips prompted me to bestow … your tenderness revived in some degree before I quitted you.'

On 7 May, Colonel Berkeley wrote: 'My heart is with you now, and where the heart is the body delights to be … the wild impetuous strokes of love burst upon me; for you have so far possessed yourself, sorceress of my soul, and when your image is before me I cease to have command of my faculties … how vehemently and passionately I love.'

In May 1819, Colonel Berkeley received an anonymous letter: 'I cannot endure that you should be here, and I do not see you; but how or where is a great consideration. I think I should contrive it some morning. I might walk up that lane … or if you could think of another spot I would endeavour to meet you. In the first time in my life, I feel that I love – fondly, tenderly and affectionately love … And oh! It is a happiness so exquisite, such an indefinable passion, so painfully pleasing, such an acute sensation of delightful agony, that I would not forego its soft pangs for any bliss this life can afford.'

On 10 May, Colonel Berkeley wrote: 'You do indeed know how to love with the most delicate ardour … think of any place, sweet love, most convenient to yourself to meet me in when I come to Charlton. No difficulty, nor danger, no weariness shall keep me from your arms.'

Mr Waterhouse returned on 10 May. On 19 May, Colonel Berkeley wrote: 'By application, I may be able to emancipate myself from heavy shackles, become free from all ties but those of love, and hasten to press thee to my fond bosom.'

On 15 June, the colonel wrote: 'Pray tell me when the departure of part of the family takes place, as you mentioned. Nothing then shall prevent my being with you.'

On 22 June, the colonel wrote: 'Write to me love, when the departure actually takes place.'

On 1 July, the colonel wrote: 'You little know the warmth and delicacy of that heart which you have so deeply wounded by hazarding such unworthy suspicions' (that the colonel was contemplating marriage with another woman). 'If I love you at all, you will be everything to me'. At the time, the colonel was secretly engaged to Maria Foote, a famous actress, and stringing her along with the promise of marriage at some time in the future.

On 3 July, the colonel wrote: 'I am uncertain whether I shall be able to come to Cheltenham … but I advise you on no account to come to London.'

On 10 July, Mr Waterhouse left home again and travelled to Jersey to visit his sister, returning on 15 August. On his return, he was dismayed to hear that there was unpleasant gossip about his wife, who was shunned by the local ladies. Mrs Waterhouse gave birth to their fourth child. Mr Waterhouse needed to find a better situation for his family. He left home for Bristol and on 14 February he set sail for Jamaica, returning in July.

The day after Mr Waterhouse left, Mrs Waterhouse took a rented house in Cheltenham. This was entirely her decision, and she had not consulted her husband. Mary Wright and Anne Creed lived with Mrs Waterhouse in Pembroke House, Cheltenham. They both told how Colonel Berkeley came to the house frequently in the early evening. Anne Creed said that Mrs Waterhouse would change into an evening dress before the colonel's arrival. Mary Wright said that Mrs Waterhouse would tell her not to go into the drawing room whilst the colonel was there. The bedroom was only a passage and three steps away. Mary Wright added that several times, when the colonel was visiting, she could hear footsteps going from the drawing room to the bedroom. Afterwards, Mrs Waterhouse's hair and frill around her neck would be 'in disorder'.

When Mr Waterhouse returned and found his wife in different accommodation, and pregnant, he left Cheltenham, vowing never to see her again. Mrs Waterhouse gave birth to a baby girl on 11 November 1820. Mr Hughes, solicitor, helped his client, Mr Waterhouse, to obtain Colonel Berkeley's letters: on 12 December 1820 they went together to Mrs Waterhouse's lodgings, where Mr Hughes restrained Mrs Waterhouse whilst Mr Waterhouse went into her bedroom and returned with a bundle of papers sealed in an envelope. It was endorsed: 'In the event of my death, let the enclosed be delivered to no other person than Colonel Berkeley, Berkeley Castle.' Mr Waterhouse unhappily questioned whether he was really the father of their child. He sued Colonel Berkeley for adultery with Mrs Waterhouse.

The Trial

The trial was before Mr Justice Park and a special jury at Gloucester Assizes. There were four advocates for each of the parties, including Mr Jervis prosecuting and Mr Taunton defending. Mr Waterhouse claimed £20,000 in damages.

Dr Wood confirmed that Mrs Waterhouse had given birth to a full-term baby girl, and the period of gestation was forty weeks (14 February 1820, when Mr Waterhouse had set sail). Mr Jervis told the jury that Mr Waterhouse last had sexual intercourse with his wife forty-two weeks and one day before the birth (30 January 1820). Mr Justice Park asked the doctor if with those dates the husband could be the father? The doctor replied, 'I have never seen such an instance.'

Mr Jervis reminded the jury that the colonel visited Mrs Waterhouse whenever the opportunity arose. During those visits they were alone together. The drawing room connected with her bedroom. Two people had been heard walking from one room to another. They were seen occupying the same sofa. And after the colonel left her lodgings, the disordered appearance of her dress was evidence of the familiarity that had subsisted between them. 'It is not necessary in a case of this sort, where such letters are produced as I have read, and which have passed between a young man and a young married woman, actually to prove that they had been seen between the sheets together.'

Mr Jervis told the jury that in assessing damages they should consider that Mr Waterhouse had been deprived of 'the wife of his bosom' at an early period of his life, as he was not yet thirty years. His four helpless infants, three of them girls, were deprived of their mother and now there was a fifth child whom Mr Waterhouse was required by law to maintain.

Mt Taunton addressed the jury on behalf of the colonel. He claimed that there was no proof that Colonel Berkeley and Mrs Waterhouse had committed the 'criminal' act that founded this action. Evidence that they had slept together, which would remove any doubt, was missing. Visits by a single man to a married woman may be improper and open to suspicion but were not conclusive. There was nothing in the letters to suggest that the colonel had 'enjoyed the person' of Mrs Waterhouse – no expressions of satisfied desire; in the letters he was the expectant lover.

If the jury had cause to consider damages, then how great an injury had Mr Waterhouse suffered because of his wife's infidelity? If he were really attached to her with mutual regard and affection, he would have shown her proper care and attention. Instead, he left imprudently and went to Jersey, leaving her outside Cheltenham, 'the vortex of fashionable gaiety and dissipation', with no female friend to take charge of her, keep her company and take an interest in her welfare. When he went to Jamaica, rather than leave her under the care of Lady Wraxhall, he deserted her, and exposed to every temptation that passions or solicitations might throw in her way. And this after he had reason to suspect that she had behaved in a way of which he would disapprove.

In addition, he had letters from Mrs Waterhouse to Colonel Berkeley that suggested she wantonly forced herself on him. The colonel would not say that he was the party seduced, but he would say that he had not seduced her. The letters were anonymous and in disguised handwriting but had been identified as coming from her.

Mr Taunton concluded, 'Only compensate Mr Waterhouse for the injury he has received, without reference to punishment of the party who inflicted it.'

The jury retired briefly and returned with a verdict in favour of Mr Waterhouse, to whom they awarded £1,000.

COMMENT

The published report of the trial for *Crim Con* (thirty-two pages) was sold for eighteen pence from all booksellers. It was copied verbatim from *The Observer*. The author wrote that 'this case, which has excited so much interest among the fashionable visitors to the town of Cheltenham and among the inhabitants of the surrounding counties ... the court was crowded to exception as early as 7 o'clock in the morning.'

Although called 'criminal conversation', the action seeking compensation for the spouse's adultery was not a criminal trial but a private civil claim for damages. The husband was considered entitled to claim compensation for the loss of services and companionship from his wife. 'Conversation' was just a polite word for intercourse. These claims were abolished in England and Wales by the Matrimonial Clauses Act 1857, which made divorce possible on the ground of adultery and created a new court of Divorce and Matrimonial Causes.

Colonel Berkeley, the eldest illegitimate son of the Late Lord Berkeley, was a busy seducer. He was the fly in the ointment in the engagement of Maria Foote and Joseph Hayne, leading to the breakdown of their engagement and the subsequent breach of promise trial in 1824.

It appears that whilst seducing Mrs Waterhouse in Cheltenham in 1819 and 1820, Colonel Berkeley was secretly engaged to Maria Foote. Mr Scarlett described him as 'an experienced and heartless designing seducer'. He was called 'a sort of tenth-rate Rochester' by the author of *The Complete Peerage* published in 1916 (Edward Fairfax Rochester was a character in Charlotte Brontë's 1847 novel *Jane Eyre*, described as romantic, passionate, impetuous, and adept at deception).

Relative values: Mr Waterhouse claimed damages of £20,000, worth £1,681,176 in 2026. The jury awarded him a mere £1,000, worth £84,058 in 2026.

Although adultery was described as a 'criminal' act by Mr Taunton, Mr Jervis pointed out to the jury, 'The crime of adultery should be punished criminally, but as the law stands the only compensation that a man might receive is damages.'

Was the colonel the father of Mrs Waterhouse's daughter? From the time that the egg is released for fertilisation, most babies will be born after thirty-eight to forty-one weeks. Fewer than 2 per cent of babies are born after forty-two weeks' gestation.

Chapter 6

The Pimlico Poisoning

Trial of Adelaide Bartlett

1886

The first known case of death by chloroform. 'How did she do it?' Sir James Paget, a famous pathologist and surgeon, asked, after she was acquitted

Adelaide Blanche de la Tremoille, aged 20, married Edwin Bartlett, aged 30, in 1875. She had only seen him once before the marriage, which had been arranged by her father. Edwin is said to have suffered from rotting teeth. After the marriage, Edwin was keen to improve Adelaide's education and sent her to a boarding school for two years, where she would only see him during the holidays. Then he sent her to a convent in Belgium for a year.

Edwin was a prosperous grocer and by 1886 he and his partner, Mr Baxter, had six grocery shops in Herne Hill and Dulwich. Several years after the marriage, Edwin and Adelaide moved to a cottage in Merton and became friendly with the Reverend George Dyson, aged 27, with 'closely trimmed whiskers and a heavy black moustache'. Edwin asked George to tutor Adelaide in Latin, History, Geography and Maths and every day, when Edwin was away on business, George would spend time with Adelaide.

Edwin and Adelaide spent one month in Dover and Edwin paid for George's return train fare so that he could travel to Dover and spend time with Adelaide whilst Edwin was out on business.

On 3 September 1885, Edwin changed his will. Previously, he had left everything to Adelaide on condition that she didn't remarry. The change withdrew the condition and George as executor and Adelaide as beneficiary knew about it.

Edwin and Adelaide moved to rooms near Embankment. Edwin paid for a season ticket from Putney to Waterloo so that George could tutor Adelaide.

The three of them visited the St Bernard Dog Show and in the evening Edwin fell ill. A doctor noticed a blue line around the edge of Edwin's gums that suggested mercuralism. When asked, Edwin told the doctor that he had not taken mercury.

The sitting room was turned into a sick room and Adelaide nursed Edwin. George would visit, as before. Adelaide told George that Edwin was suffering from an internal ailment; that Annie Walker, who had worked for them and was currently in America, had obtained chloroform medicinally for him; and that Dr Nichols had said that Edwin had one year to live. She asked George to obtain chloroform for her, to soothe Edwin and help him sleep. George bought a total of 4oz of chloroform from three chemists' shops, telling them that he needed it to remove grease spots. Adelaide tipped the contents of the chloroform from the bottles into a 6oz medicine bottle.

The night before he died, Edwin ate half a dozen oysters and a jugged hare. During the night, Adelaide slept in bed with Edwin and told how she had heard him snoring in a peculiar manner and later she had woken and found him dead. She had tried to help him by pouring brandy down his throat. Then she had called the landlady, Mrs Doggett. Mrs Doggett said that she smelt chloroform in the room. On the mantlepiece was a tumbler half full of brandy. The tumbler also smelt of a mixture of the sedative ether and laudanum.

When Dr Leach arrived, he and Mrs Doggett found an empty bottle of chlorodyne (a nineteenth-century patent medicine containing opium, cannabis and chloroform and used as a sedative). The doctor asked Adelaide whether Edwin could have obtained poison. She replied, 'He had no poison and would not have got it or had it without my knowledge.'

The postmortem was conducted in the first-floor bedroom. The contents of Edwin's stomach were removed and placed in large glass jars. When the doctors opened the body, they noticed a pungent smell, which Dr Green attributed to the presence of chloroform in the stomach.

Hearing chloroform mentioned, George asked Adelaide about the chloroform that he'd obtained for her. She said that she hadn't used it, just transferred it to one large bottle. The next morning George removed the labels *chloroform poison* from the empty small bottles and threw the bottles into gorse bushes on Wandsworth Common. George went to see Dr Leach, who told him that Dr Green was of the opinion that death was due to the contents of Edwin's stomach: the stomach and intestines smelt of chloroform and the lining was red and inflamed.

Adelaide was staying in Friern Road, Peckham Rye, with Mr and Mrs Matthews. George went to visit and was overheard saying to her, 'I am a ruined man' as he left. He returned the same evening when she asked him to say nothing about the chloroform. He replied that he would 'make a clean breast of the affair'. She said, 'If you don't incriminate yourself, I won't incriminate you.' George told Mr Matthews how he had been induced to obtain the chloroform, and Mr Matthews later told the inquest that George was 'panic stricken', having been 'duped' by a 'wicked woman'.

George had a final meeting with Adelaide in the presence of Mr and Mrs Matthews. George complained that his career was at an end and that he'd have to resign as a minister. Adelaide challenged him to accuse her: 'Do not mince matters, say that I gave it to him.' George was anxious to know what had become of the chloroform. Adelaide said that she had poured it out of a railway carriage window and thrown the bottle into Peckham Rye Pond.

Dr Stevenson sent his post-mortem report to the Home Office. Dr Leach said to Adelaide, 'I have good news for you.' He told her that Dr Stevenson had found that chloroform was the cause of death. 'That should set your mind at rest. Had it been one of those secret poisons which could be administered without the patient knowing it, you would most certainly be accused of poisoning him, by some people.'

Adelaide told Dr Leach that Edwin had strange ideas. He believed that a man should have two wives: one for companionship and the other for 'use'. She had married with the intention of companionship. They had agreed to be affectionate and loving friends, but no more. There was a time when she had longed for a child, and they had broken their rule once. She had a still birth. She explained that after they met George, Edwin had deliberately thrown her at him, anxious to promote affection 'more than platonic but less than criminal'. He told them to kiss and gave her 'affianced' to George. Later, he wanted to assert his marital rights. She told him, 'Edwin, you know you have given me to Mr Dyson, and it is not right that you should now do what during all those years of married life you have not done.' It was a duty she owed to her womanhood and to the man to whom she was practically affianced, to protest strongly against his behaviour.

She said that she had procured chloroform and had intended to wave it in his face on a handkerchief whenever he became too pressing. She said that she had told Edwin this and shown him the medicine bottle, which he put on the mantlepiece next to his bed. He wasn't angry with her.

The Inquest

Athelstan Braxton Hicks, the coroner, commenced his inquiry on 4 February 1886, after receiving Dr Stevenson's report. Inspector Marshall gave the coroner a copy of *Squire's Companion to the British Pharmacopoeia*, found amongst Edwin's effects, which had fallen open naturally on the page about chloroform. When the coroner's jury heard George's evidence, they returned a verdict of wilful murder against Adelaide and accessory before the fact against George.

The Trial

The trial opened at the Old Bailey on 12 April 1886 before the Lord Chief Justice. Sir Charles Russell, the Attorney General, prosecuted. The prosecution offered no evidence against George, who was discharged. They needed him as a prosecution witness. Adelaide, who was defended by Sir Edward Clarke KC, MP, did not give evidence, but the jury heard from George and Dr Leach about what she had told them.

Dr Stevenson concluded that the deceased must have swallowed a large dose of chloroform for it to be sufficient to cause death. And that it would not have been difficult for someone to have poured it down his throat from a medicine bottle if he were lying on his back with his mouth open. The part of the stomach lining that was red and inflamed was where the chloroform would flow to if the deceased were on his back.

There was debate about how the chloroform could have been administered. If he had first been rendered unconscious by inhaling chloroform, his reflexes would not react, and he would not swallow it. If he were asleep, because of a sedative, the introduction of a liquid at the back of his throat would have caused him to swallow it. But unusually his throat and windpipe were undamaged by the chloroform, suggesting that he must have swallowed it purposefully and quickly. Also, vomiting was a frequent but not inevitable reaction to poisoning by chloroform.

A witness said that Peckham Rye Pond was frozen on the day when Adelaide said that she had thrown the medicine bottle away there.

The jury was told how Edwin's father used to joke that a man should have two wives, 'one to take out and one to do the work'. The defence suggested that Edwin had drunk the chloroform to put an end to all his troubles: his illness; and his rejection by Adelaide.

The judge gave the jury three possible explanations for Edwin's death: that Edwin had taken the chloroform himself with suicidal intent – but there was no evidence of this; that Edwin had swallowed the chloroform by accident – but the strong sensation of burning meant that he could not have done so inadvertently; and that another person had administered it – but swallowing would cause pain and for him to cry out unless he was in a state of stupor, wholly or partially unconscious.

The jury foreman was asked, 'Do you find Adelaide Bartlett guilty or not guilty?' He replied, 'Although we think there is gravest suspicion attaching to the prisoner, we do not think there is sufficient evidence to show how or why the chloroform was administered.'

'Then you say not guilty?'

'Not guilty.'

At the announcement of the verdict there was immense cheering in the court and outside. Mr Justice Wills was angered by this and complained, 'This conduct is an outrage. A court of justice is not to be turned into a theatre by such indecent exhibitions.'

Sir James Paget, Sergeant-Surgeon to Queen Victoria, remarked, cynically 'Once it was over, and she could not be tried again, she should have told us in the interests of science how she did it.'

COMMENT

The report of the trial (313 pages) was edited by a Middle Temple barrister, Edward Beal, at the request of Sir Edward Clarke, who wrote the preface. Clarke had a large correspondence from the medical profession during the trial on matters of medical jurisprudence. The trial attracted much attention from a public who were keen to learn about the strange relationships between Adelaide and her husband Edwin, and between Adelaide and George Dyson. Julian Symons wrote a fictional account of the story: *Sweet Adelaide*.

The double jeopardy rule would have protected Adelaide Blanche de la Tremoille if, as Sir James Paget had remarked after her acquittal, she 'told us in the interests of science how she did it'. That rule prevented a person from being tried again for the same offence.

In England and Wales, following the Criminal Justice Act 2003 it became possible in April 2005 to retry a person for a serious offence providing that there was compelling fresh evidence.

Adelaide was not allowed to give evidence in her own defence. In England, Sir Edward Clarke advocated for change. He wrote that the traditional law 'often operated cruelly against an innocent person, but in nine out of ten cases it was an advantage to the guilty.' The 1898 Criminal Evidence Act changed the law in England to allow the defendant to give evidence.

Chloroform is a clear colourless volatile liquid with a characteristic sweet smell and taste. Deliberate poisoning by chloroform, while a popular theme in nineteenth-century crime fiction, was not particularly common. The question remained unanswered of how the chloroform entered Edwin's stomach without damaging his throat or his windpipe. He would need to have swallowed it quickly, preferably whilst conscious. Yseult Bridges theorised in 1962 that he had drunk it on Adelaide's instructions, believing it to be medicine that she was dispensing to him. Another theory is that Adelaide rendered Edwin unconscious by his inhaling chloroform and then immediately dosed him with the chloroform.

Chloric ether was a mixture of chloroform and alcohol.

Affianced was a common term for engaged.

The post-mortem on her husband was performed in their home. More common in the early nineteenth century, this was unusual in Adelaide Bartlette's time. As medical knowledge advanced, post-mortems became more formalised and typically took place in hospital mortuaries or dedicated facilities.

Athelstan Braxton Hicks (1854–97), the coroner, was the son of John Braxton Hicks, an English doctor best known for describing Braxton Hicks contractions: the false labour pains during pregnancy. Athelstan was a barrister, student of medical jurisprudence and Honorary Secretary of the Coroners' Society. He was renowned for his work on the investigation of suspicious deaths of children and his reforms included the professionalisation of autopsies and inquests.

Chapter 7

Child Custody

In the Matter of the Most Noble Duke and Duchess of Marlborough

1853

'Would anyone refuse to believe the oath of the Duke of Marlborough under such circumstances? ... This is just the indignation of a woman of uncontrollable passion: what a woman can do in a frenzy'

George Spencer Churchill was the 6th Duke of Marlborough. In 1817 he went through a mock marriage ceremony with 16-year-old Susannah Adelaide Law, who gave birth to his daughter in 1818. That year, Harriet Spencer also gave birth to his child. In 1819 the Duke married a first cousin, Lady Jane Stewart, aged 20. They had four children before she died in 1844. In 1846 the Duke married Charlotte Augusta Flower, aged 28. They had two children, and she died in 1850.

In October 1851, the Duke married another first cousin, Jane Frances Clinton Stewart, a near relative of his first wife. He was aged 58 and she 34. Since October 1849, the Duke had been in a state of 'decrepitude' because of gout and rheumatism. He was crippled in his arms, wrists, hands, and knees and couldn't walk or move from his chair. He was unable to take part in a church wedding, and they were married in the drawing room at his home, Blenheim Palace, where he was wheeled into the ceremony.

Sarah Licence, an 'old and faithful attendant', had been in the Duke's service for twenty-eight years. She had lived with the Duke since his first marriage. She kept the household accounts and managed and controlled the household and servants. The Duke related how before his first wife died, she had said, 'Duke, never part with Licence and Licence, never leave the Duke.' Since 1849, the Duke was obliged to have bed ropes and straps to enable him to get in and out of bed without assistance. On the first night of his marriage to Jane, and on every subsequent night, Licence helped him into bed. Licence slept in an adjoining room with an open door and was constantly summoned by the Duke during the night by a bell from his bedside to her room. She would turn him in bed and minister to his wants and infirmities. At first, Jane shared the Duke's bed whilst Licence helped him.

Following a recommendation of the Duke's doctor, since 1849 Licence had daily rubbed down the length of the Duke's spine for forty-five minutes. He would be dressed only in a flannel dressing gown when she performed this operation, passing her hand down his spine. The Duke described her 'magnetic power' which no one else could possess. At first, Jane used to sit next to Licence as she did this. There was a bolt on the outer door to his and Licence's bedrooms. This was installed because the Duke had heard noises which he suspected were from spies who came to the bedroom door to listen to what was going on when Licence was in the bedroom.

Some months after their marriage, Jane became pregnant. She complained that the Duke openly declared his disappointment and dissatisfaction at this, becoming increasingly ill-tempered. Her petition for custody stated that she had to endure 'continuous, ill-treatment, insults, and persecutions which seriously threatened her health and a miscarriage.' He continually expressed his regret at her pregnancy and made her extremely nervous, making remarks such as, 'Do you know that you may die in your confinement?' and 'Why, probably your child will be a cripple.'

The Duke's justification was, 'She knew that a man who suffers from my severe and painful illnesses, and being a cripple, absolutely unable to walk, or move from my chair, suffers from a corresponding infirmity of temper.'

Jane was suspicious of the nature of the Duke's intimate relationship with Licence and accused him of adultery with her. Jane had been sleeping separately from the Duke, and she confronted him in his bedroom declaring, 'I will not come back unless you send that woman away.' The Duke replied, 'That person is to remain there – there she is to remain,' pointing all the time at Licence's bed. Jane later wrote to the Duke: 'had I known the position Sarah Licence occupied in the establishment, never could I have married you – otherwise I'd cast my lot with you in preference to all the world.'

The Duke claimed that Jane, being his first cousin and a near relative of his first wife, knew what services Licence performed for him; that her services were an absolute necessity; and to require him to give them up would be an act of cruelty. The differences and anger between him and Jane, he said, were compounded by her temper and the unhappy suspicions that occupied her mind.

When their child was about five months old, the Duke gave Jane leave to go to Brighton for ten to fourteen days. He had admitted his errors to her brother and the clergyman and tried to pacify her, writing 'let me have the kiss of peace before you go'. Without consulting the Duke, she prolonged the visit and travelled to London to consult her solicitor. In a letter, the Duke intimated that he would seek an order of restitution of his conjugal rights. But that would have necessitated a finding about Jane's allegation of his adultery with Licence. Before she could respond, he had the child taken from her by force. She called it kidnapping.

Lady Katherine Stewart (Jane's mother) and the Marquess of Blandford (the Duke's son by his first marriage, who became the 7th Duke of Marlborough) attempted to mediate between them. The Marquess talked with Lady Katherine and Jane about the differences between the Duke and Duchess and the management of their children. The Duke had two children in his care from his previous marriage, aged 3 and 4, at the time when he married the Duchess. At first, she insisted on looking after them instead of their employing a governess, but that proved too much and so she relinquished care of them. It was arranged that the children would be the responsibility of the Duke, who would employ a governess, and the couple would reconcile. In the spirit of appeasement, Jane wrote to the Duke from a separate part of the palace: 'I wait for your permission to come and bid you goodnight'. The Duke had retired to bed early. He replied: '9pm 1 November 1852, I am in bed, and with this an aching heart and head.' He gave instructions that he would see her in the morning. She nevertheless tried his bedroom door. He thought that it was Lady Katherine coming to see him and because he was 'worried out and with an aching head', the door was bolted against her. Jane later accused the Duke of bolting the door to stop her coming in because he was in bed with Licence.

The Petition Hearing

On 7 August 1853, a Petition by the Duchess that the Duke return custody of her child to her was heard by the Vice Chancellor, Sir William Page Wood. Sir Richard Bethell, the Solicitor General, represented the

Duke and asked the Vice Chancellor to dismiss the petition saying, 'She is not legally justified to live apart from her husband, so she is not entitled to have the child.' The 1839 Act, he continued, gave the court authority, if the child was under 7 years, to deliver the child to the mother's custody. A previous court had said that it was in the best interests of such a young child to be in the uninterrupted custody of the mother, but her right must be grounded on legal grounds for separation. The object of the Act was to protect mothers who were legally separated from the tyranny of husbands who 'ill-used them'. It was envisaged that it would apply where a father who had deeply injured and sinned against a mother was withholding the child in order to pressure and compel her to return and in doing so condone his conduct.

The case here, the Solicitor General continued, was a mere, faint suspicion of adultery. The Duke had stated on oath that his wife's suspicions were entirely without foundation. 'Would anyone refuse to believe the oath of the Duke of Marlborough under such circumstances? … This is just the indignation of a woman of uncontrollable passion: *Furens quid Femina possit* (what a woman can do in a frenzy: Virgil). The wife should have brought materials before you that on the face of it would enable her to prove her right to a Decree of Separation. You will not be able to find upon these affidavits a reasonable doubt and proper cause for suspecting there has been improper intimacy between the Duke and Licence. The Duchess in her affidavit states: "I am willing to return to cohabitation if the Duke will at once and forever dismiss Sarah Licence from his house." Would a woman go back to an adulterer? The thing is preposterous.'

Vice Chancellor: 'I have known many such instances … That question (of adultery) can't be raised on the grounds of condonation if she returns to the Duke's home.'

Solicitor General: 'The Duke says that to dismiss Licence would be to admit guilt.'

Vice Chancellor: 'The Duke didn't need to take the child away from the mother. He has made these proceedings necessary.'

Solicitor General: 'The mother broke the contract to remain only for a fortnight. The Duchess made it necessary for him to take the child. The Duchess brought it upon herself by wilful refusal to abide by their agreement. However, the Duke is happy to restore the child to the Duchess without any stipulations or conditions. I invite Your Honour to make an

Order by consent of the Duke, that the child with its wetnurse shall be forthwith restored to the Duchess, to remain in her custody and care.'

Vice Chancellor: 'It is with the most unfeigned satisfaction that I hear such an arrangement has been come to – I sincerely hope it will lead to some further arrangement still more satisfactory to the parties.'

The Duke died in 1857. In his will, he left an allowance and furniture to Licence but nothing to his wife.

COMMENT

The publishers of the report of this case (123 pages) list the singular factors that make it essential reading: a lady applying to have entire custody of her child; who has withdrawn herself from his house; not by his desire; not in consequence of any conduct of his; and not refused access to the child.

The common law gave absolute rights over children to the father. A father who committed adultery and deserted his wife had the right to have custody of the children, even if they were in the care of his mistress. And the court had no authority to intervene or even grant her rights of access.

By the Custody of Children Act 1839, on the mother's application a court could order that a child under the age of 7 be delivered to and remain in the custody of the mother until reaching that age, and grant access to the father. The Act also gave the mother the right to apply for an Order for Access to a child aged over 7 who was in the sole custody or control of the father. No order could be made in favour of a mother against whom adultery had been established by judgement in an Action for Criminal Conversation by the husband or by the sentence of an Ecclesiastical Court.

Those who opposed the 1839 Act in parliamentary debates argued that if carried out to the letter and in the spirit in which it was framed, it would encourage and increase separations between married couples by 'removing the great check which the knowledge of the loss of the children imposed on the wife'. Losing the custody of their children was considered to be very effectual in checking separations. Instead of leaving her husband, the wife should make the best of her circumstances. The knowledge that a separation was attainable would only produce hatred and discord.

They replied to those in favour of the Act who said that it was for the benefit of the children, by stating that a separation of the parents was the greatest calamity that could happen to their children. 'If the mother was not well treated and she sought her child's welfare, let her endure to the end,' they argued. 'Let her bear all things for them … let her not, whatever her ability may be in mind or means, leave them an unhappy inheritance: that their parents couldn't live together. That their mother brought them up while their father was alive.'

Despite the change in the law and social policy, attitudes were slow to change. It was reported that no applications by mothers were successful between 1839, when the Act came into force, and 1848. The 1839 Act was repealed and replaced by the Custody of Infants Act 1873, which extended the relevant age from 7 to 16.

The 1839 Act did not require the mother to be legally separated from the father. The Solicitor General on behalf of the Duke had tried to persuade the Vice Chancellor to infer such a pre-condition on the basis that this had been assumed in the parliamentary debates on the bill. Although it was not necessary for the Duchess to allege the Duke's adultery and cruelty, she may have been advised that the court would see her in a more favourable light if she could portray herself as a woman who had been wronged, rather than a wife who had deserted her husband and young child. Having made those allegations, the Duke had to respond to them. The Duke was likely advised to consent to the order in favour of the Duchess because it was becoming apparent that the Vice Chancellor believed that a young child should be with its mother.

In 1819 the Duke's father, the 5th Duke, had separated from his wife, the Duchess. He then lived openly with his young mistress, with whom he had six children.

The Duke's home, Blenheim Palace, is a country house in Woodstock, Oxfordshire, which was completed in 1722. It was named after the Battle of Blenheim of 1704. It was home to the Churchill (later Spencer-Churchill) family and birthplace and ancestral home of Sir Winston Churchill. It was designated a UNESCO World Heritage Site in 1987.

Chapter 8

The Death of W.R.H. Carew and Trial of his Wife for Murder in HBM Court for Japan

1897

'Did she poison her husband? Or was it the elusive Annie Luke, his ex-fiancée?'

Edith May (Porch) Carew married Walter Raymond Hallowell Carew in St John's Church, Glastonbury, on 2 May 1889, the day after her twenty-first birthday. The *West of England Advertiser* reported that the town was gaily decorated with flags and bunting. The Porch family lived in Edgarley House, Glastonbury. Mr Porch was elected the Mayor of Glastonbury in 1879, 1892 and 1897. Walter's father was an army major. Walter had a reputation of being a womaniser.

Walter was in Government Service in the Straits Settlements, Malaysia, until he resigned in 1890 because of ill health. Edith Carew described her husband as 'always out of sorts'. She said he was invalided out because of nervous depression, due to the climate and over-work. According to his brother-in-law, he had almost died there because of his liver.

The Carews moved to Yokohama, where Walter was Secretary of the Yokohama United Club. They lived at 169 The Bluff from 15 April 1895, with their two young children Ben and Marjory and employed Mary Esther Jacob, a nursery governess, from 13 May 1895. As well as the parents and children, the family household included Rachel Greer (a Eurasian girl), Hanuya Asa (a Japanese girl), Ah Kwong (a Chinese boy), Kuroyanagi Junyu (a betto or housekeeper who lived in the betto's quarters), a coolie and a cook.

There were arguments between husband and wife over money. Edith was an heiress and received an income from her parents of £400 pa. However, the money was paid into Walter's bank account, and Edith resented having to rely upon Walter to pay her an allowance out of it.

The Inquest

Walter died on 22 October 1896 in the Royal Naval Hospital Yokohama, after an eight-day illness. An inquest opened on 1 November 1896. Mr Hall, Her Britannic Majesty's Consul in Yokohama, was the coroner and a coroner's jury of five men was sworn in. Mr Lichfield represented the Crown, while Mr Lowder and Mr Walford represented Edith Carew. Witnesses were called and cross-examined. Edith admitted buying bottles of Fowler's Solution of Arsenic immediately before and during Walter's illness but claimed that he had been in the habit of taking arsenic in small quantities for some time. She said that she had seen him take it once a day after breakfast and didn't know where he was getting it from. She obtained Fowler's Solution of Arsenic on 20 October at his request. He had said that he was in great pain and arsenic was the only thing that brought him relief. He had begged her to buy it, together with sugar of lead, and told her that if she didn't, he would obtain it by other means. She did not administer it to him. He always dosed himself, sometimes carelessly without measuring.

Friends of Walter testified about his arsenic habit. 'He told me once that when he was living in The Straits, he almost killed himself with an overdose of arsenic.' 'Some time ago at the urinal he said he was in the habit of taking more arsenic than an ordinary man could stand.' 'I was tiffining at the Club, where I generally take my tiffin, and I told him I had taken medicine containing strychnine when Walter said, "I take enough poison to kill six men – I am obliged to do so."' 'Arsenic (Walter said), I've taken tons of it.'

Edith claimed that Annie Luke, an ex-fiancée of Walter's in England, had mysteriously arrived in Yokohama at the time of Walter's illness and had written letters saying that she and Walter were 'twin spirits' and that they would soon be together in the afterlife. After his death, she claimed to have found a letter from Annie Luke, dated 13 October and addressed to Walter: 'I must see you … it makes me mad when I think of what I might have done for you … you can find me and help me if you will, for the sake of old times.' And his reply: 'I feel greatly distressed about you … I wish to and will help you … meet me this evening.' Walter went to the P & O Office in search of information about Miss Luke, who had not provided her address, but there was no trace of her coming to Yokohama.

On 29 October, a letter from 'A.L.' was received by the coroner: 'Woman is at the bottom of everything ... between us we have bamboozled the lot of you, the chemist, the doctor and last but not least that fool his wife ... I am going to join him, my twin soul ... I will exonerate that little fool from any share in helping us to meet each other ... we were divided in life, we were not in death ... I am taking good care to escape the lot of you and the law.'

On 1 November, a letter from 'A.L.' was received by Edith's barrister Mr Lowder: 'You will be acting on behalf of the wife of the man who was to me the world and more than the world. Dead men tell no tales; no, nor dead women either, for I am going to join him. Do you know what waiting means for eight long years. I have watched and waited, watched till I knew he would grow tired of her, that silly little fool, and then I came to him. What is the result? We, between us, electrify Japan ... I do not see why I should let a silly innocent woman be condemned for what she knows nothing about ... by the time you get this I shall be well on my way to join him, my twin soul.'

The expression 'twin souls' was in a book *A Romance of Two Worlds*, which was in the dining room of the Carews' house. Miss Jacob had access to it and was said to be a great reader of novels.

Dr Divers, Professor of Chemistry, Imperial University, conducted a chemical analysis of the deceased's stomach and other internal organs and found sufficient arsenic in his organs to account for the death. He concluded that the poison was given repeatedly and in increasing doses during Walter's illness, in the form of Fowler's Solution of Arsenic.

Hayashi Shiuchshiro, the assistant at Maryu's, a Japanese dispensary, claimed that he had sold Fowler's Solution of Arsenic for the order of Mrs Carew on 19, 20 and 21 October. On 19 October it was 1oz of Fowler's and 1oz of sugar of lead. He had asked what it was for, being a dangerous poison, and the woman collecting it had said it was for external use, with the sugar of lead. He couldn't recognise Mrs Carew in court as the customer, but the words *Mrs Carew* were on the order. A boy came on 20 October and bought a bedpan and 1oz more of Fowler's for Mrs Carew. Miss Jacob came on 21 October and bought 1oz of Fowler's again and sugar of lead. He admitted breaching the poisons regulations by selling Fowler's in such a large quantity.

Joseph Schadel of Normal dispensary said that he had sold Mrs Carew a half ounce of Fowler's Solution of Arsenic on 11 October, it having been prescribed by Dr Wheeler for her to use as a tonic to treat her malaria: 'a half ounce, 4 or 5 drops after meals.' That should have lasted her sixteen weeks, used medicinally. On 17 October he sold her another half ounce, refilling the original bottle. Then on 21 October, she said that she had dropped the bottle, broken it and spilled the contents, and he sold her another half ounce.

The coroner summed up to the jury. He questioned whether Walter had administered the arsenic to himself: a suicide or misadventure. But he quickly added that there was no evidence of suicide, and misadventure was improbable when at least thirty times the medicinal dose was required to be fatal. He asked: was the arsenic administered to him by somebody else? Annie Luke could not be located, and the coroner advised the jury to dismiss her as 'largely imaginary'. So, the suspicion fell on Edith Carew, having been in sole charge of nursing Walter day and night; having purchased several bottles of Fowler's Solution; and having neglected to tell Walter's physician, who cared for him during the illness that Walter was dosing himself with arsenic.

To Edith's dismay, the coroner concluded that the facts pointed to her having administered the fatal doses of arsenic to Walter and her intention must have been to kill him. The jury retired and then returned to give an open verdict: Walter had died from arsenic poisoning but there was no direct evidence as to who had fed the arsenic to him. Two local newspapers condemned the jury's verdict, accusing the jurors of violating their oaths by not accusing Mrs Carew.

The Pre-Trial Examination

On 11 November, Edith was charged with her husband's murder and given bail until the following day, when the pre-trial examination hearing began in Her Britannic Majesty's Court in Japan. The assistant judge, James Troup from the British Consulate, presided. Mr Litchfield, the Crown Prosecutor in Japan, presented the case for committal for trial. Mr Lowder and Mr Walford represented Edith.

Dr Wheeler, Walter's physician, said that he did not know Mr Carew was taking arsenic until the day before Walter's death. He asked for his statement at the inquest to be read.

> His condition worsened, and I decided to admit him to hospital. Mr Dunlop told me to speak to Miss Jacob, Mrs Carew's nursery nurse, and ask her about arsenic being taken. I asked Miss Jacob, 'What's this I hear about arsenic?' She replied,

> 'Mrs Carew told me that Mr Carew was suffering from stricture, and she asked me to get him a small bottle of arsenic and some sugar of lead.' I have never known arsenic and sugar of lead for stricture. I did prescribe a solution of arsenic for Mrs Carew on 10 October: Fowler's Solution half ounce 4 or 5 drops in water after meals.

Miss Jacob gave evidence that she lived at 2 The Bluff and was not involved with the care of Mr Carew. On 21 October Mrs Carew had written an order on a piece of paper for one bottle of Fowler's Solution of Arsenic and one bottle of sugar of lead. When Miss Jacob was served, the assistant at Maryu's had asked her why we 'bought so plenty deadly poison'. He told her that some had been bought the day before and she should warn Mrs Carew to be careful how she used it. Then, on Mrs Carew's instructions, she went to Normal, a foreign dispensary, where she was given a bottle of arsenic solution wrapped in paper by Mr Schedel. Miss Jacob gave the three bottles to Mrs Carew. She told Mrs Carew's brother, Mr Porch, what the assistant had said. Mr Porch's only reaction was to call the assistant 'impertinent'. She also told her friend Miss Christoffel, the nursery governess to Mr Dunlop, about the arsenic.

On the night of Mr Carew's death, Mrs Carew had denied giving Miss Jacob the paper with the order on 21 October. So, on 23 October Miss Jacob went back to Maryu's to retrieve it. The dispensary couldn't find it but gave her instead a paper from Mrs Carew dated 20 October requesting a bed pan and one bottle of Fowler's Solution of Arsenic.

Miss Jacob said that in the evening of 21 October, Mrs Carew asked her to take a glass of brandy and soda with cocaine to Mr Carew. He wouldn't drink it and told Miss Jacob that he'd had 'a whole chemist's shop' that day.

Mr Litchfield addressed the judge. 'On this evidence I ask for the committal of the accused for trial before a jury. The evidence is essentially, as in most cases of this kind, circumstantial. I submit there is a prima facie case for committal for trial. The evidence shows arsenic, or some other poison was the cause of death. It shows arsenic in considerable quantities was introduced into the home shortly before his death. Part of that arsenic was traced directly to the hands of Mrs Carew. It was shown that Mrs Carew had the chief duty of nursing the deceased during the time of his illness.'

Mrs Carew was committed for trial. Mr Lowder did not apply for bail. Mr Carew was buried in the Yokohama Foreign General Cemetery, where his grave carries the surprising (in the circumstances) inscription: 'Walter Raymond Hallowell Carew, in loving memory of my husband who died October 22, 1896, aged 43 years.'

The Jury Trial

The jury trial opened on 5 January 1897 in Her Britannic Majesty's (HBM's) Court for Japan. Judge Mowat presided, accompanied by Mr Troup, Assistant Judge. Five jurors were sworn in. Mr Litchfield, HBM's Crown Prosecutor in Japan, and Mr Wilkinson, HBM's Crown Advocate for China, represented the Crown. Mr Lowder represented Mrs Carew.

Mr Wilkinson opened the case for the Crown. Arsenic is sometimes taken as a solution, he explained, and the most usual form is Fowler's Solution of Arsenic. One ounce of Fowler's contained four grains of white arsenic. The medicinal dose of white arsenic was 1/12 grain to 1/60 grain, three times daily. A 1oz bottle of Fowler's would last between sixteen (1/12 grain) and eighty (1/60 grain) days, depending on the dose. A fatal dose of white arsenic was two grains, equivalent to between twenty-four (1/12 grain) and 120 (1/60 grain) medicinal doses.

The post-mortem by Dr Todd and Dr May found no evidence of organic disease. They both concluded that death was from arsenic poisoning. The stomach and intestines had been sent to Dr Divers for chemical examination, where one-sixth grain of solid arsenic was found in the liver whilst traces of arsenic were found elsewhere. Finding arsenic in the liver meant that it had been absorbed into the system and because of that and expulsion from the body, a much larger quantity must have been administered originally for one-sixth grain to have remained. Mr Carew's symptoms during his illness from 15 to 22 October suggested that the arsenic was administered in repeated doses, as his condition kept improving then worsening. The sugar of lead would have checked the bleeding from the damage caused by the poison.

Miss Jacob thought that her family should be writing to her, but she had not received any letters. Seeing torn-up letters in Mrs Carew's waste basket, she took them out, thinking that Mrs Carew might be intercepting mail sent to her. Instead, she found that they were letters from a Mr Dickinson to Mrs Carew. She passed them to her friend Miss Christoffel, who sewed them together. The letters were of the nature that no modest married woman should have accepted from a man: 'My poor darling … If you were a free woman, I would ask you to come to me … When I first Knew you, something of a passion for you would come over me … now you love me … and now too I love you … I love you utterly my dear … Love you, I think of you always, I cannot give you up now.'

Mr Wilkinson called the Crown's witnesses. Dr Wheeler said that on the evening of 22 October he had received an anonymous note: 'Maryu's three bottles of arsenic.' He was told that the letter came from 6 The Bluff, Mr Dunlop's home. The envelope, but not the note, was in Mr Dunlop's handwriting. Mr Dickinson said how Mrs Carew had told him that she was exceedingly unhappy and that her husband had ill-treated her and grown tired of her. She said that she was considering divorce. 'I know it now to be all untrue (about the ill-treatment). When I wrote to her, I believed it.'

Miss Christoffel, the nurse to Mr Dunlop's children, said that she received four letters in fragments from Miss Jacob and stitched them together. She gave them to Miss Jacob, who gave them back to her after Mr Carew's death. She then passed them on to Mr Litchfield, Crown Prosecutor.

The prosecution wished to establish who had written the anonymous 'A.L.' letters. They suspected that Mrs Carew had. They called Benjamin Mason as a witness. He stated that he had been employed for seven years in the British Postal Telegraph Department in England and for sixteen years in Japan in the British and Japanese Telegraph Department. For many years he had made a private study of peculiarities in handwriting. He had been chess editor of the *Japan Mail*, where he received correct solutions to chess problems that were published weekly. The questioning was:

Lowder:	'You received correct solutions from an individual signing himself Scacchi – the Italian word.'
Mason:	'Yes.'
Lowder:	'You were acquainted with my handwriting, and you thought I was the solver of the problems.'
Mason:	'I did.'
Lowder:	'Who was it?'
	Mason didn't answer.
Wilkinson:	'It was His Lordship, sitting on the bench.'
His Lordship:	'I hold his evidence may be received.'

Mr Mason was shown the letters in the 'A.L.' series and letters written by Mrs Carew. He stated that he recognised the characteristics and peculiarities of Mrs Carew's handwriting throughout the 'A.L.' letters. He compared the watermarks in the paper used for the 'A.L.' letters and Mrs Carew's letters and said that they were similar and he concluded that the same paper had been used in both sets of letters.

Mr Mason was shown a letter written to Sir Ernest Satow, British Minister to Japan, and signed 'A.L. Price': 'Dear Sir, I wish to call your attention to the very scandalous way in which our consul Mr Hall has conducted the inquest … Had he any right to sum up in face of evidence produced as he has done? Yours faithfully.' He described the handwriting on the letter as similar to Mrs Carew's.

The judge decided, after some contradictory evidence, that the six bottles of Fowler's Solution of Arsenic containing a total of eighteen grains of white arsenic (nine times a fatal dose) had been purchased as follows:

> 11 October ½oz from Normal Pharmacy (Mr Schedel) bought by Mrs Carew.
>
> 17 October ½oz from Normal Pharmacy (Mr Schedel) bought by Mrs Carew (bottle refilled).
>
> 20 October morning 1oz from Maruya's on Mrs Carew's order.
>
> 20 October evening 1oz from Maruya's on Mrs Carew's order.
>
> 21 October morning ½oz from Normal Pharmacy (Mr Schedel) by Mrs Carew (who said it was to replace a bottle that had broken, and the contents had spilled).
>
> 21 October evening 1oz from Maruya's bought for Mrs Carew by Miss Jacob.

During the course of the jury trial, as an extremely unorthodox move, Mr Lowder, who was of course the jury trial defence barrister, laid a charge against Miss Jacob in HBM's court on 10 January 1897 for the murder of Mr Carew. Miss Jacob was arrested on a warrant, charged with Mr Carew's murder, and appeared in court for a preliminary examination.

Mr Lowder told Jacob's pre-trial examination judge: 'I appear, Your Honour, in person, not professionally, but simply as a member of this community who considers it to be his duty to prefer this charge.' When the court attempted to fix hearing dates for the pre-trial examination of Miss Jacob, Mr Lowder explained his diary problem: 'I am busily occupied, as Your Honour is aware, in the defence of Mrs Carew (in the jury trial), whose case goes from day-to-day.'

Mr Lowder prosecuted the pre-trial examination of Miss Jacob as he was the complainant. He called Mrs Carew to give evidence and maintained that Miss Jacob was the author of the 'A.L' letters. He stated that he would not just rely on the letters but would have other incriminating evidence against Miss Jacob. At one point, Mr Lowder was sworn and entered the witness box himself to give evidence of what he knew about a box and the letters it contained.

Mr Lowder asked the judge to send Miss Jacob for trial before a jury. Mr Sidmore, the only American law practitioner in Yokohama at the time, represented Miss Jacob and argued that Mr Lowder had failed to show conclusively that Miss Jacob had written the A.L. letters and was the self-confessed murderer of Mr Carew. Miss Jacob's family was known to Mrs Carew's family, as they lived near each other, and that was how she became the Carews' nurse governess.

Miss Jacob fell ill with a nervous condition. The examination was adjourned to 12 January, then to 25 January and she was granted bail.

Meanwhile, in the jury trial of Mrs Carew, Mr Lowder presented the defence case. He reminded the jury that the prosecution case was that Mr Carew had died of Fowler's Solution of Arsenic administered by Mrs Carew. Yet there was no absolute proof that Mr Carew died of arsenic poisoning and 'not one atom' of proof that Mrs Carew had administered arsenic to him 'in any shape or form'. There were three poisons found in his body: white arsenic in solid form, Fowler's Solution of Arsenic, and sugar of lead. It was impossible to say which of those had caused his death. White arsenic in solid form was found at the post-mortem, and it was not possible to say what larger quantity of white arsenic he had originally consumed. He added that there was no evidence of Mrs Carew administering white arsenic in solid form to her husband.

Mr Lowder told the jury that Mr Carew had been in the habit of consuming arsenic since 1880. He took Fowler's in very large doses without measuring it. Mrs Carew sent for the Fowler's for medicinal use by Mr Carew, not to kill him. She was just being loyal to him when she didn't disclose his bad habit to Dr Wheeler.

He said that he attached little value to Mr Mason's handwriting analysis and asked the jury to accept that Mrs Carew was not the author of the 'A.L.' letters.

He called Dr Eldridge as a witness. The doctor said that Mr Carew's symptoms clearly indicated an irritant poisoning, but not necessarily arsenic. Another cause could be poisonous food, such as oysters or fish. Dr Baelz agreed that death by Fowler's Solution of Arsenic alone was very rare. He suggested that white arsenic in the solid form must have contributed to the death. Dr Munro agreed with Dr Eldridge that the symptoms did not exclude an irritant other than arsenic. Death could have been from a single dose of white arsenic. In cross-examination he conceded that none of the evidence was inconsistent with poisoning by either Fowler's Solution of Arsenic, or solid white arsenic, or sugar of lead.

A member of Mr Carew's club said that whilst playing billiards together, Mr Carew kept saying, at least twenty-five times, *Le moment est arrive on il fait fair la chose* (The time has come where the thing must be done).

Mr Wilkinson made his closing speech to the jury. He said that the medical evidence showed that Mr Carew's symptoms, appearances and results were all consistent with arsenic poisoning as the cause of death. He did not agree with the defence's argument that if the jury found that death was caused by the combined effects of solid white arsenic and lead (not administered by her) and Fowler's Solution of Arsenic (administered by her), then they must acquit as they were unable to say that death was caused solely by the poison that she had administered. If they found that the lead or the solid white arsenic may have contributed, but the Fowler's Solution also contributed to the death and was administered by her with the intention to kill, then they must find her guilty of murder. He quoted authorities from *Archbold*: 'If you believe that the prisoner administered antimony with the intention of killing, and that death from a natural cause was thus accelerated, that was murder and if violence hastened the death, it would be murder if the death was intended, otherwise a weakly or diseased person could never be murdered.'

Mr Wilkinson declared that there was never an Annie Luke. Mrs Carew wrote the 'A.L' letters when she was under suspicion for Mr Carew's death to cast the suspicion on 'Annie Luke' instead. Only Mr and Mrs Carew knew the name of 'Annie Luke'. At the time that the letters were written, Miss Jacob was not under suspicion and had no need to write them. Mrs Carew was also calling for sympathy from Mr Dickinson by blackening the character of her husband to him, falsely representing him as guilty of acts that would stamp him as a brute and a villain.

The judge summed up to the jury. He told them that the prosecution must prove that the Fowler's solution of Arsenic had contributed to Mr Carew's death and that the accused had administered the arsenic to him with intent to kill. There was no evidence of or motive for suicide.

The judge said that the accused had procured at least 3oz of Fowler's between 17 and 22 October. The prosecution claimed that it was 4oz. On 21 October, the purchases were at two different pharmacies because the foreign dispensary, Normal, would not have allowed more than ½oz to have been bought, so the larger quantity was bought at the native dispensary, Maryu's.

The judge reminded the jury that Mrs Carew had explained why she had bought such a large quantity of Fowler's: Mr Carew was in the habit of consuming arsenic and had begged her for more; he would use it without measuring; she didn't think that it would do any harm. But apart from what she said, the only evidence was of his use of arsenic in the past ('a year ago' ... 'some years ago' ... 'once when living in The Straits' ... 'some time ago' ... 'about one year ago').

The jury retired at 2.35pm and returned twenty-five minutes later. They found Mrs Carew guilty of her husband's murder.

The judge put on his black cap. 'The sentence is that you, Edith May Hallowell Carew be taken forthwith from the place where you stand to the British Consular Gaol, Yokohama, and therein interned, and that on a date to be hereinafter appointed by the proper authority you be taken to a place of execution, and then be hanged by the neck until you are dead and that your body is afterwards taken down and interred in the precincts of the said prison and may God deliver your soul.'

Her conviction and sentence was reported in the *New York Times* and regional newspapers throughout the UK. The *West of England Advertiser* wrote: 'The news of the result of the trial ... caused a profound sensation *(in Glastonbury)* and the deepest sympathy is felt with the Mayor and Mrs Porch ... The tragic affair has cast a gloom over the place and has brought distress and unconsolable sorrow on the family, who are held in the highest esteem in the country. Soon after it became known that Mrs Carew was involved in a serious charge, the Mayor and Mrs Porch sought retirement at Bournemouth.'

The charge against Miss Jacob was eventually withdrawn by Mr Lowder on 5 February following the conviction of Mrs Carew by the jury. Mr Sidmore told the judge: 'This charge was brought hastily, inconsiderately and heartlessly and had utterly failed, and it has been withdrawn coldly, formally and without one word of regret. This young girl has been subjected to mental and physical torture.'

Sir Ernest Mason Satow was a British diplomat, and Japanologist. He was the British Minister to Japan from 1895 to 1900. He commuted Mrs Carew's sentence of death to life imprisonment following a proclamation by the Japanese Emperor on 31 January that all Japanese subjects under sentence of death should have their death sentence remitted. Mrs Carew was transferred to Hong Kong Prison and then shipped to England in 1897. She served thirteen years in Aylesbury Prison before her release. She died aged 90 in Pembrokeshire, South Wales, where she lived with her daughter.

COMMENT

The *Japan Gazette* wrote at length about the arrest of Miss Jacob (published as a book, twenty-eight pages) and the inquest and trial (published as a book, 342 pages). The *Japan Gazette* also printed correspondence and comment about the proceedings. The *Japan Gazette* was published by Mr Black in English every evening from 1867. He also published a fortnightly summary for overseas readers. The newspaper ended publication when the Tokyo-Yokohama earthquake struck the metropolitan area in 1923. A book about the trial, *Murder on the Bluff*, has been written by Molly Whittington-Egan.

A pre-trial examination, better known as a committal hearing, was abolished in England and Wales for serious crimes in 2001. The purpose of the hearing was to ensure that there was sufficient evidence against the accused for a trial to take place. They were abolished because of the inevitable time wasting and stress caused to witnesses from the duplication of evidence. In this case, the evidence was heard three times: the inquest; the pre-trial examination; and the trial. The inquest became part of the murder investigation. In contemporary times, it is likely that there would be a murder investigation followed by a criminal trial. The inquest would be opened and adjourned until the trial had established cause of death and liability.

An accusation of a lack of independence and objectivity can be levelled at Mrs Carew's defence barrister, Mr Lowder. Whilst defending Mrs Carew, he left the advocates' bench for the witness box, where he gave sworn evidence on behalf of his client which included: 'from that time I have known them well (the Victim and the accused) – I may say intimately – I have never known them to be on any but the most affectionate terms'. In addition, he made a complaint of murder against Miss Jacob, whom he accused of being the real killer, and prosecuted her privately in court whilst at the same time defending Mrs Carew before a jury for the same crime.

The modern rule is that advocates can give evidence in their own cases only if what they have to say is essential to their case and uncontroversial.

Mr Carew died from arsenic poisoning on 22 October 1896. The inquest was held just over a week later and lasted five days. The committal hearing for Mrs Carew took place a week after that on 12 November and her jury trial followed on 5 January 1897. What would have taken at least eighteen months in contemporary times was completed within three months.

In 1896, there was a substantial British community in Yokohama, including merchants, diplomats, and expats. The Bluff is a historic district of Yokohama where foreigners lived in the nineteenth and early twentieth centuries. Many of their elegant houses were destroyed by the Great Kanto Earthquake of 1923. Yokohama was one of several Treaty ports where foreigners were allowed to trade after Japan reopened to the world in 1854. The city was a hub for trade. In the Carews' household, the betto was the housekeeper and the coolie was a low-wage unskilled labourer.

The British maintained a consulate in Yokohama. The former British consulate building was reconstructed after the Great Tokyo Earthquake of 1923. The Anglo-Japanese Treaty of Amity and Commerce of 1858 established British extra-territoriality between 1859 and 1899 and British consular officials exercised extra-territorial jurisdiction over British subjects in the area. Japan did not have a modern type of legal system, and the British had little understanding of how Japanese law operated. The Japanese did not want to be involved in disputes between foreigners. There was a system of consular courts in Japan with full-time judges. James Troup was Consul General in Yokohama (1896–98).

The British Court for Japan was established in Yokohama, in the prefecture of Kanagawa, in 1879. Between 1879 and 1900 the court had four full-time judges, including Robert Anderson Mowat (1891–97). A number of consular officials also sat as acting judge when the judge was on leave or unavailable, including John Carey Hall, British Consul-General in Kobe (1896–89) and Yokohama (1902–14). The Court for Japan heard appeals from the consular courts. Appeals from the Court for Japan were heard by the Chief Justice of the Supreme Court in Shanghai.

'At this point the court adjourned for tiffin,' occurs frequently in the report of the trial. The word is derived from 'tiffing', English slang for taking a little drink. In the British Raj in India, it meant a mid-afternoon tea. In South Asia, it came to mean a breakfast, or a home-cooked meal carried in a tiffin box and containing a midday lunch or light mid-afternoon meal, like a Bento Box.

Scacchi is an Italian name for a game of chess for two, played with thirty-two pieces on a board with sixty-four squares.

Thomas Fowler (1736–1801) published a study in 1786 on the effectiveness of his solution of 1 per cent potassium arsenite. Originally prescribed as an alternative to quinine for treating malaria, it became known as Fowler's Solution of Arsenic. By the 1880s it was used for a variety of ailments. Because of its toxicity and side effects, its use declined in the early 1900s.

In a small expat community there was always a risk that those involved in court proceedings would either know or know of each other socially. A good example is Mr Mason, who gave evidence about handwriting for the prosecution, also setting the chess problems in the *Japan Mail*, and Judge Mowat sending in anonymous entries. Mr Lowder, who represented Mrs Carew, first met Mr and Mrs Carew in 1890, when they boarded a ship in Singapore that he was on, returning to Japan.

Questions arise over the independence of the judicial officers. The British Consul was the coroner. The assistant judge was also from the British Consulate. The post-mortem doctors, Mr Todd and Mr May, were both surgeons at the Royal Naval Hospital.

In England and Wales, the Crown Prosecution Service can take over a private prosecution such as Mr Lowder's and decide to discontinue it if it is not in the public interest.

There was a jury pool of twenty-two men. Four were medically unfit; two were deaf; two had left Yokohama; four didn't answer to the jury summons and were fined $50: and five were challenged by the advocates. This left a panel of five jurors. In England and Wales, a criminal trial has required twelve jurors since the twelfth century.

Chapter 9

Scrope-Ferrers v Apthorp

A Breach of Promise of Marriage Case

1906

Married life would be a misery, 'a cat and dog's life'

Commissioned in 1875 and retired from the army in 1902, Major Dudley Richard Apthorp, late of the 19th Hussars, was visited in June 1903 by Miss Sydney Scrope-Ferrers, a lady whom he had met only once before in 1897. Dudley spent ten weeks in her company, proposed marriage, and they became engaged. He very soon discovered from things she said that she was a 'bad woman' in every respect, and he no longer wished to marry her. On 23 August he wrote her a letter saying that he strongly objected to her continually asking him for money and that it was unpardonable for her to run up bills without his agreement and that he desired their engagement to end.

His letter crossed a letter from Sydney. Perhaps sensing his coolness towards her of late, she wrote 'I am not going to be played fast and loose with; you are engaged to be married to me, and I am going to marry you, and as I have no father and my brother is away … I shall have to consult a lawyer and ask him what I ought to do.' Sydney then wrote a second letter, replying to Dudley's letter and trying to make amends regarding his complaints: 'I am so sorry you have misunderstood me, dear; believe me for your own sake as well as for mine, I am anxious to please you, and that any irritation you may feel as regards the expenditure has been owing to the fact that we never talked things over satisfactorily.'

Dudley wrote back that there was no mistake, and he meant every word that he had written. Sydney replied, complaining that articles of clothing she had ordered had not been delivered and that he must send a cheque for £50 to Mr Russell to pay for them. When Dudley refused, she wrote to him that he was being dishonourable, dreadfully mean, and didn't know what clothes cost; that she had not broken off their engagement, and he as the man could not do so. At the end of August, Dudley received a writ alleging breach of promise of marriage and claiming £3,000 damages for a broken heart.

Dudley's solicitor characterised Sydney as an adventuress whose whole object had been to extract money from him. He told Dudley that despite the undeniable breach, he had a strong defence against the damages claim because of the shortness of the engagement and lack of affection between them. Sydney's solicitor proposed a settlement, describing it as an opportunity for Dudley to repent: Dudley pays her £500 and settles the outstanding bills. He described Dudley as 'peculiar' and as having exhibited a low standard of decency. Dudley thought the letter impertinent and refused to settle. On 11 March 1904, the case was heard before the Lord Chief Justice and a special jury.

The Breach of Promise Hearing

Sydney's barrister told the court that she was 31 years old and the daughter of the late Mr George Ferrers, a barrister. She and her mother were now poor, and Sydney had pawned some of her jewellery to provide for them both; whereas Dudley, a retired major, was a man of substantial means who expected his income to double on the death of his mother. On their acquaintance becoming more intimate, he had proposed to her on 7 July 1903, and they would walk together daily in Kensington Gardens. A wedding date of 22 August had been set. He had enjoyed life in India and planned that after a honeymoon in England they would return to India for a time and travel around there.

Regarding the trousseau, he had told her to buy what she needed as his 'intended' and send the bills to him. An estimate of £100 was mentioned. He also agreed to redeem her pawned jewellery. She ordered a modest number of dresses, gowns, and other wearing apparel costing £107. The only reason that she could think of for his breaking off the engagement was that he was disgusted that marriage was so expensive.

The Lord Chief Justice commented on a very affectionate letter to her from Dudley dated 17 August that began 'My dearest Sydney'. Sydney told the court that there was no mention then of his breaking off the engagement, or of displeasure about what she had been spending. Sydney's mother said that Dudley had asked for the engagement to remain secret, and she was the only person he had told about it. The Lord Chief Justice took an interest in the bills: Delroy's bill of £6 13s 6d for boots; Mr Russell's bill of £50 for ladies' apparel; and Messrs Ludlam & Co.'s bill of £12 10s 3d for some shirts and other things.

Dudley's barrister reminded the jury of the facts beyond dispute: that they became engaged; that he broke the engagement off; that they had not been engaged for very long – so that it wasn't possible to say that he had taken a large slice out of her life and ruined her prospects for years as all the events were crowded into a period of three months; and her reputation was protected by the engagement having been kept secret. He claimed that she had actually lost little because of the lack of affection on either part. He had concluded from her behaviour and the bills that she had run up that married life would be a misery, a 'cat and dog' life. 'A very small sum would suffice to meet the justice of the case,' he concluded.

Sydney's barrister told the jury how Dudley had broken off the engagement without any excuse or justification, as though it was nothing. It would take a very large sum of money to represent the difference between the position that she was placed in now, including the humiliation of bringing the case against him and disclosing private matters, and the position in which he had promised to place her and treat her as a man should treat the woman whom he loves.

The Lord Chief Justice reminded the jury that statements made by the opposing barristers were not evidence; and that the defendant had elected not to give evidence to contradict what she said, so, they must rely upon her evidence, including what she had denied in cross-examination, to reach their decision. 'The young lady is the daughter of a barrister and would be a credit to anybody as a wife … we do not know why he really broke it off … the excuse he has given is a trumpery excuse … she has sworn to you that she told him what she was going to buy. She thought it would be £100. She spent £107. You are men of the world. Of course, it is not an extravagant figure … the defendant is not entitled to say that there was no affection. Affectionate letters, which are not meant to be in the public gaze ought not to be read in court … it is not pleasant for people who are in the position of these people, a major in the army and a barrister's daughter. There was correspondence, there had been daily meetings, they had been in the relation of lovers for something like 6 weeks. Then he broke it off. She is entitled to damages and ladies who have contracts made with them should be protected.'

The jury found in Sydney's favour and ordered Dudley to pay her £1,350. Dudley complained that up to the last moment he had thought that his barrister was going to put him in the witness box, so that he could contradict her lies. He claimed that as a result, the case was undefended and only one side of the story had been heard.

The press reported the breach of promise action and as a result, on 22 March 1904, Dudley received a letter inviting him to meet Miss Cogswell. She said that she had divorced Edgar Francis Rutter in 1902 because of his intimacy with Miss Scrope-Ferrers, who had a child; that Gladys Scrope-Ferrers was currently living with Mr Rutter at 44 Leamington Road Villas, Bayswater; and they were now married. Miss Ferrers had been married before, and Mr Rutter was named as co-respondent in her divorce in 1902. Miss Cogswell described Miss Ferrers, and the description exactly matched that of Sydney Scrope-Ferrers.

Dudley employed an enquiry agent, Arthur Bartlett Fletcher, who went to the Registry Office in Poland Street to look at the marriage certificate of Gladys Mowbray Heaton and Edgar Francis Rutter. The signature of Miss Heaton matched that of Sydney on her letters to Dudley. Dudley swore an affidavit in the Court of Appeal that Sydney was a married woman when she brought the breach of promise case. He applied for the verdict and judgement in that case to be set aside and for a re-hearing of the trial and stay of execution of the judgement in her favour. The Lord Chief Justice postponed the payment of damages to Sydney on Dudley's sister acting as security for the full amount. Dudley transferred all his stocks and shares to his sister to cover it.

On 4 June 1904, at the request of his enquiry agent, Dudley travelled to Horsham. Edith Lena Barnard (the first Mrs Rutter) accompanied him. She said that the woman she knew as Gladys Ferrers was staying at a farm outside Horsham. They drove past the farm and Dudley recognised Sydney at an open window. Dudley returned to London and swore an information at Bow Street Police Court, supported by a sworn statement that Edith had identified Sydney as the current wife of Edgar Rutter.

Martha Davis made a sworn statement that from January 1903 until May 1904 she was employed as a domestic servant by a Mrs Ferrers, at 44 Leamington Road Villas, Bayswater. Also living in the house were Miss Sydney Scrope-Ferrers and Edgar Francis Rutter, who passed themselves off as husband and wife and occupied the same bedroom. Sydney had brought several gentlemen to the house, including Dudley, who visited her there four times during July and August 1903. Sydney's mother had told Martha that Dudley was rich, and Martha was to be silent about Sydney's 'goings on' as Sydney would bring a breach of promise action against him and they would all be well paid.

Mr Fletcher swore an affidavit that he knew Edgar Francis Rutter as an associate of a gang called the Monson Mob, connected to the Ardlamont Mystery. He swore that on 6 June 1904 he went to Park Farm, Horsham, with Edith Rutter, who identified Sydney Scrope-Ferrers as the wife of Edgar Rutter and that Dudley confirmed she was also the plaintiff in the breach case.

The Appeal

On 29 July, the Court of Appeal heard Dudley's application: that the plaintiff was a married woman at the time that she brought the action. At 3.45pm, Dudley's barrister showed him five affidavits on behalf of Sydney, which had just been handed to him. Mrs Ferrers swore that she had three daughters and that Gladys, not Sydney, was married to Mr Rutter; Mr Rutter swore that he was married to Gladys, not Sydney; Sydney swore that Dudley's affidavits from Edith Rutter, Mr Fletcher and Martha Adams were all false.

Giving up, Dudley's barrister told him, 'I tell you sir, you are mad; I intend to save you from making a fool of yourself.' Dudley retorted that Sydney's witnesses were all telling lies and he wanted the appeal to go ahead. The *Morning Post* reported the next morning that his appeal had been 'snuffed out' in nine minutes. For the application to have succeeded, he needed to prove to the court that the new facts he was eliciting were capable of being conclusive in support of it. Instead, his barrister had told the court that he would not take up the court's time as the new facts were not conclusive enough. The Master of the Rolls had thanked the barrister for his very frank statement and refused to interfere with the breach of promise verdict or order a new trial. Dudley complained that Sydney's affidavits had been presented late in the day and that his barrister and his solicitor had given him away. His solicitor was later arrested over a fraudulent money transaction and served time in Wandsworth Prison.

On 17 August 1904, Dudley read in the newspapers about Edgar Francis Rutter's arrest for swindling a victim out of £50. He had kept the money as commission for organising a loan for a Royal Artillery captain that was never advanced. On 16 November, his prison sentence was reported: six months' hard labour. Described by reporters as 'a smooth tongued, well dressed, and well-educated adventurer', he was also said to be a bankrupt who owed money to all the local tradespeople.

Dudley had no funds, having transferred all his capital to his sister, partly to try and avoid having to pay Sydney. He was made bankrupt when Sydney chased the money and she petitioned Mr Salaman, Dudley's trustee in the bankruptcy proceedings, for her £1,350. In the bankruptcy court, Martha Davis had identified Sydney as the woman who lived with Mr Rutter in 44 Leamington Road Villas in 1903. Mr Salaman instructed Dudley to transfer the money back from his sister so that he could pay Sydney, but Dudley refused. Mr Salaman asked Dudley about the value of the reversionary interest in his grandfather's will and threatened to sell it on the open market. By now, Dudley was on his seventh solicitor, Mr Jolly, who applied to the Bankruptcy Registrar to stop Mr Salaman from paying Sydney. But a client of an associate of Mr Salaman had already loaned the money to Sydney on her executing a charge on the judgement in his favour. The reversionary interest was sold at public auction to a nominee of Dudley's for £4,040, paid for by a loan to Dudley of £5,000. Mr Salaman paid Sydney the sum ordered by the court.

The Summons for Perjury

The *Daily Telegraph* reported Dudley's appearance at Bow Street Police Court on 2 August 1904, where he took out a summons against Sydney for perjury. Dudley's barrister told the magistrate that the evidence that Sydney had given in the breach of promise action was false. She had described herself as a spinster, but she was married. She had referred to her 'late' father, but he was alive, a messenger in the Lord Chief Justice's Office. He asked for an adjournment so that they could collect evidence in support. The magistrate would only consider a lie about her marital status as a ground for committing the case for trial and granted an adjournment when told that evidence would be forthcoming. At the adjourned hearing, the first Mrs Rutter gave evidence about identifying Sydney as the woman who used to 'go with' Mr Rutter and also the plaintiff in the breach of promise case. Martha, whom Dudley believed was being kept out of the way, could not be found. The magistrate was not impressed by Dudley's case and dismissed the summons.

Dudley applied at the Old Bailey for a voluntary indictment alleging perjury by Sydney. The Recorder would not grant an adjournment for the case to be built and advised the Grand Jury to throw out the bill due to the lack of evidence, which they did. About one week later, Sydney commenced an action against Dudley for malicious prosecution. She did not follow up with a statement of claim, and the action was dismissed.

Dudley had one last recorded attempt to prove that Sydney had lied. He applied for a summons in Bow Street Police Court on 27 March 1906. He was armed with affidavits: a hotel night porter who witnessed Mr Rutter sharing a hotel room with a lady who was said to be his wife and whom the porter identified as Sydney; a second witness to the identification of Sydney by the night porter; an employee of Sydney's mother whom Sydney had told that she wanted the major's money, not the man, and that she was married to Mr Rutter with three children. The summons was refused.

COMMENT

Dudley Apthorp wrote the report of the trial himself (110 pages). He quoted Longfellow: 'Man is unjust, but God is just; and finally, justice triumphs.' If only justice had triumphed for Dudley. He prefaced the book, 'It must be apparent to all those who read the conduct of this case that there has been a grave miscarriage of justice … I have made up my mind to publish an account of this, and I call upon those who can give information that will assist me, to put themselves in communication with my friend and solicitor, Mr Edwin Burnett, 61 and 62 Chancery Lane, London EC.'

If a barrister is unable to follow their client's instructions, they should withdraw from the case. They should not act in the manner of Dudley's barrister and surprise their client by telling the judge that they wouldn't waste the court's time with a hopeless appeal.

For sale in 2025 by a bookseller was a page of headed notepaper from 'Edgar Francis' (alias Edgar Francis Rutter), Financial agent, 2 Marlborough Mansions, Victoria Street, London SW 27th January 1894. 'Madam, if you ever require an immediate loan from a genuine private service will you favour me with a call or a letter? The capital can remain as long as interest at £5 per cent per annum is paid. Temporary advances in a few hours – no preliminary fees or charge of any sort. Signed: E. Francis.' Edgar Francis Rutter is listed at that address in 1893.

The Ardlamont Mystery, known also as the Monson case, was the alleged murder of Windsor Dudley Cecil Hambrough, aged 20, by Alfred John Monson on the Ardlamont Estate in Argyll. Monson had hired the estate for the shooting season and taken Hamborough, whom he was tutoring. Hamborough had been having an affair with Monson's wife. Hamborough had taken out two life insurance policies on 4 August 1883 worth £20,000, naming Monson's wife and arranged by a broker friend of Monson's. Six days later, Monson took Hamborough and a third man, Edward Scott (or Edward Sweeney or Ted Davis), out shooting. Hamborough was shot through the head and Monson claimed that Hamborough had accidentally shot himself. The trial resulted in a 'not proven' verdict, despite expert evidence that the shot could not have been self-inflicted. Scott was on the run and not tried.

Relative values: the £3,000 that Sydney wanted for her broken heart would be the equivalent of £317,254 in 2026. The jury awarded her £1,350, the equivalent of £142,764 in 2026. Dudley should have bitten his lip, swallowed his pride and settled for the £500 (plus bills) that Sydney offered to accept, £52,875 in 2026.

Chapter 10

The Beattie Case

Murdered his Wife

1911

'He went automobiling with Louise and came back with her dead, resting on his arm'

Henry Clay Beattie Junior, the son of a prominent businessman in Richmond, Virginia, was accused of murdering his wife, Louise Wellford Owen, whilst in a relationship with 'the other woman', Beulah Binford.

In July 1907 Henry, then aged 23, became intimate with Beulah, then just turned 13. He paid for her to go to boarding school, but she didn't remain there long and ran away with another girl. She later said that she'd never had a chance to be a good girl. At the age of 13, when other girls were being watched by their brothers, mother and father, 'I was allowed to do just what I pleased. My mother thought that she was letting me enjoy myself. She let me stay out whenever I wanted and hardly ever asked me where I'd been. I knew right from wrong, but I didn't think of the future.' Her intimacy with Henry continued and in 1909 he fathered her child, also named Henry. Beulah abandoned the child to the care of relatives, and it died of cholera aged 11 months.

To please his father, on whom he relied for a living, Henry married Louise on 24 August 1910. They had a child. Henry had lost contact with Beulah until quite by chance in 1911 he met her at a baseball game. Their relationship was revived, and they would meet in hotels. She told him that she was now Mrs Fisher, married to a baseball player.

In 1911 Beulah wrote, 'My darling Henry, I am going to write you a little note every day in this little book.'

On 18 May she wrote: 'My Darling Henry, just a line to let you know that I still love you with all my heart.'

On 15 June she wrote: 'My Darling Baby … My Honey … I am going to be a good little girl and love you just like you want me to.'

On 16 June she wrote: 'My Darling Baby … I love you better than anything on earth. I did not mean to go out with P and I never will again … I hate him and love only you.'

On 17 June she wrote: 'My Darling Baby … please be a good boy and don't flirt with girls.'

In July 1911, Louise went to stay with her mother and uncle, taking the baby with her. On 18 July, Henry arrived at the uncle's in his automobile, a Buick tourer. Louise asked her mother to look after the baby, and Henry took Louise out 'automobiling'. He returned later, 'driving wildly at fifty-five miles per hour', steering with one hand and holding Louise's lifeless bloody body with the other. He cried out, 'My God, she's dead,' as he arrived back at the uncle's house. Louise had a wound in her left cheek, near her nose: a hole as big as a half dollar.

Henry told detectives, 'I saw a tall man with a long beard and carrying a shotgun come out from the left-hand side of the road and hold us up. I knew that if I didn't stop, I would hit him. So, I applied my brakes and as I did so he exclaimed, "What are you trying to do, run me down?" I replied, "I ought to, you are trying to use all the road." He was drunk. I didn't think that he would shoot. As I placed my hand on the clutch, the automobile jumped forward. He fired and my wife fell to my right, onto my left shoulder. I put on the brakes. On the spur of the moment, I jumped out of the vehicle. The man was standing at the rear. As I advanced towards him, he raised the gun and struck me across the nose, but I got hold of the gun. I fell down and he ran off up the road. Louise had fallen onto the floor of the car.'

The sheriff's officers had Henry take them to where the shooting happened. They saw blood spots in dust on the road surface. Reconstructing the scene, Henry placed the car on the left side of the blood spots, opposite the front seat. He positioned himself in front of the car where the murderer was supposed to have stood. The windscreen was undamaged. 'Impossible,' Detective Scherer said, 'Mrs Beattie could not have been shot from this point.' Henry then said that the man must have moved 6ft to his left before shooting. There was no blood on the car's footboard. 'If Mrs Beattie was shot from the left side', Detective Scherer remarked, 'she could not have fallen inside the car in such a way to cause the blood spots on the road.' Henry said that the shotgun was about 6ft from Louise's face when she was shot. But the detectives noted that there were no gunpowder marks on her face, as they would have expected. The angle of the gunshot wound did not match Henry's description of the position and angle of the gun when the shot was fired. Henry said that he drove all the way back supporting her body with his left arm. There were no bloodstains on the arm of his jacket or coat.

The shotgun was found about 25ft from the side of the road, along the route that Henry had taken back to the uncle's house. The sheriff's officers suspected that the gun had been thrown from the vehicle. Henry identified the gun as the one that had been used to kill his wife and said it had been shaken from the vehicle as he drove.

On 20 July, Beulah was taken into custody, where she remained until the evidence was completed in the subsequent trial. On 22 July at the inquest, Beulah gave evidence that she had been in a relationship with Henry during the last several years; that he often spent the night with her; that he was the father of her child; and that he had furnished a room for her to live in. She was asked, 'Do you love Beattie?' She replied, 'Certainly, and rather than see him electrocuted I would confess that I had killed his wife myself.' Paul Beattie, a relative of Henry's, confessed that he had bought the shotgun and shells for Henry, at Henry's request.

The coroner was of the view that she had been shot outside the vehicle where the blood spots were found, not whilst sitting inside. The verdict of the coroner's jury was that Henry was guilty of murdering Louise. Henry was arrested and held in custody awaiting trial at the same jail as Beulah. They communicated with each other through a 'trusty'. To prevent this, Beulah was moved to a jail in Richmond. It was reported that Henry looked unconcerned in custody and spent his time smoking cigarettes and strumming his guitar.

The detectives told Beulah that Henry was just using her as a cloak with Louise, who knew about Beulah, to hide his conquest of a third woman. Beulah made a written statement to the detectives. She claimed that she was the motive for Louise's murder as Henry had frequently told her that he wished to 'get rid' of Louise. She said she hoped that she would never see him again.

The Trial

The trial began on the first anniversary of his wedding. The court room was hot, like an oven, and the judge chewed relentlessly.

Henry maintained his claim that a stranger had shot Louise whilst she was sitting in his car. Under cross-examination, he admitted to his illicit relationship with Beulah; that he was furnishing a flat for her; and that in the week before the murder he had spent three evenings with her, as well as being with her until midnight on the night before Louise's death. He told the jury that Beulah was a 'woman about town: she told me that other men were running around with her'. He said that he'd made a clean breast of his relationship with Beulah before he married Louise and that he and Louise had never spoken a cross word, were both of an affectionate nature and as happy as could be.

He admitted writing a letter to Beulah a short time before the killing: 'As soon as the old man dies – say, kid, you and I will run away together. I don't know whether we can get married or not, but we will take a chance anyway.' He dismissed many expressions of affection for Beulah as 'only taffy or gush, such as a man gives to a woman of that kind'. He claimed that the words *will be good* that he wrote were *well, be good*, and not a reference to them being together after Louise's death. The detectives believed that the fear of Louise telling Henry's father about his renewed indiscretions with Beulah prompted him to kill her.

Paul Beattie told the jury that a week before the killing, Henry had asked him to buy a single-barrelled shotgun. He had given Paul $2 to pay for the gun and 5 cents for cartridges. On the evening following the killing, he met Henry, who told him, 'I wish to God, I hadn't done it. I would not have done it for a million dollars, but she (Louise) never loved me; she only married me for my money.' Henry asked Paul to find Beulah and tell her that, 'If she opens her mouth or says anything about this thing I'll kill her if it takes a hundred years to do it.' Paul gave Beulah the message and she responded, 'I reckon Henry Beattie will marry me now.' Paul later said to reporters, 'I hated testifying against my kith and kin. What I did … I did for a sense of duty … was hard at first, to nerve myself to tell all I knew, but I am relieved that I have done it.'

The prosecutor told the jury, 'Here was an innocent wife, untouched in sin, vice or shame, and proud in her motherhood. But this man, filled with venom, corruption, vice and sin, left the innocent woman with his own child at her breast and took to his arms a woman off the streets. There is the motive.'

It took the jury only fifty-eight minutes to reach a verdict of guilty of murder. The judge sentenced Henry, 'On 24 November, between the hours of sunrise and sunset you must forfeit your life to the community. May God have mercy on your soul.' Henry's father had paid expensive lawyers to defend Henry, and he spent more on an appeal, but on 10 November the Supreme Court refused a new trial. On the morning of his execution, Henry wrote and signed a confession: 'I Henry Clay Beattie Jr desirous of standing right before God and man, do on this day … confess my guilt of the crime charged against me.' He was executed in the electric chair just four months after the murder. Under the heading *Sleeps By the Wife He Slew,* a newspaper reported that he was buried next to his murdered wife.

On 7 September, one thousand people gathered outside the jail as Beulah packed her clothes and her toilet accessories, entered an automobile and sped away from the jail. A theatrical agent announced that she would make her first appearance at the aptly named Liberty Theatre, Philadelphia, in one week's time.

COMMENT

The book of the trial (128 pages) announces *The Sensational Story of the Life of Beulah Binford, the Woman in the Case,* while the author writes 'A great history of a great crime, the most highly sensational tragedy of the century.' He prefaces the story with 'it is doubtful if any crime of the twentieth century *(it is only 1911)* marked thus far by crime and bloodshed has stirred the country to the extent of this latest and most sensational one.'

At least seven local newspapers reported the trial. One newspaper, under the sub-heading *Like the Thaw Case*, reported that before the trial 'an insanity plea was being strongly considered … to show that Beattie had an abnormal fondness for women, and that he was an excessive smoker of cigarettes. The Washington Times' claimed that the prosecution would have preferred to call evidence about Henry's relationship with Beulah by putting her in the witness box, but they didn't dare to do this because they believed that she was too unreliable.

Beulah, although just a witness, was detained during the trial. The Federal Material Witness law in America permits the arrest and detention of a material witness in a Federal criminal case whose testimony is considered vital, if there is a risk that they might flee or be tampered with. There is no such law in England and Wales.

After her release, the National Board of Censorship forbade her from appearing as herself on stage or screen and a silent film, *Beulah Binford's*

Own Story, portraying her downfall, was pulled from circulation. The Board of Censorship made the following statement:

> The Board has carefully viewed and discussed the Beulah Binford motion picture, and the released picture is condemned because of the feeling that the sole and only appeal is directed to morbid curiosity, this being true regardless of the merits and demerits of the actual picture. The picture intrinsically fails to teach any lesson except one of sentimental toleration for the girl who takes easy opportunities to go wrong. We consider that the picture, although containing no positively indecent scene, would have a demoralizing tendency even if it were not known as the Binford picture. When to this fact is added the present notoriety of Miss Binford and the way in which the picture would be advertised, it seems to this board that the interests of the public and the interests of the motion picture business demand the suppression of the film.

A commentator in the *Movie Pictures* magazine in 1911 took a kinder approach to Beulah's problems: 'Instead of the case-hardened woman of the world, I found a slip of a girl, who never has had a chance. The girl should have a helping hand extended to her. It is a blot upon Christian Ministry and Christian Brotherhood that for forty-five days since her story first became public, she has received no offers of aid or sympathy. She has never had a mother's care and surely, she should not be held responsible for missteps taken when she was thirteen years old. As a matter of fact, her story instead of being one to damn her is a rebuke and an indictment against a Society that enables such things to be.'

In 1927, Kelly Harrell recorded a folk song, *Henry Clay Beattie*, in which the singer confesses to his father, brother and sister, as they say their farewells, that he has killed Louise.

> Yes I confess that I killed her
> I've taken her sweet life away
> But oh how greedy and brutish
> I was for taking it away.

In 2019 Amy Stewart, an American novelist, published a book in her Kopp Sisters series, which featured Beulah. Michael I. Shoop wrote in a review on The Historical Novel website:

> It's World War 1 and the Kopp sisters attend The National Service School for Women at Camp Chase to learn military discipline and preparedness. At the Camp are a lively mix of fun-loving debutantes and serious military-minded women. One of the Kopp's tent mates is the notorious Beulah Binford, a woman fleeing her scandalous past under an assumed name. Beulah is worried that her shocking secret will be discovered.

Buick is one of the oldest automobile brands, with the first example made for sale in 1904. Only thirty-seven were made that year. The Buick Four, available as a touring car, was introduced in 1909.

Chapter 11

The Trial of Henry Stanton v Louisa Stanton

For Perjury

1815

What a roller coaster. Happily married one day, she has him bound over to keep the peace the next, then he sues her for perjury for making false allegations about him to the court

Henry Stanton met his future wife Louisa by chance in Whitehall in May 1814. They were soon dining and drinking tea together. Henry lived with his aunt and Louisa came to visit him at his aunt's house. Henry remembers his aunt saying to Louisa, 'He has no fortune but his half pay as a subaltern officer. … nor can he maintain a wife without she brings a fortune with her.'

With Louisa's approval, Henry rented a house with a shop front and storage, to start a business. Henry told how Louisa was pressuring him to marry her: *she* offered to marry *him*. She told Henry that she lived in miserable slavery at home, with a cruel mother and brother who would stop her father agreeing to the marriage. She said that Henry didn't need to get her parents' approval, she was above age and without a fortune in her own right.

Henry said that he was under the influence of passion, love and cupid assisted by her 'beguiling fascinations', which blinded his senses. They married on 13 August 1814. Henry wrote about himself as a husband: 'We had not even the slightest cause of quarrel, dispute, altercation or argument … I never laid a hand on her in wrath, never uttered a threat or even an angry word, nor held a thought to her prejudice … I displayed very ardent love to her at all times.'

On 21 August, they were out with friends, celebrating their marriage, when without warning Louisa said to the group, 'Mr Stanton has been saying he will sell me at Smithfield's.' Henry replied, 'I am not yet so soon tired of her, but if I do, I shall not set her up for less than a guinea and I shall have a silken halter for her.' Everyone treated this as a jest. That day Louisa told Henry, in a jocular way, that she was pregnant. He knew that he could not be the father and told himself that what she'd said couldn't be true. He remembered her embracing him that night. The next day she left, never to return.

On 22 August, Louisa went to the Public Office in Marlborough Street, supported by her father and brother, and asked the court to protect her from him by binding him over with securities to keep the peace. Before justices and under oath she claimed that: he had represented himself as having considerable property in India; he had asked her twice to take a letter to her father asking for an advance of £35 as he hadn't a farthing to buy dinner; he had treated her several times with cruelty and barbarity; he had threatened to take her to Smithfield and sell her with a halter around her neck; he had told her that he wouldn't keep her if her father didn't; he had conducted himself in such an alarming manner by his threats and actions that she apprehended that her life was in danger; he had squeezed her throat; she had found a razor lying open on the table and believed that he had placed it there to terrify her and make her believe that he would murder her unless her father advanced the money.

Henry denied all the accusations: there was always plenty of food and drink in the house; she never complained to his aunt who was present in the house much of the time, nor to anyone else who had visited them; he had paid for a great variety of articles that week; he had adequate means for their maintenance in a plain way; on 22 August in the morning he had given her a few shillings pocket money and had offered her more but she had declined.

Henry spent seventeen hours in detention at the Marlborough Street Public Office and Marylebone Watch House until he could raise £240 bail. On 25 August, he was bound over in the sum of £400 to keep the peace for one year. His barrister Mr Ally told Henry, 'Mr Stanton, I can do nothing for you, they have sworn the articles of peace against you – indict them all for perjury. It is your only remedy.' Henry recalled the conversation:

Henry: 'Can I indict my wife for perjury?'
Mr Ally: 'Most certainly.'
Henry: 'Then I most certainly shall.'

For the first time, Henry noticed her pregnancy. Louisa claimed that he had violated her by force in a public field next to Edgeware Road at about 6pm at the end of June 1814. Henry strongly denied this and pointed out that it was a busy thoroughfare. He declared, 'I will never acknowledge this child who is not mine. If I am required to support the child, I will have it reared in the workhouse. Better to stigmatise the child than have people think it's mine.' The child was born in early March 1815, almost seven months after the marriage.

Henry wanted to have the bind over removed, to restore his good reputation. He justified the necessity of an open trial as the only sure means of exonerating his character from the 'false and villainous aspersions' so unjustly cast upon it. He relied upon Mr Ally's legal opinion that he could prosecute Louisa for perjury and had his solicitor prepare an indictment, which was laid before justices at the Clerkenwell Sessions House on 13 September 1814. The preamble to the indictment read:

> The said Louisa Stanton not having the fear of God before her eyes, but being moved and seduced by the instigation of the devil and wickedly and maliciously contriving to deprive Henry Stanton of his good name, fame and credit, cause him to be reputed a man of brutal and abandoned principles, being sworn as aforesaid did falsely, maliciously and corruptly say, depose and swear amongst other things in substance and to the following effects.

It then listed all the wrongs that Louisa had claimed in the articles of peace. Henry's name was on the back of the indictment as the first and main witness. Henry instructed Mr Ally again as the barrister to prosecute his case.

The Perjury Trial

The trial of The King (as nominal prosecutor) v Louisa Stanton took place on 10 January 1815 at the Clerkenwell Sessions House. An advocate did not represent Louisa. The day did not start well when Henry tried to give Mr Ally three letters from Louisa where she offered to return home to Henry. One letter read, 'You have always treated me with the greatest kindness.' 'Mr Ally refused to take them from me', Henry complained, 'saying to me in a loud voice in the presence of Louisa, her family and her solicitor's clerk, "I want no more of your bits and scraps."'

Things got worse when Mr Ally told Henry, 'You must prepare your mind to lose. However, I shall do my best for you and propose an arbitration. I know the whole affair. It is an infamous conspiracy. You must get rid of the child at any rate.' To Henry's surprise, Mr Ally told the court that he had researched the law and found that he had unhappily fallen into a fatal error. He had found that it was the rule and practice of the courts not to admit the evidence of parties prejudiced in cases of perjury or conspiracy. That would mean that Henry Stanton would not be a competent witness in the trial. Mr Ally admitted that he was raising an objection to his own case. He thought it extremely unfair that in such cases the wife could give evidence, but the husband could not counteract with his own testimony.

Mr Ally told the court that if they agreed with him that it would be unfair to exclude Henry Stanton from the witness box, then he was ready to proceed with all the evidence against Louisa Stanton. But if the court felt obliged to follow the current rule and practice of the courts and exclude Henry Stanton, who was his main witness and named on the back of the indictment, he was not prepared call any evidence. The court thanked Mr Ally for his candour and declared that Henry Stanton was not a competent witness in this case. Henry instructed Mr Ally to proceed and call his other witnesses. He said that he had a dozen respectable witnesses. Mr Ally declined to do so. The case was put before the jury with no evidence being called and the jury returned a verdict of not guilty.

Henry felt very wronged by Mr Ally. 'It is the duty of an advocate', he wrote, 'to either return his client's brief and fee or to defend him with all the energy, right or wrong, legal or otherwise, rules of court and each 'fatal error' of every description.' He said that if he had known what Mr Ally was going to do, he would have paid 5 guineas for another barrister to represent him. Mr Ally's justification was that after making the 'indict them all for perjury' remark to Henry, he had not been instructed to advise on the proceedings, just briefed for the court appearance.

Henry thought it was evident that Louisa and her family had been told about the 'fatal error' and that was why they had not wasted their money by instructing a barrister for the hearing. Mr Ally's behaviour reminded Henry of King Pippen in *The Play*:

> The King of France went up the Hill
> With twenty thousand men
> Oh did he so, what happened then?
> Why, he marched them down again

COMMENT

The book, price one shilling and six pence (seventy-four pages), which reported the trial calls it *Extraordinary and Unprecedented.* It claimed that 'this interesting case had already occupied the attention of almost every newspaper editor in the British Empire.'

A plaintiff in a perjury case had a direct and clear interest in the outcome and was believed to be inherently biased and unreliable as a witness. That is why Henry was not a competent witness in his trial against Louisa Stanton.

A barrister has a duty to present relevant legal authorities to the court, even if they may be detrimental to their client's case. The barrister prosecuting Louisa Stanton for perjury reminded the judge that the evidential rules prevented his client Henry Stanton from giving evidence. When the judge agreed, he gave the fact that Henry Stanton was his main witness as the reason for his refusal to call any other prosecution witnesses, despite Henry having instructed him to do so. The jury, with no evidence to consider, had no option but to find Louisa not guilty.

A subaltern was a junior commissioned officer rank in the army, below captain. The word means 'subordinate'. After the Napoleonic wars, there was a necessary reduction in the size of the army. Instead of being dismissed, many officers were placed on half-pay. They were not on active duty but had to return to their regiment if summoned.

Smithfield was a large open space close to the City of London. It was also a livestock marketplace for many centuries. The livestock market was moved to north London in 1852, and Smithfield became a market for cut meat. The grade II listed market building opened in 1868.

Relative values: 1815 compared to the values in 2026. The one shilling and sixpence book would now cost about £6.50. Henry's joke about not taking less than 1 guinea for Louisa at the livestock market would be the equivalent of £74. The £5 he would have paid for another barrister, instead of Mr Ally, would be £370. The £35 he asked Louisa's father to advance him would be the equivalent of £2,607.

In 1815, the Public Office at 21 Great Marlborough Street was a Justice of the Peace Office. It was also the Police Court, established in the eighteenth century. It later became Marlborough Street Magistrates' Court.

The Marylebone Watch House had accommodation for the constables of the watch and was also Marylebone Vestry Courthouse.

Pippin was a musical. King Pippin was a reference to the son of King Charlemagne, heir to the throne in the Middle Ages, who sought glory on the battlefield.

Chapter 12

The Killing of Stanford White by Harry Kendall Thaw

1906

Stanford White, Voluptuary and Pervert, Dies the Death of a Dog

Born on Christmas Day 1884, Evelyn Nesbit was known as the most beautiful artists' model in the world. She first performed in public when she was 5. On the death of her father, Evelyn and her mother were destitute. At the age of 13, they moved to New York, where she was sought by and frequented the studios of famous artists.

One day, she was about to leave the studio of Charles Dana Gibson, having sat as the artist's model, when she met Stanford White, a famous architect. 'By Jove Gibson, who is this little vision of empyrean blue?' Stanford asked. 'Tell me, I must know this little sprite, whether she is of this world or just a fairy from out of wonderland.' In August 1901, when she was 16, she met Stanford again at a lunch party in a studio on West 24th Street. He was in a room with a large velvet swing. Stanford put her on the swing and swung her very hard. Her foot crashed through a large Japanese umbrella that hung from the ceiling. He later sent a carriage to take her to a studio in Madison Square Tower. She attended several parties there. Stanford visited Evelyn's home and told her mother that he would look after her.

Stanford gave her pretty trinkets and flattered her – this ingenious, luxury-loving little model with the eyes of a Madonna and the smile of a siren. Soon she was ensconced in a high-class apartment house where Stanford paid the bills and was a frequent visitor. He brought his male friends to see her and boasted that she was 'his by discovery'. A stage career was mapped out for her by Stanford, who managed it.

In September 1901 she went to a photographic studio in East 22nd Street. She drank a glass of champagne and posed for the photographer wearing only a kimono. The next night she went with Stanford to the studio on West 24th Street. He took her to a bedroom and persuaded her to drink a glass of champagne, despite her complaining that she didn't really like it because it was bitter. After the drink, she felt a pounding and thumping in her ears and the room went black. When she came to, she started to scream. She was in bed with nothing but a little shirt on and Stanford was in bed next to her, naked. There were large blotches of blood on the bedding. She sat up and saw mirrors all over: on the walls, the floor and the ceiling. She started to cry. Stanford said that he had finished and threw the kimono over her. She screamed even louder at the realisation of how she had lost her virginity.

Stanford took her home and she cried all night about the mirrored room in Stanford's hidden lair; the drugged wine; and the awakening. He made her swear that she wouldn't tell her mother what had happened. He said it was all right, that everybody did these things, which was all people were born for and lived for and that there was nothing so nice as young girls and nothing so loathsome as fat ones. Stanford had intercourse with her a further eight or nine times, plying her excessively with wine and exercising his strong personality over her.

Her stage career was brief but brilliant. She was an actress in musical comedies, described as *the most beautiful woman behind the floodlights*. With the stress of her giddy life, she fell ill, and it was doubted whether she would dance again. She went on a European trip with Stanford, and they returned to New York after a few weeks.

Harry Thaw met Evelyn after a play when she was 17. They were at a supper party of young stage girls in an exclusive restaurant. Harry had been left part of his deceased father's $40 million estate and received an annual allowance of at least $40,000.

Stanford chose to have Evelyn educated at Henry C. De Mille's School, where Stanford and Harry and other men of their type would visit her. One day, Stanford took some of the pupils for a ride in a big touring car. His risqué conversation was such that three of the girls insisted on getting out and walking back to the school. As a result, Evelyn was asked to leave the school, but she fell ill before she could do so. Whilst she was getting better, Harry was in constant attendance on her. Stanford had deserted her and refused to pay her school fees of $3,000.

The *Girl-in-the-Pie* affair contributed to Stanford's bad reputation. A dinner was given for several artists and men about town with notorious fashionable women in attendance. At the approach of dawn, four men entered bearing a huge pie, which they placed on the table. An orchestra struck up the nursery jingle:

> Sing a song of sixpence, a pocket full of rye
> Four and twenty blackbirds baked in a pie

The pie burst open, and a beautiful young girl emerged clad in black gauze. She posed as a bird about to fly and released two dozen golden canaries, which flew around the room. Stanford then helped the young girl, a 15-year-old model, down to the floor.

The young girl lived with her mother, but on the night of the banquet she disappeared and remained in hiding for two years, despite the police looking for her. She said, 'When I was lifted from the pie to a seat at the table, I found myself queen of the revel. It was dazzling at first but soon became a sad queendom. Stanford was kind for a time but when he went to Europe, he instructed his clerks to get rid of me with as little trouble as possible. I never saw him again. Not yet 18, turned onto the street to live, I got married to a man who left me when he found out about my part in the Pie banquet.' She died soon after. In 1884, Stanford married Bessie Springs, aged 22.

When Evelyn was recovered, she left the school, and Harry paid her debts and expenses. The reputational damage to the school, from the inappropriate goings-on with young girls, forced its closure. Evelyn confided in Harry about what Stanford had done with her.

Harry married Evelyn in 1905. In 1903 she had refused his request because she feared that it would cause a separation between Harry and his mother. His mother had said that she would never accept Evelyn and if they married she would disown him. Rumour had it that Evelyn had turned down an offer of $250,000 to give him up and leave America. She'd said, 'My heart is not for sale.' Finally, his mother had accepted the marriage, and a secret ceremony took place with both families present.

A doorkeeper at the Madison Square Theatre told how a few nights after Christmas 1903, Stanford was looking for Evelyn. When he was told, 'She's gone home', he pulled out a pistol and said, 'I'll find and kill that **** before daylight.' The doorkeeper told Harry about that.

Stanford had created the Pleasure House on the roof top at Madison Square Garden. On 25 June 1906, a new play called *Mam'Zelle Champagne* was playing at the Madison Square Theatre there. Evelyn was present in a group with Harry. The group appeared to have been drinking and were restless. Harry got up from the table several times. At 10.30pm Stanford came in and sat on his own about five tables in front of theirs.

Harry said, 'Suddenly I saw my wife grow pale and shiver. I thought she was ill. She sent me a note *the dirty blackguard is here*. Then I saw the fat scoundrel sitting there, big and healthy. That poor delicate little thing, all nervous and shaking like a reed. And there he was, the big healthy scoundrel, God.'

During the show's finale, whilst the chorus were singing 'I could love a million girls', Harry's group went to leave. Harry, lagging back, walked behind some artificial shrubbery a few feet from Stanford, pulled out a revolver from his pocket and fired three shots. The first bullet entered Stanford's right eye and penetrated his brain. Stanford upset his chair as he rolled to the floor and bled profusely. The three shots sounded clearly above the music of the orchestra and dance chorus. Ordered by the stage manager, the chorus girls continued singing and dancing whilst Stranford lay prostrate. Harry broke the gun, emptied the remaining shells and held the gun aloft. Women screamed to be let out. Harry walked away calmly but was detained by a fireman.

A policeman took hold of Harry and asked him, 'Did you do it?' Harry replied, 'Yes, I did it. That man ruined my life (or wife). I guess he won't ruin anymore homes. Is he dead?' The policeman said he was, and Harry said he was glad that he'd 'made a good job of it'. Evelyn ran over and said, 'I didn't think you'd do it that way. Look at the fix you're in.' She threw her arms around him and kissed him. She said, 'Oh Harry, why did you do it?' He kissed her back and said, 'It's all right dear wife. He ruined you and I fixed him. It's alright. I have probably saved your life.'

Vanity Fair announced in a headline: 'Stanford White, Voluptuary and Pervert, Dies the Death of a Dog.'

The Trial

At his trial, Harry claimed to have been insane at the time of the killing, due to hereditary reasons and the stress of circumstances at the time. He claimed that he had suffered from temporary or emotional insanity for years and that he did not know the nature or quality of the act at the time that he committed it. He also claimed self-defence, believing that Stanford had made threats to him and Evelyn.

The police evidence included a search of Stanford's studio. They found a mirrored room and securely locked drawers built into the wall that contained evidence that this was indeed a den of vice.

In the witness box, Dr Wiley was asked what sort of man could have behaved in the way that he did when he shot Stanford. The doctor replied that he must be insane. The defence advocate was very persuasive and made the jurors regard Stanford as a fiend, whose slaying was a noble deed; made the jurors thrill with sympathy for the fragile pale face of little Evelyn; and showed that Harry had lost his reason.

The jury was unable to reach a verdict (seven voting guilty and five not guilty). After the second trial in 1908, Harry was found not guilty by reason of insanity and incarcerated in Matteawan Hospital for the criminally insane in New York. In 1913 he escaped to Canada but was extradited to America and finally released from hospital in 1915. In 1916, he was arrested for the sexual assault, kidnap and beating of a teenage boy. He was found to be insane and hospitalised again until 1924. Harry died in Miami, Florida, in 1947. He left an estate worth $1 million with a bequest to Evelyn of $10,000.

COMMENT

The published book of the trial *The Great Harry Thaw Case or A Woman's Sacrifice* (297 pages) was written by Benjamin. H. Atwell. He described it as 'a graphic and truthful narrative of the most sensational case in modern jurisprudence … the talk of America and Europe: the unusual degree of heart interest underlying the tragedy; the startling and sensational disclosures of life in the great metropolis; and the legal precedents established.'

A further book, limited to 250 copies, was written by William Travers Jerome and Francis P. Garvan (thirty-nine pages). It posed *The Famous Hypothetical Question in the Trial of Harry Thaw for the Murder of Stanford White*. They claimed it was 'one of the most noteworthy productions of its kind in criminal jurisprudence.' Assuming that expert evidence can only be an opinion that is based on a set of hypothetical facts, as the ultimate facts are only decided by the jury, the famous hypothetical question was asked by Judge Fitzgerald of Doctor Wiley: on the night of 20 June 1906, when he shot and killed the person described as Stanford White, did Harry Thaw know the nature and quality of the act he was doing and that such act was wrong?

Charles Dana Gibson (1867–1944) was an American pen-and-ink illustrator who created the Gibson Girl in 1890, an embodiment of the new woman: sophisticated, athletic, elegant, beautiful, and independent. He lived in New Rochelle, New York, a popular colony amongst artists, actors and writers. He became the editor and then the owner of *Life* magazine.

Stanford White (1853–1906) was an American architect, a partner in the architectural firm Mead and White, one of the most significant Beaux-Arts firms at the approach of the twentieth century.

Harry Kendall Thaw (1871–1947) was the son of the American coal and railroad baron William Thaw.

Empyrean blue is a vibrant, sky-like, rich deep blue.

Madison Square Garden opened its doors in 1879 and was located at the corner of East 26th Street and Madison Avenue. An arena that seated 10,000 spectators, it was demolished in 1890 because of a leaky roof and collapsing balconies. A new Madison Square Garden was designed by Stanford White and built on the same land. It featured a thirty-two-storey tower, the city's second tallest building, a 1,200-seat theatre, 1,500-seat concert hall, the largest restaurant in New York, the largest main hall in the world, and a roof garden cabaret. The building cost $3 million and dominated Madison Square Park. The tower was demolished in 1925.

Relative value compared to 2026. Harry Thaw's deceased father's estate of $40 million is the equivalent of $1.5 billion. Harry's $40,000 annual allowance would be the same as $1.5 million. Evelyn's school fees debt of $3,000 would amount to $114,807. The sum of $250,000 allegedly offered to Evelyn to leave the US would be the equivalent of $9.5 million. The $3 million that Madison Square Garden cost to build would be $114,807,000.

Henry Churchill de Mille (1853–93) was an American dramatist, actor and educator. He was also a playwright. His wife, Beatrice de Mille, founded the Henry C. de Mille Preparatory School for Girls in Pompton, New Jersey, after the death of her husband. She converted her home into the school. The school closed in 1907 when Evelyn Nesbit's affair with Stanford White became public, leading to a decline in enrolments.

The Matteawan State Hospital for the Criminally Insane, established in 1892, was located in Fishkill, just outside the city of Beacon, New York. The Superintendent of State Prisons had control over the hospital. The first female law enforcement officer to be killed in the line of duty, Nellie Wicks, was stabbed by an inmate there in 1906.

Chapter 13

Re Fynn

Custody of Infants

1848

'I will be fully prepared to meet and expose this infamous and diabolical conspiracy to rob me of my own darling, noble and splendid boys'
'As to Jane Ainsworth ... I would sooner see my boys dead at my feet than in the custody of that fiend'

Robert Nicholas Fynn, barrister and Lieutenant in the 2nd West York Militia, married Emily Harriet Fynn on 29 March 1843, when she was aged 17. Robert worked in London as the Secretary to the Galway and Ennis Grand Junction Railway company, until its dissolution in February 1846. On 1 December 1846, against his will and under pressure from Emily, he took her and their sons Robert and Alfred, aged 1 and 2, to Brussels to visit her mother Jane Ainsworth, a widow. Robert then returned home to London to look for work, leaving his family in Brussels with Jane.

On 26 May 1847, Robert obtained a bracelet on credit from a Parisian jeweller, worth £165. The payment was due within six months. Four days later, he sold the bracelet for £30 so that he could travel to Brussels in June to be with Emily, who was due to give birth to baby Emily. Robert told Emily that she should travel with him to Turin, where he was to be foreign correspondent of *The Times* newspaper. But Emily refused, saying that she needed to be in Brussels for her sister's wedding in September.

Robert left for Turin on 26 July 1847, taking his sons with him. He later complained that Emily wrote an 'abusive, slandering and lying' letter to Robert's father, who was already ill. He claimed that her letter had hastened his father's death and caused him to make a new will dated 3 August 1847, in which he only left Robert the 'trifling' annuity of £60 per year. Robert left Italy in December 1847 as the foreign correspondent position had been offered to someone else because of his delayed arrival in Turin, the result of his trying to persuade Emily to travel with him.

Robert took his sons to Paris. The jeweller was aggrieved that Robert had sold the bracelet and had not paid for it. Robert was insolvent and told a bankruptcy court in Paris that he expected to be paid £200 on the administration of the railway company and to earn £300 per year as a foreign correspondent. In fact, he only received £60 from the railway company, which he used to pay other debts and send some money to Emily. Robert was arrested and imprisoned as a debtor. Robert was convinced that the jeweller had only acted to bankrupt him because of pressure from Emily and Jane.

Whilst Robert was in prison, the boys lived with Emily and Jane and baby Emily. Robert complained that his sons were only brought to visit him twice. Robert was released from prison on 24 February 1848 and returned to London to bring proceedings for the return of his sons to his care and to make Emily resume married life with him. On 10 June he served a citation on her in the Ecclesiastical Court to compel a restitution of conjugal rights but later did not proceed with it when Emily agreed to be reconciled with him and accepted a ring from him in commemoration of that. Emily returned to London with the children in June 1848, but to Robert's surprise she went to live at a different address, which she wouldn't disclose to him.

On 10 June 1848 Robert petitioned to recover possession of his sons and accused Emily and Jane of hiding them from him. The Queen's Bench Division issued a writ of habeas corpus for their production. The parties appeared in Chambers on 23 June 1848 before Mr Justice Patteson. The judge ordered that the boys be handed over to Robert within one month unless Emily and Jane made an application in the meantime for them to stay with them. Robert was given access to the boys from 1pm to 6pm daily and they were not to be removed from the jurisdiction. Within that month, Emily and Jane petitioned, on behalf of the children, for their custody, care, maintenance, and education to be committed to a person (the grandmother) appointed as guardian and for the father to be prohibited from making a habeas corpus application. The custody hearing was fixed for 23 July 1848 before Vice-Chancellor Bruce. The entire case rested on the petition, supported by joint affidavits from Emily and Jane, and affidavits in answer from Robert.

The Custody Hearing

In his affidavit, Robert requested the court to order the delivery of his sons to him. He had a settled residence and ample means to educate and support his infant sons. He could earn £150 per year from his literary accomplishments. He would allow Emily daily, unaccompanied access to them. Motivated by kindness and affection towards his wife, he was not applying for the return of his daughter. Emily was now aged 22 years and 7 months and Robert claimed that due to her inexperience and youth she was unfit to have custody and management of his sons. Her income was only £90 per year, barely sufficient to support and clothe herself and their 13-month-old daughter and pay for a nurse, let alone support their two boys as well. He stated that his young wife was a tool in the hands of her designing mother. If her mother was chosen as a guardian for the children they would be taught to hate, loath and despise him. Emily had instructed them to call him 'bad man' and 'naughty papa'.

He described himself, on the other hand, as a kind, attentive, faithful, fond, attached and devoted father. He and Emily had lived happily and harmoniously together. He was never violent or abusive towards her, except once: in October 1844 he threw the contents of a glass of wine at her head because she taunted him about an 'insolent' letter her mother had written to him.

Jane's petition, supported by Emily, was for the return of the boys to their mother until they reached 7 years old, and Jane to be appointed a guardian responsible for their maintenance and education. They complained about Robert's reckless extravagance; insufficiency of means; neglect when the boys were in his care; and cruelty towards his wife. They claimed that Robert had misleadingly introduced himself in Brussels to Jane and her five daughters as the 'late Chief Justice of Tobago'. In truth, he had only served in that position for two months in 1840 until he was forced to resign. In January 1843, when he had proposed to Emily, he had said that he was receiving an allowance of £300 per year from his father. In fact, this was not a fixed sum but a gratuity.

Emily stated that Robert had been violent towards her: throwing her on the floor with her infant child as she tried to protect their 60-year-old nurse from him. When in 1844 she complained about his waste and extravagance, he had struck several blows to her head, kicked her, threw a glass containing hot spirits and water at her head and face so that the glass broke against her head, and thrust her head into the fire. He had no occupation; often drank to excess; called her a 'bitch ... whore ... hypocrite ... liar' and other names. When he left for Turin with their boys, he had to pawn possessions to pay for his going. On New Year's Eve 1847, he had written from Paris that he'd pawned his gold pin and the boys' spoons to buy bread. The next day he had written: 'My children are without even their night clothes and have not a morsel to put in their mouths. The day after he wrote: You say you cannot assist me, and that I know it: it is false. Pray, why cannot you pawn your watch, dressing case, or tabinet gown? Any wife with a particle of real love would do more than this for a husband.'

When the boys were handed over to Emily at the prison, they were in poor health and had been badly neglected, with filthy bodies and lacking clothes. Their nurse complained that they called her a 'bitch' and a 'beast'. If they were returned to their father, their morals would be 'contaminated and corrupted'.

At the court hearing, Robert Fynn represented himself. Mr Malins, Mr Southgate and Mr Robinson represented Emily Fynn and Jane Ainsworth. Robert addressed the judge, 'She has abandoned her duties as a wife, which disentitles her to any favour from this court ... let her support and educate my daughter whom I consent to leave in her custody ... As to Jane Ainsworth ... I would sooner see my boys dead at my feet than in the custody of that fiend.'

Robert argued that the Custody of Children Act 1839 envisaged only an application by the mother for the delivery of infant children to her from the custody of the father. In this case, the children were already in the mother's care and the mother's rights under the Act to make application did not cover those circumstances.

Robert claimed that, 'A host of cases, decisions founded on the law of nature, as well as the law of the land, justify Your Honour granting me a decree for the sole custody of my boys.' He then read from authorities for that proposition.

Mc Pherson on The Law of Infants: 'There is a right inherent in the father ... to act as guardian of all his children, by nature and nurture.'

Lord Chancellor King [Ex parte Hopkins]: 'The father is entitled to custody of his own children during their infancy, not only as guardians by nature, but by nurture.'

Lord Eldon admits [De Manville v De Manville]: 'The legal natural right of the father to have the custody of the person of his child, even while at the breast of the mother.'

Blackstone's Commentaries: 'The father possesses sufficient power over his child to keep him in order and obedience … the legal power of a father – for the mother as such has none, for she is only entitled to respect and reverence – does not cease over his children until they arrive at 21.'

Vice-Chancellor Bruce [Ex parte Bartlett 1846]: 'Where the wife in consequence of an act of violence, separated from her husband, the court gave her the custody of her daughter aged between 1 and 2 years, but refused to give her custody of her son who was aged 5 years, although allowing access to him.'

Vice Chancellor of England [Blake v Wallscourt]: 'Notwithstanding there may have been certain improprieties, and occasionally violent outbreaks, exhibited on the part of father towards his children, the court will not take from him the custody of their persons, which is given to him by common law and the law of nature, especially where the alleged grievance has been suffered to exist for a considerable time without any application for the judicial interference of the court.'

Robert then produced a letter that he wrote to Emily the day before and said that he hadn't received a response to his warm-hearted, generous overture: 'Notwithstanding … all that you have wickedly and designedly done to ruin and blast the present prospects of the father of your children, I hold out to you the hand of peace and reconciliation, and I do so for the sake of my darling, angelic, innocent children. Let not your hatred and animosity towards their father stifle those feelings which ought to activate you as their mother. For their sake, we ought to make mutual sacrifices; for their sake and future prospects we ought to bury the past in oblivion and try once more to live happily together. If this praiseworthy overture is rejected, I will be fully prepared to meet and expose this infamous and diabolical conspiracy to rob me of my own darling, noble and splendid boys.'

He asked the judge, 'What will Your Honour think of the heart of such a woman – so callous – so ossified – so dead to all noblest feelings of our nature?'

Vice Chancellor Bruce gave his judgement on 9 August 1848. He noted that Robert did not ask for custody of baby Emily, just the young sons. Robert wanted a reconciliation, but Emily may have a good defence to the restitution of conjugal rights.

He explained that a father may be negligent, injudicious, and at fault, a person from whom you may well wish your minor child to be removed for their own sake. But before the court could interfere with that father's rights it must be satisfied that it was not merely better for the child, but essential for their safety or their welfare in some profoundly serious and important respect.

Emily took care of the boys when Robert was imprisoned in Paris for debt, having acted discreditably. Emily's actions were beneficial, as had she not taken charge then the boys would have been in danger. The separation of the boys from him in January 1848 was for their benefit and of greatest importance.

Before being imprisoned, the father had sole charge of the boys in various parts of Europe. He was unable to take proper care of them or provide for someone to do so. The Vice Chancellor could not conceive of how the father, lacking the means then and in the future, would educate and provide the care so important for the boys' welfare. To restore the boys to the father would be consigning them to an unsettled and irregular mode of living, adverse to culture and discipline and an opportunity to occupy a middle or higher rank in society.

The Vice Chancellor referred to letters that the father had written to the mother. On New Year's Day 1848 he had written about Jane: 'The vengeance of God will overtake the murderess of your father, and my children will curse her to the end of time.'

On 8 January 1848 he had written: 'All your lies and meanness and unnatural and heartless conduct will only make me bitterly make you suffer … I shall most assuredly … take my daughter also from you.'

The Vice Chancellor ruled that: 'Before the jurisdiction of the court could be called into action, it must be satisfied, not only that it has the means of acting safely and effectually (alluding to property), but also that the father has so conducted himself, and has shown himself to be a person of such description, and is placed in such a position to render it, not merely better for the children, but essential for their safety, or to their welfare, in some serious and important respect that his right should be treated as lost, or suspended, or interfered with.'

The Vice Chancellor described Robert as a person to whose guardianship or care every reasonable man, having an option, would strongly object to entrust children. He was clearly unfit to be the guardian of his children. He said that it was incumbent on the court, for the sake of the children, to interfere against their father.

He agreed with Robert that the petition by Jane supported by Emily was not under the 1839 Act, but if just because of that he were to place the boys in Robert's custody, Emily would have the right to present a petition the next day under that same Act and probably gain custody back.

The Vice Chancellor stated that he proposed to make an order, in which property would be part, with a scheme for the custody, residence, maintenance and education of the boys which provided for limited access by the father. He adjourned the hearing until 19 August, making an Interim Direction on Jane undertaking to provide for the proper care and maintenance of the three children until further order: the children to remain with Emily and Jane, and Robert to have four hours' access daily at a convenient place in the neighbourhood.

Further Hearings

On 14 August, at a private hearing, Jane offered to undertake and covenant to educate and maintain the children. The Vice Chancellor commented that he ought to require either an actual appropriation of property or income, or security.

On 18 August, nothing changed. The Vice Chancellor declined to grant the petition. Instead, he discharged his 9 August Direction and Jane's 14 August undertaking and covenant. He directed that the infant Emily remain in the custody of her mother and grandmother. He ruled: the court was satisfied that the father was unable to maintain the boys; it was undesirable, because of his character and habits for them to be in his custody; the grandmother would undertake to educate and maintain the boys; but the court could not appoint the grandmother as their guardian in place of the father as the court could not make a distinct settlement of property for that purpose as the grandmother's covenant to pay an annual sum to her daughter for her daughter and the children was personal and would die with the grandmother and so was insufficient.

He would not direct, as Jane had requested, that Robert be prohibited from bringing habeas corpus proceedings for the return of the children to him without leave of the court. This was after Robert undertook that if he obtained custody of the boys he would provide for their maintenance and education until further order and allow Emily access for six hours daily at her place of residence and without him being present. It is not known if the boys were ever returned to Robert's custody.

Out of court, but within the sight and hearing of the judge, a melee ensued as Jane abused Robert and then his barristers for acting for him;

Emily repeatedly struck Robert; and Alfred, his brother-in-law, struck Robert in the eye and knocked his hat off. The judge declared that he had never witnessed such a dreadful scene in all his legal career.

Robert went immediately to Bow Street Police Office and made a complaint that Alfred had assaulted him in Vice Chancellor Bruce's court. Alfred appeared before a magistrate to show cause why he shouldn't be bound over. Mr Thomas, representing Alfred, argued that Robert should be bound over as well: for threatening to pursue Alfred's mother to hell; threatening to placard the affairs of Alfred's family in every part of St John's Wood, where they lived; and taking lodgings at the back of Jane's house, just to annoy her family. Alfred was bound over to keep the peace with two sureties of £250 each.

COMMENT

The case was reported to have 'excited a great deal of interest in the legal world on account of the novelty of the points for the first time raised – to deprive a father of the custody of his children.' Vice Chancellor Bruce explained that the case had been argued in public as neither party had expressed a wish to the contrary, and neither party had asked for judgement to be given privately: 'I have conceived it right to state my views in open court.' This was one of the earliest reported child custody decisions. A barrister of the Middle Temple wrote *a Full Report of This Important Case* (112 pages). There was also a full report of the case in *The Law Times* on 18 November 1848.

The judge agreed that the petition by Jane and Emily was not under the 1839 Act and considered that if he gave custody of the boys to the father, Emily could present a petition under the 1839 Act 'tomorrow' and probably get them back. Emily could, following the judge's reasoning, present a petition under the 1839 Act the next day for the boys' return to her care.

A writ of Habeas Corpus requires the custodian of a person in custody to produce them before a court so that their detention can be reviewed.

A remedy available to a deserted spouse was to obtain a Decree of Restitution of Conjugal Rights. This would order the deserter to return home and render conjugal rights. Originally only available in the Ecclesiastical Courts, it was later available in the Court for Divorce and Matrimonial Causes. Disobedience to the Decree was punished by excommunication until the Ecclesiastical Courts Act 1813, which substituted imprisonment not exceeding six months. Conjugal rights referred to companionship, cohabitation, and sexual relations.

By the Matrimonial Causes Act 1884, failure to restore conjugal rights ceased to be punished by imprisonment. Instead, it was classed 'statutory desertion', entitling either spouse to an immediate Decree of Judicial Separation and, if coupled with the wife's adultery, divorce.

In 1965–67 there were 110 petitions, 65 by husbands and 45 by wives. A wife may want to be allowed to return home or compel the husband to provide maintenance if she couldn't. The action was abolished in England and Wales by the 1976 Matrimonial Proceedings and Property Act.

In India, restitution of conjugal rights was continued in the 1955 Hindu Marriage Act and remains today. As middle-class Hindu women became more independent and often had jobs before marriage, a woman may take a job in a different town in order to support the family. It was considered that enforced companionship and cohabitation would help prevent marriage breakdown. A 1977 judgement held that only the husband had the right to choose and establish the matrimonial home.

Robert claimed that he could earn £150 per year from his literary accomplishments, but he had only one book published, *The British Consuls Handbook*.

Relative values: By 2026 values, the bracelet that Robert bought on credit for £165 would cost £17,881; the £300 per year that he hoped to earn as *The Times* foreign correspondent in Turin would be worth £36,425; and the £60 per year left to him and to Emily in his father's will would be worth £7,285.

A tabinet gown is made of a silk and worsted fabric, similar to poplin.

Chapter 14

The Trial of William Sawyer for the Wilful Murder of Harriet Gaskell at Campo Grande, Lisbon

1814

A suicide pact. Or was it, when one person died and the other didn't?

The death was the outcome of a love triangle between Mr Rickord, Harriet Marshall (later Gaskell) and William Sawyer, who lived together in the British Army quarters in Campo Grande, about 3 miles from Lisbon in the Kingdom of Portugal. Sawyer and Rickord both worked for the British Army as Assistant Commissaries in the Field Train of Artillery at the Royal Artillery's base in Lisbon.

Rickord was married to Harriet's sister, who lived with their children in Woolwich, London. To complicate matters, Rickord was also having an affair with Harriet and had provided lodgings for her in London where he would stay when he was not with his family and where Harriet was known as his wife. When Rickord was serving abroad, he would write to Harriet and send her money. Harriet worked as a tailor in New Hoxton Town, London, and from 1813 her employer rented a room to her, where she lived instead.

On this occasion, before Rickord was sent back to Portugal, he lived with Harriet for a week before returning to his family. Harriet's employer found out that the man she had been living with was in fact Harriet's brother-in-law. Shocked by this, she told Harriet to quit. She searched Harriet's room and found a loaded pistol and two bullets under her bed.

Not wanting to be left to fend for herself, Harriet insisted that Rickord take her to Portugal with him and threatened to kill herself if he didn't agree. She changed her name to Gaskell and joined Rickord in his house in Campo Grande. Rickord agreed to a colleague, Sawyer, sharing their accommodation. Sawyer, who also had a wife in England, repaid him by having an affair with Harriet behind Rickord's back. Harriet promised Sawyer that when they returned to England, she would dump Rickord and live with him. Rickord became suspicious of their closeness and questioned them both about what was going on. Harriet told him of her and Sawyer's plan for the future.

Rickord was distressed and angry and told Harriet that he would kill himself unless she pledged not to live with Sawyer. Harriet did as he asked, explaining to Sawyer that otherwise her sister and children would be left destitute by Rickord's death. Harriet announced that she would not be breaking her word if she died with Sawyer instead, 'I have promised Rickord that I will not live with you, I may still without breaking my word, die with you.' From their suicide pact, Harriet died on 27 April 1814, but Sawyer survived.

The Special Commission Trial

Harriet's death in Portugal led to the trial of Sawyer in London by the process of a Special Commission Court that sat at the Old Bailey in the presence of Lord Ellenborough, Mr Justice Chambre, Mr Baron Wood and a jury. The Attorney General prosecuted with Serjeant Best; Mr Ally and Mr Curwood defended Sawyer. Mr Ally objected to the trial taking place, stating that although the court had authority to try offences committed in foreign countries, this did not extend beyond the colonies to separate and independent kingdoms, which had their own competent laws and procedures to try such cases. Lord Ellenborough agreed to consider Ally's submission, but only after the evidence had been heard.

The court heard how Sawyer was unwell the day before the death and stayed in bed late on the morning of 27 April. When Daniel Tolin called on him, he asked Tolin to go and look at a house and grounds with him, which he wanted to rent instead of living with Rickord and Harriet. They were gone for about two hours. Rickord, Sawyer, and Harriet then went out riding together before they all sat down for dinner in Rickord's house. William Green chatted with Sawyer, who was attentive and rational. Witnesses said that Rickord, Sawyer, and Harriet appeared agitated at dinner and Rickford and Sawyer left their food.

About half an hour after dinner, Sawyer and Harriet left the group. Rickord and Green were concerned for them and went to find them. Whilst searching the garden they heard two pistol shots, then a third shot. Rickord was ahead of Green and saw what looked like two people on the ground in the garden. Green could see the bodies in the distance and Rickord called out to him that they needed to get medical assistance. They ran to Tolin's house for help.

William Fiander had heard the pistol shots and spotted Sawyer at about 7.30pm with a handkerchief tied around his head. He followed Sawyer to a table in Rickord's house where pistols were kept. He struggled with Sawyer to stop him taking a pistol, but Sawyer got the better of him and thrust Fiander away. Fiander ran to get help.

Fiander, Green, Rickord, and Tolin ran to Rickord's house, where Sawyer was lying on the parlour floor in a pool of blood, next to a packet of razor blades, having cut his throat and with a wound to his temple. Tolin asked Sawyer where Harriet was. Sawyer, unable to speak, was handed a pen and paper and wrote down where Harriet's body lay. Tolin went to where Sawyer had indicated and found Harriet with a fatal head wound where a pistol ball had penetrated her temple.

Dr Donnelly, Assistant Surgeon to the Royal Artillery, Lisbon, examined Harriet in the garden where she lay. The wound to her temple from the pistol ball had killed her. Dr Donnelly examined Sawyer late that evening. Tolin questioned Sawyer, who had difficulty speaking because of the wound to his throat, and Tolin wrote down what he understood had happened. He read it back to Sawyer, who signed it:

> From the unfortunate circumstances of my laying violent hands upon myself and upon Harriet Gaskell, in justice to mankind and the world in general, I do think it proper to declare and attest, while being of sound mind, that the death of Harriet Gaskell was owing to her taking part of a phial of laudanum and shooting a pistol at her head … I then took the residue of the laudanum and discharged two pistols at my head which were not effectual … It was agreed that we should destroy each other, but that she subsequently requested that I should destroy her first … This was at the back of the house where I endeavoured to do so without any person being an accessory to it.

Tolin went to see Sawyer again on 30 April and inserted the word *my* so that it read 'and my shooting a pistol at her head.' Sawyer wished to make it clear that Harriet had not shot herself. He made an endorsement about the change on the paper, read it to Sawyer, who also read it, before signing it in the presence of Dr Donnelly and other witnesses. Sawyer told Donnelly that he would sign anything to exonerate Rickord from any imputation on Rickord's character. He said that Rickord had been generous and kind and had let him live in his house; that Rickord and Harriet had been happy together until she had given in to his entreaties. It appeared to Dr Donnelly that Sawyer admitted what he had done in the belief that he was dying and seemed indifferent to any living consequences.

Despite efforts to locate Rickord for the trial, he could not be found and did not give evidence. Sawyer told the jury that Harriet was determined to commit suicide and for him to follow her example. His mental derangement was such that he could not remember what had happened and he could not remember admitting to killing her. He wanted to die and would have said anything.

Witnesses who knew him, testified about Sawyer's excellent character, humanity and good temper and they were convinced that he had signed the admissions when he was not in a fit state to do so. Dr Donnelly said that no man in his right mind would sign a paper like that. But when he was asked if he believed Sawyer was insane, he said, 'no'. Tolin said that he was sure that Sawyer understood what he had written. He thought that Sawyer had replied, 'yes' when asked whether he consented to the admissions, but as his throat had been sewn up Sawyer could not articulate properly.

The judge summed up for the jury. He told them that if the mind of a man was so disordered as not to be able to distinguish between right and wrong, to judge good from evil, in law he was not guilty of the crime of killing another. In this case he had contemplated his own destruction – which showed he was conscious of what had just happened. There was no proof of a deranged mind. He had been out riding, joined a dinner party, gone to view a house and grounds, and requested a pen and ink to write down where Harriet lay. His own confession was signed with a steady hand.

The jury's verdict was that Sawyer was guilty of Harriet's murder, although they did ask the judge to be merciful. Mr Ally raised his objection again to the court's authority to try the case. Lord Ellenborough postponed the sentencing so that he, with a panel of judges, could decide if the court did have jurisdiction. Later, Lord Ellenborough confirmed that the court's

Right: Oscar Wilde was arrested at the Cadogan Hotel on 6 April 1895 after the failure of his libel case. (*Illustrated Police Budget*, 13 April 1895)

Below: Oscar Wilde arrived at Bow Street Police Court to boos from the crowd. (*Illustrated Police News*, 20 April 1895)

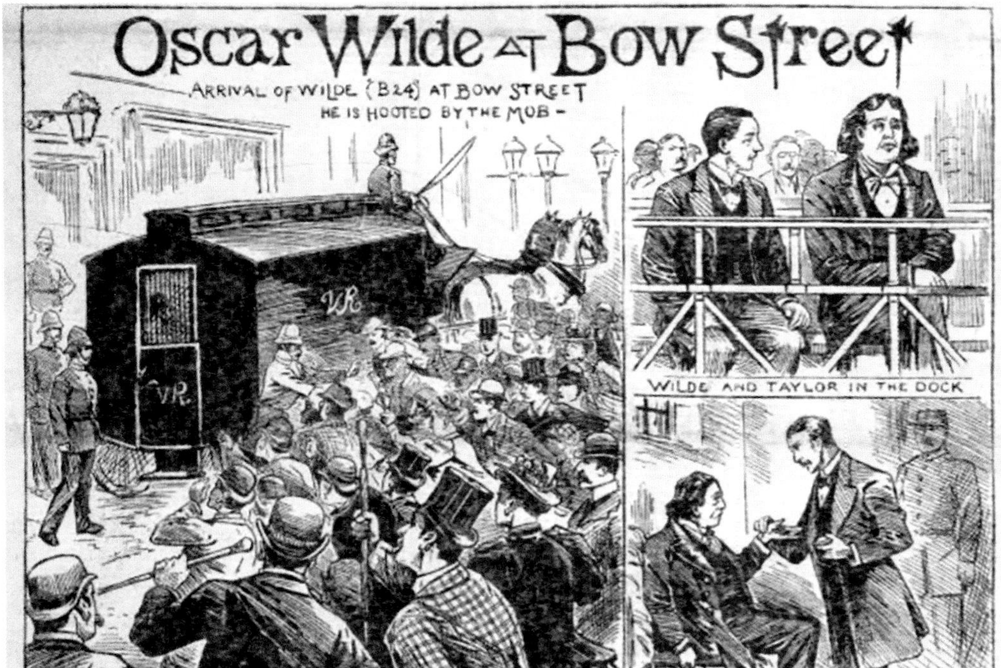

Left: Oscar Wilde in the dock alongside Alfred Taylor at the Old Bailey during the first gross indecency trial. (*Illustrated Police Budget*, 4 May 1895)

Below: Oscar Wilde in New York, 1882. (Photographed by Napoleon Sarony, The Library of Congress)

Above: The trial of Her Majesty Queen Caroline in the House of Lords, 1820, drawn by George Cruikshank. The Queen is seated at the table in the centre. (Library of Congress)

Right: Evelyn Nesbit, 1901, at age 17. 'The woman' in the Stanford White killing. (Photographed by Rudolf Eickemeyer Jr., Smithsonian Institute)

EVELYN NESBIT AS "THE SUNBONNET GIRL"
when 16 years old.

Evelyn Nesbit at age 16, 'The Sunbonnet Girl', taken just before she met Stanford White. (From the collection Studies in Scarlet – Marriage and Sexuality in the US and UK 1815-1914, in the Harvard University Law School Library)

William Treavers Jerome, the New York County District Attorney cross-examining Evelyn Nesbit Thaw, 1907, in the trial of Harry Thaw, drawn by Nell Brinkley. (From the Studies in Scarlet – Marriage and Sexuality in the US and UK 1815-1914 collection, in the Harvard University Law School Library)

HARRY THAW KILLS STANFORD WHITE IN JEALOUS RAGE OVER ACTRESS WIFE

INSANE PATIENT FOUGHT FIERCELY WITH 3 GUARDS

MISSOURI FORBIDS TRUST TO COLLECT ADMITTED CLAIMS

TRAGIC CLIMAX ON ROOF GARDEN BEFORE CROWD

Millionaire Slayer Claims Famous Architect Ruined His Wife Before His Marriage to Her—Held for Murder by Coroner.

Thaw Tells Own Story Of the Killing of White

MRS. THAW ALONE WALKS TO COURT

The sensational trial of Harry Thaw was the talk of America and Europe. (The Library of Congress)

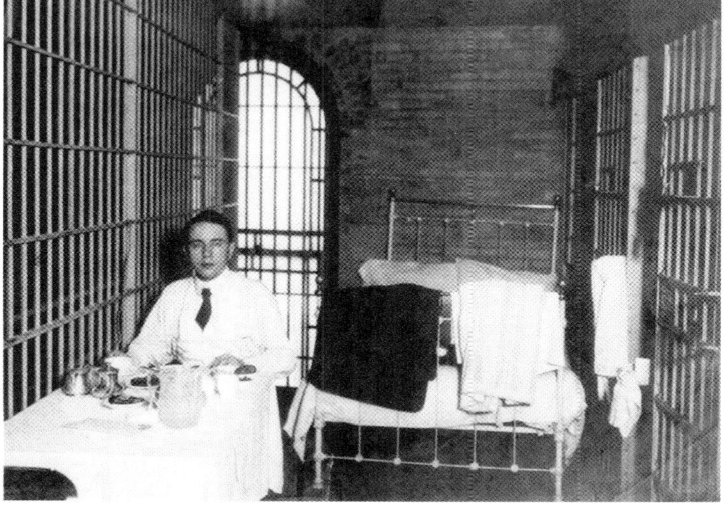

Harry Kendall Thaw in Tombs jail, seated at a formal table setting laid for a breakfast provided by Delmonico's Restaurant 1906. (*The Plain Speaker*, Hazleton, Pennsylvania)

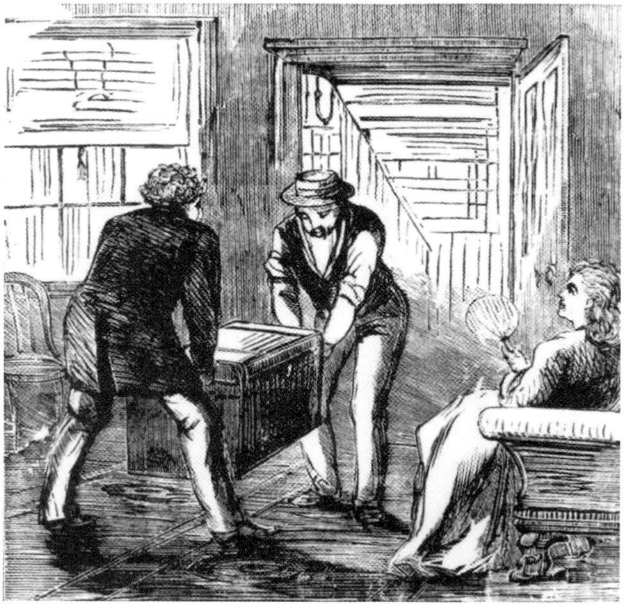

Jacob Rosenzweig removes the trunk containing the body of poor Alice Bowlsby. (From the Studies in Scarlet – Marriage and Sexuality in the US and UK 1815-1914 collection, in the Harvard University Law School Library)

Opening of the mysterious trunk and horrible discovery of the body of Alice Bowlsby. (From the Studies in Scarlet – Marriage and Sexuality in the US and UK 1815-1914 collection, in the Harvard University Law School Library)

Right: The arrest of Jacob Rosenzweig for the murder of Alice Bowlsby. (From the Studies in Scarlet – Marriage and Sexuality in the US and UK 1815-1914 collection, in the Harvard University Law School Library)

Below: Police traced the sender of the mysterious trunk to Jacob Rosenzweig's house on Second Avenue in New York City. (From the Studies in Scarlet – Marriage and Sexuality in the US and UK 1815-1914 collection, in the Harvard University Law School Library)

Correct View of Rosenzweig's house on Second Avenue, New York City

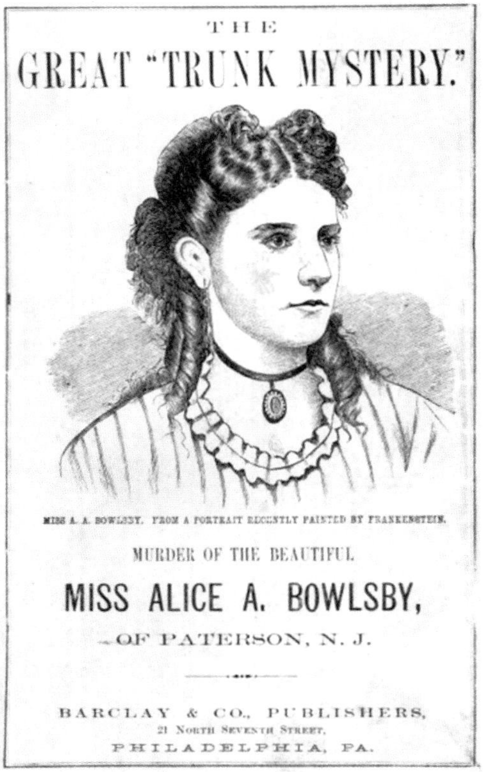

THE

GREAT "TRUNK MYSTERY."

MISS A. A. BOWLSBY, FROM A PORTRAIT RECENTLY PAINTED BY FRANKENSTEIN.

MURDER OF THE BEAUTIFUL

MISS ALICE A. BOWLSBY,

OF PATERSON, N. J.

BARCLAY & CO., PUBLISHERS,
21 NORTH SEVENTH STREET,
PHILADELPHIA, PA.

Front cover of book about the Great Trunk Mystery, published in 1875 by Barclay & Co with woodblock engraving of Alice Bowlsby.

RELEASED FROM JAIL, SHE NOW WILL POSE FOR MOTION PICTURES

Newspaper cutting of Beulah Binford September 1911, the 'other woman' in the trial of Henry Clay Beattie. It records her on her way to New York for moving picture productions.

Above: Members of the jury inspect Henry Clay Beattie's automobile, Beattie is marked with an X. (From the Studies in Scarlet – Marriage and Sexuality in the US and UK 1815-1914 collection, in the Harvard University Law School Library)

Right: Front cover of the book published by The Phoenix Publishing Company. (From the Studies in Scarlet – Marriage and Sexuality in the US and UK 1815-1914 collection, in the Harvard University Law School Library)

Above: Picture of Henry C. Beattie and Beulah Binford in 1911 before his trial for murdering his wife Louise. (*Rocky Mountain News*, Denver, Colorado 21 August 1911)

Below: Nannie Dickey riding with John Tytus whom she accused of seducing her on a buggy ride after dark. (From the Studies in Scarlet – Marriage and Sexuality in the US and UK 1815-1914 collection, in the Harvard University Law School Library)

Edward Gibbon Wakefield, 1826, before his abduction of Ellen Turner. (Photograph by Benjamin Holl, National Library of Australia)

James Greenacre sketched from life at the Old Bailey on 12 April 1837 before his murder trial. (From the Studies in Scarlet – Marriage and Sexuality in the US and UK 1815-1914 collection, in the Harvard University Law School Library)

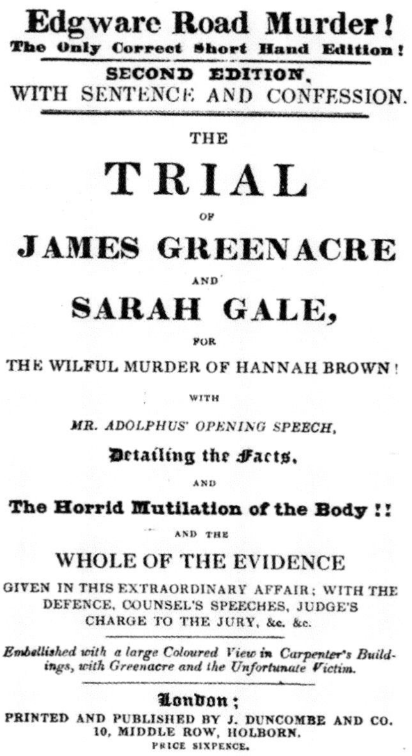

Edgware Road Murder!
The Only Correct Short Hand Edition!
SECOND EDITION,
WITH SENTENCE AND CONFESSION.

THE
TRIAL
OF
JAMES GREENACRE
AND
SARAH GALE,
FOR
THE WILFUL MURDER OF HANNAH BROWN!
WITH
MR. ADOLPHUS' OPENING SPEECH,
Detailing the Facts,
AND
The Horrid Mutilation of the Body!!
AND THE
WHOLE OF THE EVIDENCE
GIVEN IN THIS EXTRAORDINARY AFFAIR; WITH THE DEFENCE, COUNSEL'S SPEECHES, JUDGE'S CHARGE TO THE JURY, &c. &c.

Embellished with a large Coloured View in Carpenter's Buildings, with Greenacre and the Unfortunate Victim.

London;
PRINTED AND PUBLISHED BY J. DUNCOMBE AND CO.
10, MIDDLE ROW, HOLBORN.
PRICE SIXPENCE.

Front cover of the booklet published by J. Duncombe & Co. (From the Studies in Scarlet – Marriage and Sexuality in the US and UK 1815-1914 collection, in the Harvard University Law School Library)

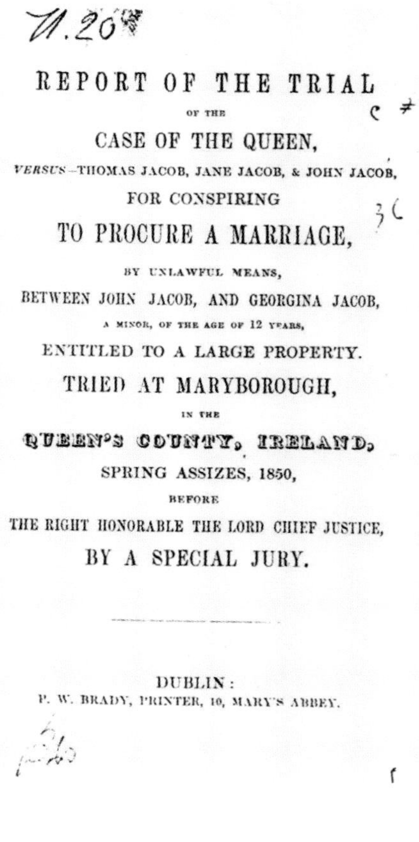

REPORT OF THE TRIAL
OF THE
CASE OF THE QUEEN,
VERSUS–THOMAS JACOB, JANE JACOB, & JOHN JACOB,
FOR CONSPIRING
TO PROCURE A MARRIAGE,
BY UNLAWFUL MEANS,
BETWEEN JOHN JACOB, AND GEORGINA JACOB,
A MINOR, OF THE AGE OF 12 YEARS,
ENTITLED TO A LARGE PROPERTY.
TRIED AT MARYBOROUGH,
IN THE
QUEEN'S COUNTY, IRELAND,
SPRING ASSIZES, 1850,
BEFORE
THE RIGHT HONORABLE THE LORD CHIEF JUSTICE,
BY A SPECIAL JURY.

DUBLIN:
P. W. BRADY, PRINTER, 10, MARY'S ABBEY.

Front cover of the booklet about the Jacobs' trial, printed in 1850 by P.W. Brady. (From the Studies in Scarlet – Marriage and Sexuality in the US and UK 1815-1914 collection, in the Harvard University Law School Library)

Front cover of the pamphlet about the Mortimer Smith libel trial, published in 1847 by Castigator Press. (From the Studies in Scarlet – Marriage and Sexuality in the US and UK 1815-1914 collection, in the Harvard University Law School Library)

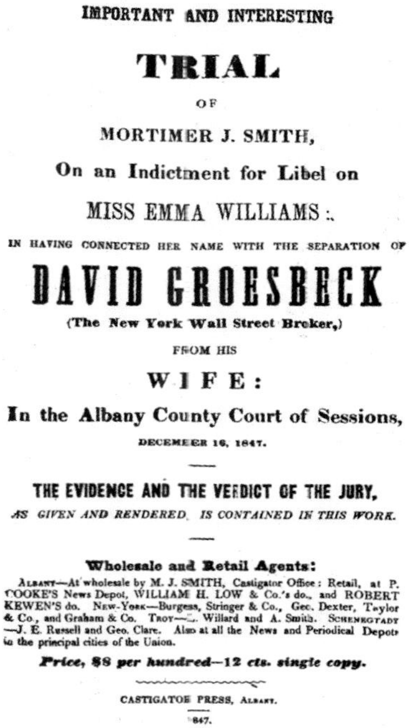
IMPORTANT AND INTERESTING

TRIAL

OF

MORTIMER J. SMITH,

On an Indictment for Libel on

MISS EMMA WILLIAMS:

IN HAVING CONNECTED HER NAME WITH THE SEPARATION OF

DAVID GROESBECK

(The New York Wall Street Broker,)

FROM HIS

WIFE:

In the Albany County Court of Sessions,

DECEMBER 16, 1847.

THE EVIDENCE AND THE VERDICT OF THE JURY,

AS GIVEN AND RENDERED, IS CONTAINED IN THIS WORK.

Wholesale and Retail Agents:

ALBANY—At wholesale by M. J. SMITH, Castigator Office: Retail, at P. COOKE'S News Depot, WILLIAM H. LOW & Co.'s do., and ROBERT KEWEN'S do. NEW-YORK—Burgess, Stringer & Co., Geo. Dexter, Taylor & Co., and Graham & Co. TROY—L. Willard and A. Smith. SCHENECTADY—J. E. Russell and Geo. Clare. Also at all the News and Periodical Depots in the principal cities of the Union.

Price, $8 per hundred—12 cts. single copy.

CASTIGATOR PRESS, ALBANY.

1847.

FIFTH EDITION!!!

Report of the Trial

OF

Waterhouse v. Colonel Berkeley,

FOR

CRIM. CON.

Which was tried at the Glocester Lent Assizes,

On Saturday, April 7, 1821,

Before Sir J. A. Park, and a Special Jury.

Copied verbatim from the Observer of April 15th.

Cheltenham:

PRINTED AND SOLD BY TURNER AND HADLEY, QUEEN'S BUILDINGS, AND MAY BE HAD OF ALL BOOKSELLERS.

Price Eighteenpence.

Front cover of the pamphlet about the adultery trial of Colonel Berkeley published in 1821 by Turner & Hadley. (From the Studies in Scarlet – Marriage and Sexuality in the US and UK 1815-1914 collection, in the Harvard University Law School Library)

TRIAL

FOR

CRIM. CON.

BETWEEN

GILL, Esq. v. AUBREY, Esq.

TRIED AT THE LATE

WORCESTER ASSIZES,

IN WHICH MANY

CURIOUS CIRCUMSTANCES

ARE DEVELOPED.

"This was the time when a hole was to be bored from an empty house adjoining Mr. Aubrey's, for the purpose of watching Mrs. Gill, but it was found impracticable, as the wall was hollow. Mr. Gill was assisting in this boring scheme." *See Harris's Evidence.*

London:
PRINTED AND PUBLISHED BY
G. MORGAN, 42, HOLYWELL-STREET, STRAND;
And to be had of all Booksellers and Newsmen.

PRICE TWO-PENCE.

1820.

Front cover of the pamphlet about the adultery trial of Mr Aubrey, published in 1820 by G. Morgan. (From the Studies in Scarlet – Marriage and Sexuality in the US and UK 1815-1914 collection, in the Harvard University Law School Library)

Front cover of the book about the divorce trial involving Sir Charles Dilke, published in 1886 by F. Henning, who personally made the woodcut portrait of Sir Charles. (From the Studies in Scarlet – Marriage and Sexuality in the US and UK 1815-1914 collection, in the Harvard University Law School Library)

Too late to admit him to debtor's jail, Wildes Walker was detained overnight with Sheriff's Deputies in a brothel in Mercer Street, New York, locked in a bedroom with one of the residents. "The Gentleman's Companion", a vest pocket guide to brothels in New York in 1870, included references to Mercer Street.

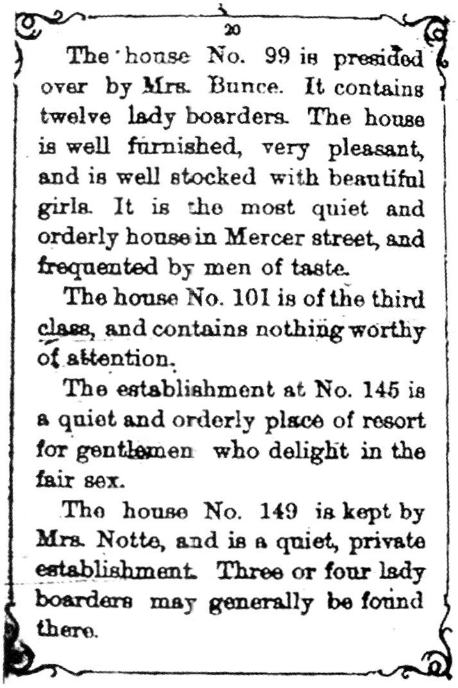

20

The house No. 99 is presided over by Mrs. Bunce. It contains twelve lady boarders. The house is well furnished, very pleasant, and is well stocked with beautiful girls. It is the most quiet and orderly house in Mercer street, and frequented by men of taste.

The house No. 101 is of the third class, and contains nothing worthy of attention.

The establishment at No. 145 is a quiet and orderly place of resort for gentlemen who delight in the fair sex.

The house No. 149 is kept by Mrs. Notte, and is a quiet, private establishment. Three or four lady boarders may generally be found there.

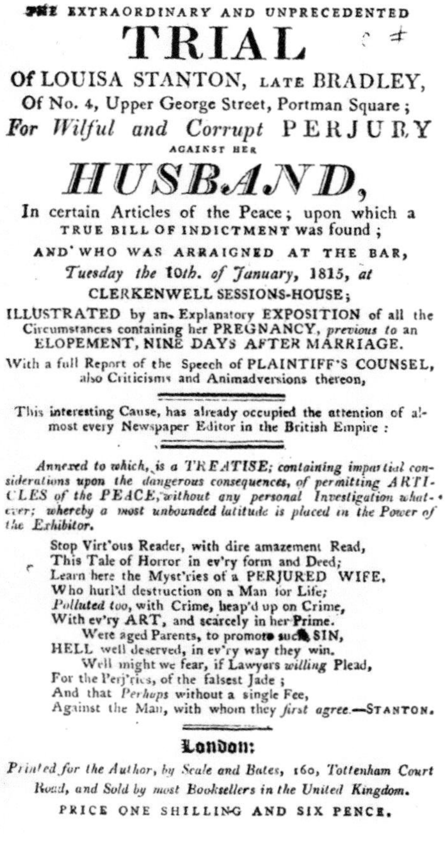

THE EXTRAORDINARY AND UNPRECEDENTED

TRIAL

Of LOUISA STANTON, LATE BRADLEY,
Of No. 4, Upper George Street, Portman Square;
For Wilful and Corrupt PERJURY
AGAINST HER

HUSBAND,

In certain Articles of the Peace; upon which a
TRUE BILL OF INDICTMENT was found;
AND WHO WAS ARRAIGNED AT THE BAR,
Tuesday the 10th. of January, 1815, *at*
CLERKENWELL SESSIONS-HOUSE;
ILLUSTRATED by an Explanatory EXPOSITION of all the Circumstances containing her PREGNANCY, *previous to* an ELOPEMENT, NINE DAYS AFTER MARRIAGE.
With a full Report of the Speech of PLAINTIFF'S COUNSEL, also Criticisms and Animadversions thereon,

This interesting Cause, has already occupied the attention of almost every Newspaper Editor in the British Empire:

Annexed to which, is a TREATISE; containing impartial considerations upon the dangerous consequences, of permitting ARTICLES of the PEACE, without any personal Investigation whatever; whereby a most unbounded latitude is placed in the Power of the Exhibitor.

Stop Virt'ous Reader, with dire amazement Read,
This Tale of Horror in ev'ry form and Deed;
Learn here the Myst'ries of a PERJURED WIFE,
Who hurl'd destruction on a Man for Life;
Polluted too, with Crime, heap'd up on Crime,
With ev'ry ART, and scarcely in her Prime.
Were aged Parents, to promote such SIN,
HELL well deserved, in ev'ry way they win.
Well might we fear, if Lawyers *willing* Plead,
For the Perj'ries, of the falsest Jade;
And that *Perhaps* without a single Fee,
Against the Man, with whom they *first agree.*—STANTON.

London:

Printed for the Author, by Scale and Bates, 160, *Tottenham Court Road, and Sold by most Booksellers in the United Kingdom.*

PRICE ONE SHILLING AND SIX PENCE.

Front cover of the booklet about the Stanton perjury trial, printed in 1815 by Scale & Bates. (From the Studies in Scarlet – Marriage and Sexuality in the US and UK 1815-1914 collection, in the Harvard University Law School Library)

Cartoon published by J. Fairburn 1824 depicting Colonel Berkeley, Maria Foote and Joseph Hayne. Colonel Berkeley: "I have been there before you my boy, take her if you like." Maria Foote: "Hush thee baby, hush thee thy mother is here – Thy father's a bastard who once was a peer – Hush thee baby hush thee smooth all thy pain – Thy mother will marry the simpleton H__ e." Joseph Hayne: "I'll not have the Colonel's left off piece, that's flat." (From the Studies in Scarlet – Marriage and Sexuality in the US and UK 1815-1914 collection, in the Harvard University Law School Library)

PRICE FOUR-PENCE.

£1500 DAMAGES!!!

TRIAL

OF

Viscount Glerawley, v. Captain Burn,

FOR

CRIM. CON.

Tried in the Court of King's Bench, June 30, 1820,

BEFORE

LORD CHIEF JUSTICE ABBOTT,

With the whole of the

EXTRAORDINARY LETTERS

Which passed between the Defendant and LADY GLERAWLY!!

DISCLOSING MANY

CURIOUS LOVE SCENES!!

" He was aware that a great prejudice would be raised against his client by these " letters, and that they would place him in a very ridiculous light, when to- " morrow there would be nothing in any one's mouth, but young Burn's letters, " and he deserved to be punished for his nonsense, in order to deter others from " being guilty of the like absurdities."

LONDON:
PRINTED AND PUBLISHED BY G. MORGAN,
No. 42, Holywell Street, Strand;
AND MAY BE HAD OF ALL BOOKSELLERS AND NEWSVENDERS.

Front cover of pamphlet about the adultery trial of Captain Burn, published in 1820 by G. Morgan. (From the Studies in Scarlet – Marriage and Sexuality in the US and UK 1815-1914 collection, in the Harvard University Law School Library)

authority extended to all felonies committed beyond the seas. Sawyer was executed by hanging in Newgate Prison on 15 May 1815 and his body taken to St Bartholomew's Hospital for use by medical students. 'The Newgate Calendar describes how he was dressed in a suit of black, and (it) was not ironed.'

COMMENT

Reports about the trial for the *Wilful Murder of Harriett Gaskell* (thirty-four and thirty-five pages) were written and published.

In 1814, a suicide pact was not a specific legal concept and to kill another person by such agreement, as William Sawyer did to Harriet Gaskell, was regarded as murder. The 1957 Homicide Act amended the law in England and Wales so that a person who kills another in pursuance of a suicide pact is charged with manslaughter, not murder.

Sawyer was tried in London because a law passed by Henry VIII in 1541 allowed the trial in England of a serious crime such as treason or murder committed in a foreign independent kingdom by a British citizen against another British citizen. It authorised the King's Bench to issue a Special Commission to try such individual. The Special Commission Courts were outside the regular courts system and comprised either a panel of judges or a jury. These special courts sometimes deviated from the evidential rules in normal criminal trials and Sawyer was able to testify on his own behalf.

Currently, the 2003 Sexual Offences Act allows the prosecution of British citizens for certain sexual offences committed abroad. The 1978 Suppression of Terrorism Act, 2000 Terrorism Act and the 2003 Crime (International Co-operation) Act provide for extraterritorial jurisdiction over terrorist offences, including murder. The 2021 Domestic Abuse Act extends jurisdiction to certain forced marriage and domestic abuse offences committed abroad by British citizens. The 1988 Criminal Justice Act allows for the prosecution of torture committed abroad.

The British Army was in Portugal in 1814 as part of the Peninsular War against Napoleon's forces, following the French invasion of Portugal in 1807. Britain sent an expeditionary force to aid Portugal and Spain in their fight against the French. By 1814, the war was nearing the end. A commissariat in the Field Train of Artillery, although a civilian, played a vital role in the Peninsular War, being responsible for the transportation, maintenance and supply of ammunition and artillery pieces to the front lines.

Hoxton New Town was the development of Hoxton Fields in the late eighteenth and early nineteenth centuries.

Laudanum is a tincture of opium and contains 10 per cent powdered opium by weight. Suicide by laudanum overdose was common in the nineteenth century.

Chapter 15

Gill v Aubrey

Trial for Criminal Conversation at Worcester Assizes

1820

'Never were more pains taken to procure evidence, and never with less success, and I never knew a weaker case'

Mr Gill suspected that his wife was secretly meeting with Mr Aubrey. To his mind, his suspicions were confirmed when in October 1817, in disguise, he watched Mrs Gill take Mr Aubrey into an apartment at an inn where she was staying. He refused to listen to Mr Aubrey's explanation, told her to leave their house and called her relatives to take her away. She refused to go.

He was determined to gather further evidence against her. A witness described how she and two others had seen Mrs Gill look around her before walking along a dirty lane to the back door of Mr Aubrey's house and then go inside. Ellen Lewis, in the service of Mrs Wainright, lived opposite Mr Aubrey. In January 1818, Samuel Harris, the keeper of the turnpike gate, helped Mr Gill spy on his wife by giving Ellen a telescope and asking her to watch the Aubrey house and look out for Mrs Gill. In January or February 1818, she saw Mrs Gill and Mr Aubrey together in the front room behaving in a 'familiar' way with each other. On one occasion, she saw Mrs Gill sitting in a chair when Mr Aubrey leant forward to kiss her. Mrs Gill didn't move away but Ellen couldn't see if they actually kissed.

Ellen admitted that she had waited more than a year to tell Mr Gill what she'd seen. She also agreed that Mr Gill had paid for her lodgings in Worcester for two weeks, waiting for the trial to commence, and that he had called on her there about three times. She had taken tea with him in a public house, had drunk a glass of rum and water with him and had taken his hand.

When questioned by the judge about the delay before she informed Mr Gill, she said that Mr Harris kept asking her if she'd seen anything and she would say that she'd seen something, but not say what. That was because her sister had told her not to speak about it.

Harris told how Mr Gill had asked him to watch Mrs Gill. In January 1818, he saw Mr Aubrey walk 20 yards past Mr Gill's cottage, then double back and go in. Mr Harris hid in a laurel bush, from where he observed Mrs Gill and Mr Aubrey in a room together behaving in the same familiar way with each other that Miss Lewis had described. Mr Harris's wife told him not to tell Mr Gill what he'd witnessed.

Mr Gill became more desperate to catch his wife in a compromising situation with Mr Aubrey. In June 1818, he procured a boring instrument and with the help of Mr Watkins, they tried to bore a hole, to use as a spy hole, through the wall of an abandoned house next to Mr Aubrey's, but were defeated by the construction of the wall. In December 1818, Mr Gill disguised himself in a great coat, red ruff and wig and waited in Mr Harris's house to watch for Mrs Gill. Finally, Mr Gill procured a 'curious device which he proposed could ascertain the guilt or innocence of his wife', but the nature of it was 'unfit for the public eye'.

The Trial

The trial before Mr Justice Park was prosecuted by Mr Scarlett and defended by Mr Raine.

The jury heard all about Mr Gill's suspicions. Cross-examined, Mr Harris said that Mr Gill had only paid his expenses. When asked by the judge why he had remained silent after what he'd seen from the laurel bush, he replied, 'My own wife told me not to tell.'

Mr Raine rose to address the jury for Mr Aubrey, but they told him that he didn't need to. They retired briefly and returned to announce that Mr Gill had failed to make out a case against Mr Aubrey.

Mr Justice Park told the parties: 'Never were more pains taken to procure evidence, and never with less success, and I never knew a weaker case.'

COMMENT

This trial was reported in a short pamphlet (eight pages) advertised teasingly as *Trial for Crim. Con.* It was price two-pence (equivalent to about 50 pence in 2026) to be had at booksellers and newsmen.

Mr Scarlett should have known that he did not have any of the types of evidence that would convince a jury that the alleged act had taken place. An eyewitness would be hard to find as this was an act that would be conducted in private. But there were no passionate letters between the couple; no confession of infidelity to the husband; and no pregnancy by another man.

We do not know precisely what the nature of the ‘familiarity’ observed between Mrs Gill and Mr Aubrey was. Either the witnesses were too embarrassed to say, the publisher was too discreet to write about it, or it did not amount to anything more than the usual meaning of the word: that they were casual and relaxed and used to each other’s company.

How would the hole in the wall not have been discovered? Not least by the noise made when boring it. The ‘curious device’ that was ‘unfit for the public eye’ is best left to the reader’s imagination.

Chapter 16

The Great Trunk Mystery of New York City, 1871

The Murder of the Beautiful Miss Alice A. Bowlsby

A clear-cut case against the murderer. How did he escape justice?

On 26 August 1871, a 12-year-old boy selling candy and newspapers outside the Hudson River Railroad Depot in New York saw a horse and cab arrive there. There was nothing unusual about that. He ran and opened the door and helped a young lady aged about 19 to get out. He showed her to the ticket office, where she paid $22 for a ticket to Chicago. A wagon came down the street and she said, 'Here comes my man.' The boy helped her man to carry a travelling trunk to the baggage room. She showed her ticket to Chicago and asked for the trunk to be sent there. The trunk was taken to the platform and placed in the baggage car.

This everyday scene changed quickly when such an unpleasant smell came from the trunk that the Baggage Master insisted the trunk was removed and opened. It was found to contain the naked body of a young woman. The trunk measured 2ft 8in, yet the woman was over 5ft tall and had been literally crushed into it. She looked about 20, with blonde hair and blue eyes. The body had been distorted in an effort to pack it into such a small area and was covered by a bed quilt. The police were called and had the body removed to Bellevue Hospital, where it was placed on ice in a patent ice coffin.

The pathologist calculated that the woman had been dead for about three days, and decomposition was advanced. There was a placenta, and he concluded that the cause of death was metroperitonitis from a medical mishap during childbirth. He reported that she could not have been squeezed into the trunk after her body was stiff with rigor mortis, which would have set in soon after death, and must have been crushed into the trunk whilst she was still alive or very shortly after her death.

The police hunt was on to find the truckman and the young lady who had brought the trunk to the station. The killing featured in the New York press and William Pickett read about it in the morning newspaper. He told the police that he had been hired by a woman, who called herself Julia Sidney, to take the trunk to the station. He had collected the trunk from the basement of a three-storey house at 687 Second Avenue owned by Jacob Rosenzweig, who lived there with his wife and daughter. Jacob had helped him to load it on the truck. The police went to the address and after a struggle they detained Jacob nearby. He denied ever having met the truckman and claimed that he knew nothing about the trunk.

Jacob was held in Sing Sing Prison whilst the police started to build a case against him. They found a scrap of paper in his house which showed that Jacob advertised his services in the *New York Herald* and *Sun*, calling himself Dr Ascher: 'Ladies in trouble guaranteed immediate relief. No fees until perfectly satisfied; elegant rooms etc provided Dr Ascher 8 Amity Place.' It was reported that he used to run a lager beer salon but to earn more money had paid $40 for a diploma in medicine and was a professional abortionist.

A local undertaker reported that Jacob had asked him how much he would charge to bury a woman. Jacob told him that a servant girl had died, that he was poor and only had $10 and he didn't mind how she was buried. The undertaker told Jacob to provide a certificate from the doctor who had attended the girl so that he could get a permit from the Board of Health. Meanwhile, people queued at Bellevue Hospital to view the 'trunk woman', despite the body's decrepit state, claiming that they were there to attempt to identify her.

A *New York Times* reporter had been investigating professional abortionists, and he reported that in July 1871, he had taken a lady with him, so as not to look suspicious, to Dr Ascher's office. The doctor had asked for $200 in advance, 'to release the lady from difficulty'. He was able to provide a marriage or a burial certificate. He would take care of the 'result', 'a resort to the sewer or river at night, who is the wiser?' And if the mother died, she could be 'disposed of (as well) without trouble'. When the doctor realised that the reporter was not a genuine client, he threatened to kill him and he only escaped by pulling out a revolver. The reporter claimed that whilst he was at the doctor's office he saw a young woman who resembled the woman in the morgue.

A servant at Jacob's house told the police that a woman had died whilst giving birth assisted by Jacob. She had been buried under a false name and the child, who survived, given to a foundling hospital. The death certificate gave the cause as dropsy. She later added that she had seen the dead 'trunk woman' in Jacob's house; and recognised the quilt that had covered the body.

The body was positively identified by Dr Kinnie, her family doctor, as Alice Augusta Bowlsby. He recognised a scar on her left arm below her elbow where he had vaccinated her. The family dentist, Dr Parker, examined the mouth and teeth of the corpse and identified her from dental work that he had carried out on her. Miss Bowlsby had left her aunt's address in Newark and had not been seen since.

Police searched Jacob's house again and Officer Larne found a handkerchief. The letters *A.A. Bowlsby* were visible under a magnifying glass. The press reported that when she left her aunt's house, she had waved adieu with the same handkerchief. They also found an abortionist's instruments and blank certificates for cause of death and stillbirth. On a large white sheet of paper were 'recipes' and a list of their principal ingredients, including calomel, opium, belladonna, laurel-water, and Fowler's Solution of Arsenic, all of which could help induce an abortion. One recipe, for example, was '4 scruples (measures) extr opii (purified extract of opium) and belladonna equal 10 grains.'

Alice's aunt, Mrs Williams, went to the police and told them that Alice was pregnant, and Walter Conklin was the seducer. She said that they had been very intimate, and friends believed that they were about to be married. When Alice left her house, she had said that she was going to meet Walter in New York. Local gossip was that Walter had refused to marry Alice when he found out that she was pregnant and that he had brought her to New York to visit Jacob. Mrs Williams went on to identify her niece. The local press in Alice's hometown reported her death and Walter killed himself by shooting himself in the head. Dr Wallace was called to the deceased, who had lived for a further ten minutes after the doctor had reached him. The doctor described a wound from a pistol shot behind Walter's ear, 'I passed my finger into the wound as far as I could and found it penetrated the scalp and went upward, forward and towards the opposite side. The wound was the cause of death.'

The Inquest

An inquest was held. The coroner had the body removed to an undertakers, where it was placed in an ice coffin. The jury were brought to the undertakers, where they took the oath and then viewed the body by the light of two kerosene lamps.

Deputy Coroner Cushman conducted a further post-mortem examination of the body. He found evidence of a laceration caused by a sharp instrument and the expulsion of a foetus from a large womb. He concluded that death was caused by metroperitonitis, following an abortion. This was also the jury's verdict, and they added that the abortion had been carried out by Jacob Rosenzweig between 23 and 26 August 1871 at his home, 687 Second Avenue. A false bosom was found in a further search of Jacob's house, and it was identified as Alice's by her mother.

The Manslaughter Trial

Jacob's trial in the Court of General Sessions began in October 1871. The prosecution case was overwhelming as there was proof that: an abortion had been performed on Alice; the trunk containing the body had been removed from the house in Second Avenue; Jacob had helped the truckman to load the trunk onto his vehicle; Alice had been positively identified by her doctor and dentist; her handkerchief had been found in the Second Avenue house; the quilt in the trunk was identified by a servant as having come from that house; Jacob had made enquiries of an undertaker about burying a girl; and he was a professional abortionist with suspicious practices.

His defence tried to muddy the waters: calling witnesses who said that he was of good character; producing a witness named Anne Bowlsby from Brooklyn who said that she had visited Jacob's house and left her handkerchief there; claiming that Walter could have killed Alice and sent her in the trunk to New York; disputing that an abortion had taken place and that Alice had ever set foot in Jacob's house; Jacob insisting that he had never met Alice; Jacob challenging the jury, 'Who saw me kill her?' They even disputed the identification of the body and inferred that the doctor and dentist who had identified Alice were 'hired' for that purpose.

The prosecutor made what later turned out to be a bad error. Late in the trial, and without giving disclosure to the defence, he called Nellie Willis as a witness. She gave evidence that she had an abortion with instruments carried out by Jacob and she had suffered bleeding that was so bad she was admitted to hospital.

The jurors retired for only two hours before returning a verdict of second degree manslaughter by causing death by abortion, and the judge imposed the maximum sentence of seven years' imprisonment. Jacob was returned to Sing Sing Prison.

The Appeal

The defence appealed the guilty verdict on the ground that the late evidence of Nellie Willis, for which the defence was unprepared, was inadmissible and prejudicial as it raised a fresh criminal allegation against Jacob. The appeal court agreed and ordered a new trial to take place in November 1872. The defence argued that it was not possible to try Jacob again as the law under which he was prosecuted had been repealed, the new law was not retrospective and there was no provision in the new law to govern the transition. On 13 November 1873, Judge Sutherland of the Court of General Sessions reluctantly agreed, and Jacob was discharged.

COMMENT

There were at least two reports written about this crime. *The Trunk Tragedy or The Late Mysterious Murder in New York of The Young and Lovely Miss Alice Bowlsby*, 'Full and Terrible Details of the Tragedy' (sixty pages) claims to be 'the only reliable account published'. A second (103 pages), advertises itself as 'One of the Most Startling Revelations of Crime that Ever Was Developed, Even in the Crime-Saturated City of New York.'

Until 1829, abortion was legal in New York up to the 'quickening', the time when the foetus starts to move. It was also quite common as a method of contraception and considered by some as safer for the woman than pregnancy and childbirth. Doctors were not licensed and for a woman without financial support, an abortion by a reputable doctor was very expensive. The deaths of such women from medical malpractice was already a scandal.

In 1829, legislation made pre-quickening abortions a misdemeanour and post-quickening abortions a felony. In 1869 the New York legislature passed a law making any abortion an offence of manslaughter. In 1872, abortion was prohibited by a new law that repealed the 1869 statute under which Jacob had been tried, with no transitional provisions. Legislators were under pressure to stop the killing of young women, such as Miss Alice

Bowlsby, by unqualified 'doctors' like Jacob Rosenzweig. The licensing of physicians was introduced in the 1880s.

Being unmarried and pregnant was shameful and immoral, so that an unmarried pregnant woman would hide her condition, possibly by going away, rather than be ostracised by her family and social circle.

The Sing Sing correctional facility is a maximum-security prison for men in the village of Ossining, New York. It was completed in 1828. Its name comes from the Native American tribe from whom the New York colony purchased the land in 1685 – the Sintsink.

Rigor mortis typically begins within one to two hours after death and becomes fully established within six to twelve hours.

A patent ice coffin, which displayed the murdered body, incorporated a refrigeration system using ice to slow decomposition. An ice chamber with ice blocks was attached to the coffin and the cold air from the melting ice would circulate around the body. Popular in the nineteenth and twentieth centuries, it allowed a longer viewing period for the body.

Jacob already had a system for disposing of bodies 'without trouble'. The real mystery is, why did he try to send this body by train to Chicago? As the report writer comments, 'once in the depot at Chicago, the trunk would have lain there until discovered by someone, in the same way it was in that of the Hudson River Company.'

Metroperitonitis is the combined inflammation of the uterus and the peritoneum.

Chapter 17

The Trial of Mortimer J. Smith for Libel

1847

Castigated by the Castigator. *A frolic in the hay barn ends in divorce*

Mortimer J. Smith was the proprietor and editor of the *Albany Castigator*, a Democratic newspaper. In an edition of the newspaper, he claimed that Emma Williams had encouraged the 'alienation' of David Groesbeck from his wife Mary Groesbeck by allowing him to show improper affections towards her and take liberties with her. The outcome was that Mortimer was prosecuted by the District Attorney for Albany, on behalf of the people, for the libel of Miss Emma Williams.

David and Mary were married in November 1837 and lived together until October 1846. During that time, she had five children with him, one of whom died. Mary said that she had known Emma since childhood. In 1841, from mid-June to the end of July, Emma came to visit them in their house in New York. On the first night of Emma's visit, Emma and David slipped out together in the evening and went alone to Vauxhall Gardens, were they were gone for about one hour. On the second evening, David sat beside Emma all evening, talking with her closely, leaning towards her with his head by her bonnet and devoted to her. The next day they went to Hoboken and David paid particular attention to Emma, who was at his side all the time.

On 3 July they all left New York to celebrate on Independence day, the following day. In the afternoon of 4 July, David and Emma sat facing each other, on a hay cart in a barn. Emma wore a 'low-necked' dress. A witness later described how, 'It came to the tip of her shoulder and straight across.' Watched by Mary, they were frolicking together and covering each other with hay. David was putting hay around Emma's neck. The witness told how, 'I saw him put a handful of hay between Emma's dress and her bosom … the hay could not have got into her bosom unless his hands had put it there … I saw his fingers between her dress and her skin.' She was meanwhile wrestling with him and putting hay on him. Mary watched unhappily and walked off in disgust. Minutes later she saw that Emma's hair was dishevelled, and her dress was torn. David lay with his head on Emma's lap during a bus journey to a fair. He was also seen holding her hand. Mary watched Emma take David's arm on the way to dinner.

Emma didn't visit again until 1844, when David gave her a diamond ring costing $33. Mary saw Emma wearing it.

In 1846, Mary called Emma to her house and confronted her about Emma writing a letter to David and receiving the ring from him. David said in front of them both that he was so angry with Mary for accusing him and Emma that he could kill Mary, and he slapped her face. He also gave Emma books and large hooped earrings. A miniature of Emma was seen in a trunk in his bedroom.

Mary Brennan, a chambermaid at Emma's family's home, said that she saw a miniature of David in Emma's possession. Emma's sister produced a miniature of the man she was about to marry and asked Mary which of the two men was the more handsome. Mary said David was and Emma agreed that he was handsomest, describing him as her beau. When David called at the house, Emma would take him into the parlour and lock the door.

The Trial

Mr Jordan's summing up for the prosecution lasted a remarkable seven and a half hours. He outdid Mr Wharton for the defence, who could only manage six and a half hours. The jury deliberated for eight hours and found Mortimer J. Smith not guilty, the libel being justified and true.

Divorce

Mary sued for divorce from David in the Supreme Court of Equity, New York, in November 1847, on the ground of David's repeated acts of adultery. She had separated from him in October 1846.

A 20-year-old woman, Frances Fleming Charles, gave evidence that she lived in rooms furnished by David, who also paid her rent and supported her financially. He visited her there often in January and February 1847, slept in her bedroom, where there were two beds, and stayed all night, leaving after breakfast. She was regarded as a woman of 'ill fame'.

The court found that during 1847 David committed adultery and had carnal knowledge with diverse other persons whose names were unknown; and that in January and February 1847 he had committed adultery with Frances Fleming Charles. The court granted Mary her divorce decree; ordered David to pay $600 pa maintenance for her and $700 pa maintenance for the children; and awarded Mary care and custody of their children. The marriage was dissolved so that she was free to marry again but he could not remarry until after her death.

COMMENT

The first report of the trial was a pamphlet priced 12 cents (sixteen pages), predictably by the *Castigator Press*, Albany, in 1847. The pamphlet's author, Mortimer J. Smith, writing about himself in the third person, sought to justify giving yet further publicity to the immoral goings on: 'The Publisher would briefly remark, that his object in reporting and publishing this trial is not for the gratification of malice *(if you say so)* or to please the morbid taste of the community *(which sells copies)*, but it is to lay the facts as they have been developed on the trial before the public, as well as to somewhat indemnify him for the heavy expenses which he has incurred in defending himself from the charges set forth in the indictment *(fair enough)*.'

The *Albany Castigator* was produced every Sunday and devoted to sporting and dramatic intelligence, general news, gossip and the suppressing of vice and immorality.

The second report (thirty-eight pages) was published in New York in 1870, twenty-three years later, but not by Mortimer J. Smith. David Groesbeck, head of a well-known Wall Street broker's firm, had been appointed to the position of Receiver of the Erie Railway Company. The railroad was built with public funds, and at the time it began operation it was the longest single railroad in the United States.

The 1870s publisher's motivation, so long after the event, was to embarrass David by contrasting this *onerous and responsible* appointment (of Receiver), diligently sorting out mismanagement, substantial debts, and warring financiers with the irresponsible and risky behaviour he had demonstrated in his youth. The 1870s publisher also wished to cast David as a hypocrite. They wrote: 'The evidence taken on the important and intensely interesting trial of Mortimer J. Smith *(by)* the fearless editor of that remarkably interesting sheet, the Albion Castigator … throws considerable light upon the early life of a gentleman who has recently undertaken the tremendous task of improving the morality of Wall Street.'

They continued, 'A quarter of a century ago, the individual … with hot blood of youth running riot in his veins, he neglected his loving wife to frolic on a barn floor with the fair object of an unlawful passion, even going so far as to take indecent liberties with the gushing Emma in the presence of his outraged wife.'

They also compared Mortimer J. Smith to *people in glass houses who should not throw stones*, but it is not clear what Smith was in danger of by his fearless reporting.

Albany lies in the upper Hudson Valley, at the head of the Erie Canal and in the State of New York. As the state capital, it was a cauldron of political thought and action. Known as 'Newspaper Town', with the first steam printing press and many local newspapers, gazettes and magazines, it was one of the most important publishing centres in the United States.

Vauxhall Gardens in New York was a popular eighteenth- and nineteenth-century landscaped pleasure garden inspired by Vauxhall Gardens in London. By 1805, the gardens had moved to Lafayette Street. A travel writer described them as a poor imitation of the gardens in London: a neat plantation, with gravel walks adorned with shrubs, trees, busts and statues. There was a theatre staging vaudeville comic operas and displays of fireworks. The area became a fashionable upper-class residential district.

In 1841 Hoboken, New Jersey, was a growing town on the banks of the Hudson River.

Independence Day has been celebrated by Americans since 1776. In 1841 it was not yet a federal holiday, but towns and cities would organise patriotic displays.

Relative values: the ring that David gave to Emma cost $33, the equivalent of $1,414 in 2026.

Chapter 18

Nannie A. Dickey v John B. Tytus, 1878

Sued for Bastardy and Breach of Promise

'She loved not wisely but too well' and the Dickey Bird was born

Nancy (Nannie) Dickey's brother Joe was surprised to receive a letter in November 1877 from Dorothy Dixon (called Mrs Ducker) in Cincinnati. Mrs Ducker told him to get Nannie Dickey's child, a girl, born at Mrs Ducker's home, 'I have kept it for four years and never been paid for my troubles. Either you come and get the child and pay me or I will bring it to you.' The child had been kept a secret by Nannie from the Dickey family and Nannie's social circle.

On 7 December 1877 Nannie Dickey filed an affidavit and complained on oath that on 8 December 1873 she was 'delivered of a bastard child' and that John B. Tytus was the father. Miss Dickey was 28 and John Tytus four years her junior when the child was born. She was the daughter of a wealthy farmer and described as 'voluptuous … a dashing, queenly looking woman (with a) … fine physique', and the reigning belle in her social circle. He was a member of the Tytus Paper Company, highly connected, 'handsome, almost effeminate'. He was said to be a member of 'the same bright circle of friends … a most enviable exemplification of what constitutes a pure life and perfect manhood … educated with great care and cultured in all the arts of elegance requisite to the dignity of his position in society … four years married, an affectionate father and devoted husband.'

The Preliminary Examination

There was a Preliminary Examination on 12 December 1877. Nannie claimed that she only had intercourse with John because he had promised to marry her when he was 25 years old. John's attorney claimed that their first intercourse was as early as 1865, when John was 16 and she was 20, 'to a boy of sixteen from a woman of twenty, you surrendered up the dearest jewel of your womanhood – your virtue'.

She called John a villain. She denied that Gordon Shillito was really her child's father and that Gordon had told her to accuse John and claim that she and John were engaged. She said that although she was very well acquainted with Gordon, there was no special intimacy between them, he had never proposed to her, had never given her a present, had never appeared as a lover companion, but had only paid attention to her as a friend. She admitted that she had been alone in a room with him several times.

The parties could not agree a settlement. Nannie demanded that John admit to being the father. John refused to do so but was willing to support her financially. John made a Proposition of Compromise to prevent a trial. He agreed to pay Nannie $1,000 and promissory notes: one for $100 due after one year and twelve notes of $300 each due from two to thirteen years' time 'in full satisfaction of all claims and demands whatever'. He had told his attorney, 'The child is not mine, but I would rather pay something than have such a horrible scandal come out against me (in a trial).'

The Trial

Nannie declined John's proposed settlement, and a breach of promise trial began on 25 February 1878. In her petition, Nannie complained that on 8 March 1873 John had promised to marry her, but in June 1874 he had married Minnesota Ewing instead. She asked for $20,000 damages and his Proposition of Compromise was read to the court. In an amendment to the petition, she accused John of debauching her and having illicit intercourse with her, causing the birth of their child on 8 December 1873.

Nannie told how she had known John since they were children. She had started 'going' with him since 1872, when she went to live with her uncle, Mr Bonnell. John lived just five minutes away and would call to see her most days and they would go driving together in a buggy. He had talked about marrying her ever since they were together. They first had intercourse in 1872 on the public road, after dark, near her uncle's, after he agreed to marry her. They had intercourse six times. In February 1873 he made a 'positive' promise to marry her 'soon'. She prepared for the marriage by making underclothes.

John had told her that it was best to delay the wedding and persuaded her to have an abortion. On two occasions he obtained medication from

Dr Linn, who had since died, and herbs from the drug store to make into a tea. She took the medicine and drank the tea but to no effect. He then arranged for her to see Dr McCarthy and John paid him $40. The doctor persuaded her not to abort the baby. She agreed with John to have a secret birth and marry afterwards.

Dr McCarthy took her to Mrs Ducker, and he was present when the girl was born there. John told the doctor to see that she had everything she needed. John came to see her and the baby two days after the birth. He cried when he saw her, put his arms around her neck and told her that he had acted the part of a villain and asked her to forgive him. He said that he was afraid of visiting her there again in case people suspected that he was the father. Nannie remained with Mrs Ducker for six weeks.

Then Nannie went to live with her uncle, Mr Bonnell, leaving the baby with Mrs Ducker. John came to visit her at her uncle's. He said that he'd deal with everything and still promised to marry her until two months before his marriage to Minnesota. There was a meeting in autumn 1877, where Nannie, John, John's father, and Mr Bonnell were present. Nannie told John, 'You must acknowledge the paternity of the child.' He replied, 'I can't. I have a wife.'

Dr Corson told the court how in September 1873, when Nancy was in an advanced state of pregnancy, John came to his office and told him that he had a lady friend in a pregnant condition, a lady whom the doctor knew. The lady was of high standing in society and had, in an unguarded moment, 'loved not wisely but too well'. He asked the doctor for help. Dr Corson told him that he couldn't do anything of the kind and that money couldn't buy him.

Mrs Ducker told how Dr McCarthy had asked her to take a lady boarder and that Miss Dickey then came to live in her house after the birth. John visited once, when the baby was two days old, saying that he was a friend of Miss Dickey. She received $160 from him to support Miss Dickey, not the child, although Miss Dickey said that John was the father. Nannie did mention Gordon Shillito to Mrs Ducker, saying that he was a very dear friend and she thought more of him than any man, but he was not the father. Mrs Ducker had custody of the child for a little over four years, during which time Nannie only came to visit her daughter once, at two months old. Mrs Ducker had seen John three years ago, when she asked him if he was going to do anything more for the child. He told her that the child was not his but gave her $100. Dr McCarthy told her it was 'Gordon Shillito's child and we should make him pay something for it'. When Joe Dickey came looking for his sister's child, Mrs Ducker hid her at another address, giving her up when Joe handed over $100 cash and a cheque for $200.

John's attorney remarked that the child, Miss Dickey Junior, was in court with a nurse and the court could see that she had ears that stood out, resembling Nannie's cousin Dan Bonnell. His attorney asked for the child to be placed next to John, for the jury to compare them. The judge wouldn't allow this and said that the jury had already seen the child. Mrs Ducker was asked if the child, named 'the Dickey Bird' by the press, bore a resemblance to any of the gentlemen John, Dan, or Gordon. She said that the child bore a closer resemblance to Gordon than to John. John's attorney also alleged, through the evidence of Dr Heron, that the child was suffering from scroflitic abscesses on the head, which could be hereditary and that Dan Bonnell's children had died of scrofula.

John said that he had met Nannie in 1868 when she lived at Mrs Mitchell's house. Between spring 1871 and autumn 1872 he called to see her three or four times. She then went to live with her uncle, Mr Bonnell. John denied that he had sexual intercourse with her, 'not in any place, at any time, under any circumstances'. He had never made a promise of marriage, 'never mentioned it, not one word was ever mentioned on the subject between us'. His only relationship with her was like that of a younger brother with an elder sister. When she got into serious trouble, she had called on his assistance despite not being the father of her child and he had made no secret of paying for her. He denied sending her to see Dr McCarthy and had only seen the doctor himself at Nannie's request. He was flattered by her confiding in him and paid Dr McCarthy $125 and Mrs Ducker $160. He had paid Dr McCarthy to stop him betraying Nannie and in a letter in August 1894 had accused the doctor of trying to blackmail him. He denied obtaining medicine and herbs for Nannie to attempt an abortion. He agreed that he had gone to see Nannie after the birth and had sent $250 with Dan Bonnell for Mrs Ducker.

Colonel Snelbecker, the ex-Chief of Police, stated that the doctor's bill for the birth was $1,200. The colonel said that five letters written to the doctor by Miss Dickey between February and December 1873 were stolen in a burglary from the doctor's home at night by a man who had threatened him with a pistol. Those letters had come into the colonel's possession. He had made copies before returning them to the doctor. The doctor had asked the colonel to collect the money from John and give the letters to

John in return. The doctor said that he'd take $750 and the colonel could keep the rest. The colonel said that he visited John, who refused to pay or have anything to do with the matter. John told the colonel that he wasn't the guilty party and wouldn't be blackmailed or have any money 'squeezed out of him'.

One letter from Nannie had mentioned 'Mr T' (Tytus) and another had mentioned Gordon, but Gordon had visited the doctor with his father and obtained that letter from him. John had written to the doctor on 25 August 1874, 'I had nothing to do with this thing, only as a friend of Miss Dickey. I have no fear of any legal process. I am not the man, and you know it.' In the doctor's opinion, it was not possible to know who the father was.

The jury found in favour of Nannie and ordered John to pay her $6,000 in damages.

COMMENT

The report of the trial (176 pages) claims on its cover to be 'Illustrated with Photographs and Autographs'. The author writes that the trial implicates 'persons belonging to the first families of Ohio' and that his object in presenting the facts to the public is not only to 'give a full and impartial statement of the facts of the case' but also to 'supply an almost gluttonous demand for the full proceedings in court.'

The trial was commented on in thirteen different newspapers. The following are a selection of the comments. 'Miss Dickey received several eligible offers of marriage during the trial and that she decided to accept one of them': *Portsmouth Tribune.* 'By the time Mr Tytus is through with the courts he will wish he married Miss Dickey and killed her the next day. It would have been cheaper for him in the end': *Chicago Post and Mail.* 'The Dickey-Tytus breach of promise case shall continue to be the subject of comment by the press. In sensationalism, it only falls short of the Beecher-Tyler scandal. A new trial is moved by Mr Tytus. It should be granted. First, because there was no evidence to sustain the finding of the last jury; second, because we think the dear public of Porkopolis and Miami Bottoms generally would like to hear the youthful merchant prince, Gordon Shillito, do a little swearing. The fact is we were not satisfied with John's swearing. Now let's hear Gordon': *Washington Post.* 'The Tytus-Dickey trial developed a strange phenomenon in the people of Middleton. Their ears stick out. But for the trial, this peculiarity would never have been noticed': *Lebanon Patriot*. 'Since Miss Dickey struck her bonanza, breach of promise cases are developing all over the country, and buggy riding has lost its prestige': *Hocking Valley Gazette*.

In the United States, the law regarding the maintenance of an illegitimate child varied from state to state. In Virginia, for example, in the nineteenth century, if a single mother were incapable of looking after her illegitimate child, there could be a trial to determine the paternity, and the court could set the amount and the duration of the father's contribution towards the child's upkeep.

In the late sixteenth century in England and Wales, justices of the peace had power to order a mother or father of an illegitimate child to pay for the child's maintenance, either directly or through the parish officials. Under the Bastardy Act 1733, a man could be imprisoned until he gave security to indemnify the parish from the cost of looking after the child or he agreed to marry the mother. The mother could be imprisoned until she named the father.

The Poor Law Amendment Act 1834 made it harder for unmarried mothers to obtain financial assistance from fathers and shifted the responsibility for poverty relief from the Parishes to the newly established workhouses in which mothers where housed and their children schooled, in exchange for work.

The Poor Law Amendment Act 1844 and later the Bastardy Laws Amendment Act 1872 gave power to the mother of an illegitimate child to summon the putative father to the Petty Sessions, within twelve months of the birth, or twelve months of the father's return from overseas, where the justices could compel him to support the child. Before 1872, the maximum maintenance that could be ordered was two shillings and sixpence per week. That was amended to the actual cost of maintenance of the child. The maintenance cap of two shillings and six pence per week in 1872 is equivalent to £19 per week in 2026. Before agreeing in 1872 that the cap should be the actual cost of maintaining the child, Parliament had considered twelve shillings, the equivalent of £90 in 2026, as a more realistic weekly cap.

Relative values: To avoid a trial, John offered Nannie a total of $4,700, spread over thirteen years, the equivalent of $143,884 in 2026. The jury awarded Nannie $6,000, the equivalent of $183,694 in 2026. Dr McCarthy's bill for the birth was $1,200, the equivalent of $36,738 in 2026.

Chapter 19

The Trial of James Greenacre and Sarah Gale for the Wilful Murder of Hannah Brown

1837

He was after her money. Then became angry when she didn't have any

Hannah Brown was aged about 47. She lived in rooms at 45 Union Street, Middlesex Hospital, where she spent the day washing and mangling for a living. She was a widow, her husband having died two years after their marriage. He had left her and sailed to Jamaica but was washed overboard during the journey. She was rumoured to have saved a considerable sum through arduous work and a frugal lifestyle.

She was courted by James Greenacre, having met him through a Mr Ward. Evan Davies, a friend of Hannah's, told how he met Hannah and Greenacre together about nine days before Christmas 1836, when she introduced Greenacre to him as her 'beau'. Davies went for a drink with Greenacre, who claimed to have a 1,000-acre farm in Hudson's Bay, America, having arrived from there about four years ago and due to return three weeks after Christmas.

Hannah didn't know about Sarah Gale, who had been living from time to time with Greenacre in 6 Carpenter's Place, Camberwell, since 1835, when her husband had deserted her. She was known to neighbours as Mrs Greenacre. Sarah gave birth to their son in February 1836. Henry Wignell and his wife described how on Thursday, 22 December 1836, Sarah came to their house, 55 Poland Street, Walworth, asking to use the back parlour as a lodger. Greenacre helped her to move in and slept with Sarah for two nights during the Christmas week.

On Thursday, 22 December, Davies met Greenacre for a drink in the Queens Head public house. Afterwards, they went back to Davies's house.

Hannah Brown was there already, and she and Greenacre sat on the sofa together. Greenacre told Davies that he and Hannah were to be married at St Giles-in-the-Fields church on Sunday, Christmas Day 1836. The banns had already been read on 27 November and 4 and 11 December. Greenacre asked Davies to give Hannah away and for Davies's eldest daughter to be a bridesmaid. They arranged to meet before the ceremony at The Angel public house near the church. Hannah Davies was Evan's wife. Hannah Brown had invited her to spend the day following the ceremony at Greenacres's house. Hannah Brown had told her, 'We are going to America.' Evan Davies described Hannah as the most sober, agreeable and pleasant woman in London.

On Saturday, Christmas Eve, Greenacre came to see Sarah at Wignell's house, and she went off with Greenacre at 9.30 or 10.0am. Mr Edmonds saw Sarah in the front garden of 6 Carpenter's Place between 10 and 11am that morning. Elizabeth Corney was Hannah Brown's landlady. She last saw Hannah that day. Hannah had sold most of her possessions, including her mangle, saying that it was Greenacre's idea for pocket money. Greenacre was waiting for her outside sometime between 12 noon and 3pm. Hannah took her remaining possessions packed in boxes and Greenacre and the coachman helped her to load them onto a hackney coach to take to Greenacre's house. Hannah Brown told Corney that there were a few small things in her room that didn't belong to her, and she would return for them on Monday, Boxing Day, and return the key then and pay the last of her rent.

Later that day, Greenacre told Hannah Davies that the marriage was off as he had found that Hannah Brown had no property and was attempting to spend his money. It wouldn't be good to plunge them into poverty. Catherine Gill, a friend of Hannah Brown, had arranged that Hannah would spend the Christmas Eve night in her accommodation in Windmill Street, off Tottenham Court Road. Hannah said that she'd get there at about 9pm. Hannah never arrived.

On Christmas Day, Greenacre called to see Sarah at about 1pm and they dined together. He stayed until 9 or 10pm. On Boxing Day, Mr Edmonds saw Sarah again at No. 6. Sarah was out all night on Boxing Day, in very inclement weather, returning between 7 and 8am whilst she left their son, under a year old, locked in her Poland Street room. She finally left the lodgings with Greenacre on New Year's Day 1837, when he helped her to remove her possessions back to 6 Carpenter's Place.

On Christmas Eve, Mr Higgins had placed a flagstone against a wall in Edgeware Road. On 28 December, PC Pegler found a sack behind the flagstone. It contained the trunk of a human body. He found mahogany shavings on the sack. An inquest was held on the body on 31 December, and the jury returned a verdict of wilful murder against some person unknown. On 6 January 1837, a bargeman at Johnson's Lock in Stepney, which links the Regent's Canal to the Thames at the Limehouse Basin, complained that the lock gates on the canal wouldn't close. Mattias Rolfe, the lock keeper, used a long wooden pole with a hook on the end to fish out a human head, by its hair. The right eye had been knocked out, and the left jawbone was broken. He wrapped it in a cloth and took it to the 'bone house'. On 2 February, James Page was working at an ozier bed in Coldharbour Lane, Camberwell, when he found a sack containing the legs and thighs of a human body. PC Wood took these remains to the police station and then to the Paddington Poor House.

The head, preserved in spirits, was identified at the Poor House by Hannah's brother, Mr Gay, as Hannah Brown. His identification was confirmed by other witnesses, who all remarked that she had a mark on her left ear caused by a fellow servant having forcibly pulled her earring from her ear lobe. When laid out, the head, trunk, thighs, and legs were all aligned. Thomas Higgins, who worked for Mr Ward, told how his boss knew Hannah Brown and Greenacre. Greenacre had visited their workshop a week before Christmas and afterwards a sack went missing. Higgins identified the sack by the mahogany shavings he used to carry in it, and by a string attached to it that he'd taken from his apron. It was the sack that had contained Hannah's trunk.

On 23 January, Greenacre advertised for a partner to invest £300 in a patent for an apparatus to wash linen. A woman responded and met with him several times. He wrote to her inviting her not only to invest, but also to be his female companion, describing himself as a widower, without any incumbrances.

On 8 February, Mr Birtwhistle and Mr Girdwood, both surgeons, examined the head at the Paddington Poor House. The deceased had received a blow to the right eye causing the loss of the eye and bruising around it. That injury was from a blow of great force before death, such as from a fist, and would have knocked her out. There was a wound to the back of the head that was only visible from inside the skull. That could have been caused by her falling against a blunt object or from the blow to the eye. The neck had been sawn through at the joint and the fleshy part cut with a knife. The head was entirely devoid of blood, suggesting that her throat was cut whilst she was alive, but unconscious, as blood would not have flowed after death. Mr Lane, a chemist, examined her stomach contents. He found gin, but not sufficient to cause intoxication.

Meanwhile, Greenacre had moved. Mr Edmonds described how before they moved out and 6 Carpenter's Place was advertised 'to let', he went to view it. The house smelt of brimstone, as if it had been fumigated. Sarah was there with her son.

On 26 March, Inspector Feltham went to 1 St Albans Street, Kennington, where Greenacre was living. He had a warrant to arrest Greenacre for Hannah's murder. When he entered the bedroom, Greencare was putting on his trousers. The inspector saw a woman in the bed. He asked who she was, and Greenacre replied, 'A woman that's come to sleep with me.' It was Sarah and the inspector told her to get up and dressed so that she could accompany him as well. A rattling sound from her hand was from a watch, which the inspector took from her, together with two rings on her fingers. He also recovered two cornelian earrings set in gold, some money in her pockets and pawn tickets for a pair of shoes and two veils. There were five boxes of possessions, including a boa, a dress, a small neck shawl with drops of blood on it, a collar and other articles identified as belonging to Hannah Brown. He also found a saw, a French knife, and some bullets.

Sarah said: 'There is a child in the next room. I can't go without my boy.' Greenacre said to the inspector: 'It's lucky for you that you came today, for I should have been on my way to the sea tomorrow morning.'

They were taken to Paddington Police Station and placed in separate cells. Sergeant Michael Callow Brown described how Greenacre tried to kill himself. He looked dead when he was found in the cell. He had tried to strangle himself by tying a noose with a silk handkerchief around his neck and attaching the other end to his right foot. The surgeon came and bled him, and he recovered after three hours. 'I don't thank you for what you've done,' Greenacre said. 'Why didn't you let me die? I want to die. Damn the man who is afraid to die. I am not.'

They were moved to the Marylebone Police Office. The road from Paddington Police Station was crowded with people trying to get a glimpse of them. From there they went to New Prison in Clerkenwell, where prisoners were held awaiting examination by magistrates.

The Pre-Trial Examination

On 27 March, their pre-trial examination took place, to establish if there was sufficient evidence to commit them for trial before a jury. That day, Inspector Feltham had returned to 1 St Albans Street and found a child's frock that matched rags found lying near the sack in Edgeware Road.

At the pre-trial examination, Greenacre told how Sarah lived with him and used to wash and cook for him, but on becoming acquainted with Hannah, he had told Sarah to leave, which she did. Hannah had come to his house at about 7pm on Christmas Eve, 'fresh', having been 'treating' (buying food and drink) and drinking with some coachmen. She insisted upon having rum for tea and he had thought it a good opportunity to press her for a statement of her circumstances as she had repeatedly said that she could get £300 or £400 at any time. She refused to answer his questions, and he was convinced that she was deceiving him. He told her that he had found out that she had tried to obtain silk gowns in his name. She feigned a laugh at that and retaliated by saying that he had misrepresented the state of his property. She was rocking backwards and forwards in her chair and he had put his foot against it to stop her. She fell backwards and hit her head with great violence against a clump of wood. She died suddenly. He panicked, thinking that he would be imprisoned for her murder and decided to dispose of the body.

He emphasised that Sarah had played no part in what he did and had no knowledge of where the items identified as belonging to Hannah had come from.

On 1 April, PC Thomas Tringham was in a cell with Greenacre:

Greenacre:	'Many people run away with the idea this was moved in a cart.'
Tringham:	'You mean the body?'
Greenacre:	'Yes, it was not in a cart, but in a cab.'
Tringham:	'Was it on the same night that the affair happened?'
Greencare:	'No, it was not. It was in the morning; on the Monday morning I believe (Boxing Day).'
Tringham:	'Was it after daylight?'

Greenacre: 'No, it was between the hours of 2 and 5am. There was a great deal of mystery about the head. People ran away with the idea that it was thrown over the tunnel at Maida Hill. However, I don't want to satisfy public curiosity.'

The Murder Trial

The trial took place in 1837 before Lord Chief Justice Tindal, Justice Coltman, Recorder Coleridge, and a jury at the Central Criminal Court. Mr Greenacre was charged with the wilful murder of Hannah Brown. Miss Gale was charged that with knowledge of Greenacre's act, she continued to aid, comfort, and assist the murderer. They both pleaded not guilty.

Mr Adolphus, Mr Clarkson, and Mr Bodkin were the prosecution advocates. Mr Price represented both defendants and addressed the jury on their behalf. He admitted that Greenacre was the killer but claimed that the crime was manslaughter rather than murder. He told them that on Christmas Eve, the blow on the eye was inflicted by hand. He asked the jury, 'Is it possible to believe that any man would have struck such a blow without great provocation?' He described Greenacre's action as the 'frantic fury of a frenzied mind, a madman almost'.

He told the jury that there was no evidence to link Sarah with the murder, or the concealment of the body. She had been 'turned out' of Greenacre's house so that he could receive Hannah Brown there. Following the killing, his intention was to share his exile with Sarah, who would comfort him through life, and he had hidden knowledge of what he'd done to Hannah Brown from her.

For the charge against Sarah, the jury would draw their own conclusions from what was known about Sarah's movements at the time. Sarah was seen at 6 Carpenter's Place in the morning of Christmas Eve. The murder had taken place there in the evening. Greenacre spent most of Christmas Day with Sarah in her lodgings. The body remained at 6 Carpenter's Place until it was moved early on Boxing Day morning. Sarah was seen again at No. 6 on Boxing Day. She was found with articles identified as belonging to Hannah Brown.

The Lord Chief Justice summed up for the jury. He asked them to consider whether Greenacre had committed wilful and premeditated murder, or manslaughter: 'an accident from a wanton act.'

Whilst in prison before his trial, Greenacre had written and had published a brief outline of his history, 'in the hope of counteracting the vindictive feelings and public prejudice which have been excited against me, through falsehood and exaggerated statements that have appeared in public newspapers'.

The jury retired for fifteen minutes. Greenacre was guilty of murder. Gale was guilty of helping Greenacre to conceal the body and escape justice.

At the sentence hearing, too late to assist her evidentially, Greenacre protested Sarah's innocence, 'Standing as I do upon the verge of the grave, this woman is as innocent of the offence charged as any lady, or gentleman, in this court. Indeed, she did not know anything of it until we came together at the police office before the magistrates. I feel it, my Lord, to be a religious duty to exculpate her from all participation in this unfortunate affair. With respect to the articles disposed of and possessed by her, she never knew by what means I got them.'

The Recorder sentenced Greenacre first: 'Let me now entreat you to turn to the contemplation of the great change which awaits you, and to occupy every moment of the short interval in applying to the throne of Grace; so that by penitence and prayer you may seek – happily find – through the mention of your Redeemer, the accepted sacrifice for the sins of erring mortals, that forgiveness in another world which you cannot receive in this.'

His Lordship faltered and shed tears. Recovering, he continued, 'It only remains for me to pronounce the awful sentence of the law, which is that you be taken to the gaol from whence you came to a place of execution, and that you there be hanged by the neck until you are dead.'

The Recorder then sentenced Sarah to transportation for life.

Greenacre was taken to the cell for the condemned in Newgate Prison. There he confessed to two Sheriffs of London (who sometimes sat as judges) that in the afternoon on Christmas Eve, he quarrelled with Hannah Brown about how much property each of them possessed. She accused Greenacre of deceiving her about his wealth and used bad language towards him. He took a piece of wood and struck her violently in the right eye. Whilst she was stunned, he cut her throat, collecting the blood in a bucket, and killed her. He dismembered the body and that night had thrown her head into the Regent's Canal.

Before his execution, Greenacre wrote to Sarah: 'It will all be over by 9 o'clock tomorrow, and I hope you will not make yourself unhappy about me. I should advise you to make a good use of your time when abroad, for there females are very scarce, and a good wife is a great treasure and thought more of than in England.'

Greenacre was hanged on 2 May 1837. Sarah was deported on 17 July 1837 on board the ship *Henry Wellesley.* She arrived in New South Wales on 22 December. She married Job Noon in 1849 near Maitland and worked as a bonnet maker. She died aged 81.

COMMENT

A pamphlet, *The Life of James Greenacre* (twenty-eight pages) was published and on sale for sixpence. Another pamphlet, *The Edgeware Road Murder – The Trial of James Greenacre and Sarah Gale* (thirty pages) – *Finding the Head, Trunk and Legs of the Murdered Woman* was also priced sixpence, and advertised as 'the only correct edition, taken in shorthand, detailing the singular manner in which the dreadful and mysterious transaction was discovered.'

The editors were intrigued by the accidental discovery of the head in the canal in Stepney and the legs and thighs in the osier bed in Camberwell; and how together with the trunk from Edgeware Road, providence had enabled all parts of the body, found in the north, south and east of London, to be united and aligned.

The defence of provocation, claimed by James, was a common law concept, not contained in a statute. It could reduce a murder charge to manslaughter. It required the defendant to have been provoked by another's actions or words to such an extent that they temporarily lost self-control and the accused was not 'master of his own understanding'. The provocation had to be such that a reasonable person of the defendant's sex and age might have lost self-control and acted in the same way. This defence was codified in the Homicide Act 1957. It was abolished by the Coroners and Justice Act 2009 and replaced by a requirement of a qualifying trigger in addition to the previous requirements of loss of self-control and passing the reasonable person test. Sexual infidelity can never be a qualifying trigger.

There is a potential conflict of interest on the part of their defence that was ignored. Sarah Gray helped James Greenacre to conceal the crime after he had murdered Hannah Brown. They were both represented by the same barrister, Mr Price. Greenacre's previous history of violence towards women and his cold-blooded murder of Hannah would have made it possible for Sarah's defence to claim that he had threatened her to make her help him conceal the murder and escape justice and that she took those threats seriously, giving her the defence of duress. Duress has been a defence since the thirteenth century. The rationale is that a person should not be punished for an act which they did not do freely and where the alternative was that they feared death or serious injury if they didn't do as instructed. Duress is never a defence to murder but could have been a defence to her charge of harbouring him and concealing the body.

Before 1837 the sentence for an accessory after the fact to murder was death. The 1837 Punishment of Offences Act removed the death penalty for that offence and certain other offences and substituted transportation for life. The aim of the Act was to reduce the use of the death penalty for many offences. Sarah Gale escaped death and was transported instead to the usual destination of Australia. The 1861 Offences Against the Person Act removed transportation and substituted imprisonment for life for being an accessory after the fact to such a grave murder.

In England and Wales, in 1837, when there was no more space in a burial ground, bodies were exhumed and burnt in a 'bone house'. The Stepney Church Yard bone house where the head of Hannah Brown was taken by the police officer was likely at the large graveyard surrounding the parish church of St Dunstan and All Saints. There was also a bone house at the Stepney Meeting House burial ground, and Spitalfields Charnel House.

Hannah's body was pieced together and taken to the Paddington Poor House. It was usual to bring unclaimed bodies there for anatomical dissection, primarily for medical training. The Anatomy Act 1832 allowed the dissection of bodies of people who died in workhouses provided that they were unclaimed. The Poor House was able to profit from medical schools, which used the cadavers. Burial grounds were attached to the workhouses.

The jury was not told about Greenacre's violent history. If the fact of a defendant's previous bad character is not disputed and is of a similar nature to the current allegation, then by the 2003 Criminal Justice Act it may be admitted in court to show that it is more likely that the defendant committed the current offence.

Greenacre's mother was killed and his sister wounded in a sparrow shooting accident. He mistreated his first wife, and she died. He tried to seduce a 16-year-old girl who kept house for him. His second wife was a farmer's daughter with whom he had two children. She was unhappy and tried to poison herself. She died of 'brain fever'. He married his third wife and treated her in a cruel way. He left her in London, where she later died of cholera. He was made bankrupt and travelled to New York with his son, where Greenacre was imprisoned for libel. He married his fourth wife in New York. She was a 19-year-old dressmaker who had emigrated to America with her sister. Needing to hide from some people in New York, Greenacre took his son to Boston. He returned to New York some months later, leaving his son behind. Soon after he returned to London alone, leaving his pregnant wife in New York after relieving her of her savings. He moved into 6 Carpenter's Place, Camberwell. In 1835 Sarah Gale came to live with him.

Osier beds in Coldharbour Lane, where the sack containing the legs and thighs was found, were places where osier willows were grown. The flexible stems were harvested for use in basket weaving and other crafts.

Chapter 20

The Queen v Thomas Jacob, Jane Jacob, and John Jacob for Conspiring to Procure a Marriage by Unlawful Means

Poor Georgina, tricked into marrying at 12 years old, for the sake of her inheritance

Mrs Charlotte Jacob was the widow of Vickers Jacob and Georgina was the only one of their four children to survive. Vickers had settled his estates in Wales, worth £29,000, with an annual income of £1,208, on his widow Charlotte and after her death on Georgina.

Georgina spent the Christmas holidays in 1847, after her twelfth birthday, with Miss Joly at Roscrea in County Tipperary, Ireland. Thomas Jacob (her father's first cousin) arrived and took Georgina to stay with him at his family's home, Mountrath, in County Laois. By March 1848, Georgina was still living with the Jacobs: Thomas and Jane and their children, Alicia and John.

Thomas was interested in Georgina's inheritance and at his request, Charlotte gave Thomas a deed showing the rental values of the Welsh estates. Charlotte said to Jane, 'Mrs Jacob, it is not improbable that in a few years Georgina may become the wife of one of your sons, and I should like John.' Jane replied that it would be an honour that she could not expect. But there would be many plans laid for Georgina, as she was such a fine girl and had such a property.

Thomas proposed a contract of marriage between Georgina and John, who was also underage. Thomas said that of course they wouldn't live together as husband and wife until they were older, and that it would protect Georgina against a whole lot of bad people who were after her inheritance.

Charlotte had doubts about whether she was doing the right thing. She asked Thomas to consult her solicitor, Mr Wolfe, in Dublin about the legal implications of the marriage contract. Thomas called him an 'off-handed fellow' but agreed that he'd go to see him. Thomas didn't call on Mr Wolfe. Asked by Mr Wolfe later why he hadn't consulted him about the marriage contract, Thomas had told him, 'It is too good a prize to be lost, and I knew that you would stop it.'

Charlotte received a letter from Thomas on 6 April 1848, saying that he'd consulted Mr Stephens, a solicitor, on their proposal for the union of John and Georgina. Mr Stephens had confirmed that a proper settlement and contract of marriage before the Registrar would fully and perfectly meet their wishes. Mr Stephens suggested that the estate be settled one half on Georgina and one half on John, and on the children of the marriage after their death. There were two trustees for Vickers' settlement, the Reverends Thornhill and Carpenter, but neither of them were consulted.

On 7 April, Charlotte wrote a letter to Thomas: 'Dear Mr Jacob, I think what you propose *(the marriage settlement)* is quite reasonable. If they enter into a contract before a suitable age, it must be worded that neither will be bound to fulfil it, if they do not feel a true relish and affection for each other, on the expiration of 5 years from the time they enter in the contract, but I am sure there is no fear *(about that)*.' Thomas did not reply.

Thomas objected to the *neither will be bound to fulfil it* and said that he wouldn't enter into a non-binding contract: 'You might as well give it up and go.' Thomas and Jane told Charlotte that her relative, Dr Jacob, was a tyrant and worked at a hospital for the insane, and that he would lock Charlotte up in his madhouse to get at Georgina's inheritance. Thomas claimed that Miss Joly had a young man visiting Roscrea and she would sell Georgina to him for £300 or however much she could get. He said that Charlotte shouldn't refuse to consent to the marriage contract and all they had to do was serve notice of the marriage and go before the Registrar. Charlotte believed that the contract was advantageous for Georgina and would protect her inheritance.

Thomas and Jane urged Charlotte to speak to Georgina and get her consent. They said many times that Georgina and John would not live together until they had married in a church and meanwhile their family would guard, protect and educate her.

Charlotte spoke to Georgina in her bedroom in Mountrath and warned her that her inheritance was in great danger. She asked Georgina to enter into the contract of marriage with John, to protect herself and her property. Georgina was concerned that she didn't know whether she liked John or not. Charlotte told her that it would save her from a plan by Dr Jacob; it was only a contract; and at the age 21 Georgina could marry John or whoever else she pleased. Georgina agreed to do what Charlotte wanted. She asked if she would be bound to John forever. Charlotte told her 'no'. She asked again if she would still be 'free'. Charlotte said that she would. Charlotte later admitted that she knew she wasn't telling Georgina the truth and that it would be binding. Georgina later said that if she had thought it was binding in law, she would not have consented. The Jacobs confirmed to her that she need not 'have' John when she grew up and she believed them.

Charlotte told the Jacobs that Georgina had consented to the contract. John said that he would 'lay himself out' to gain her affections. Thomas said that she was a good girl for being so obedient and she could have a white pony.

Thomas had a marriage settlement drawn up. Charlotte said that she'd like the Attorney General's opinion on it. Thomas replied, 'Poo, pooh.' Charlotte said that the two trustees should sign it. Thomas said that it was useless to trouble the trustees and get their consent. Georgina spotted the words *intermarriage of John and Georgina Jacob* on the back of the deed. She said, 'surely I'm not to be married to John Jacob?' Jane said that it was not a marriage, just a contract. Charlotte reconsidered and thought that what she was doing was wrong. Thomas said it was too far gone to stop it.

Meanwhile, the Registrar of Marriages, John Ince, had been contacted about the ceremony to be performed with him. A Notice of Marriage dated 12 April 1848, had been given showing both parties were underage. Ince contacted the Registrar General, who replied: 'There is not any objection to the marriage of two minors by a District Registrar, provided they have the consent of their parents. But it is to be supposed that no parent … would consent to the marriage of a minor at an improper age.'

The marriage was to take place on 22 April. This was less than the three weeks required from service of the notice. John Ince had been ill for some time and was bedridden. The ceremony was to be conducted in his bedroom. Thomas had written out the words that Georgina was to say in front of the Registrar and had rehearsed it with her. On 22 April morning they went to Ince's house. Two witnesses were found, Mr Turpin and Mr Hill. The Deed of Marriage Settlement was signed in a small parlour off the hall. Charlotte told Mr Turpin that she was extremely glad to get her daughter married into such a respectable family. He thought that Georgina appeared like a noticeably young girl, but as her mother was with her, he wasn't concerned. When Charlotte saw Ince, she though that he looked 'deplorable' and declared, 'this man is dying'.

Ince asked Georgina if she knew what she was doing. She said that she did. He then asked Charlotte if she consented to the marriage. She said 'yes'. Thomas handed Georgina the paper he'd written, and she read it out. John and Georgina signed the Marriage Book. Georgina was very cheery but declined to take John's arm as they left.

Ince died later on the day of the ceremony, having solemnised their marriage on his death bed. It was suggested that Thomas had been anxious for the marriage ceremony to take place before Ince died as another Registrar may have asked the children awkward questions.

After the ceremony, Georgina stayed with the Jacobs in Mountrath. Charlotte visited her constantly. She had a pony that was bought for her before the marriage and John tried his best to please her. During her visits to Mountrath, Charlotte and Georgina shared a bed. One night, Georgina threw her arms around Charlotte in bed and asked her to take her away until she was old enough to be married or to free her if she could. In August, Georgina complained about how she was being treated at the Jacobs. Charlotte became ill and Georgina went home to visit her and didn't return to Mountrath. She implored Charlotte, 'Mamma, now that I am with you, keep me.' John contacted Georgina and said that his father would be very angry if she didn't go back to Mountrath.

Mr and Mrs Jacob visited Charlotte and declared that they had come to bring Georgina back to Mountrath. Georgina said that she wouldn't go with them and hid upstairs. Thomas claimed, in front of Charlotte's brother-in-law, Mr Kehoe, 'John has slept with her.' Neither John nor Jane denied that. Charlotte replied: 'No, and if that's the case I will keep her now and go to the utmost to punish you.' Thomas said that he'd take her if he liked. Charlotte declared, 'Don't you dare go upstairs and touch her.' John and Jane told Thomas they'd hold Charlotte whilst he dragged Georgina down. Mr Kehoe said, 'No violence in this house,' and eventually the Jacobs left.

Charlotte consulted Mr Wolfe in Dublin the next day. He confirmed that Georgina was legally united with John for life.

The Trial

The trial was held at the Spring Assizes, Maryborough in Queen's County, Ireland in 1850, before the Lord Chief Justice and a special jury of twelve men. Francis M'Donogh QC prosecuted. Mr Hayes defended. Thomas Jacob, Jane Jacob, and John Jacob were charged with conspiring to procure a marriage by unlawful means between John Jacob and Georgina Jacob, a minor aged 12 entitled to a large property.

The prosecutor told the jury that it was illegal to conspire to procure a marriage by unlawful means, such as false representations, fraud and deceit. Each of the defendants must have contributed to the unlawful means. It was enough if each conspirator had, by his acts or expressions, shown that he was cognisant of the conspiracy and contributed somehow to its success. Thomas was a practising lawyer and would have understood the legal implications of what he was doing. He also commented that Charlotte became a plotter against Georgina's best interests, so that Georgina was completely alone.

The Marriage Certificate stated that the marriage was solemnised in an office, instead of at Ince's deathbed. The defence argued that his whole house was his 'office'. The Lord Chief Justice told the jury that this was not like the Wakefield case. The validity of the marriage was not disputed and was not in issue at this trial: 'Your verdict will leave it (the marriage) where you find it.'

The Lord Chief Justice summed up the case to the jury and told them to focus on the charge: that they falsely and wickedly represented to Georgina that the contract wouldn't bind her until she was 21; if she didn't like John Jacob she could marry whom she pleased; and she wouldn't be his wife until they married as grown-ups in a church. Did they intend to deceive her and was she deceived? She was only 12 years and 3 months old at the time of the marriage and without a father to protect her.

The jury retired for only thirty minutes and then returned to find all three defendants not guilty.

COMMENT

The judge told the jury that Charlotte became a plotter with the Jacobs against Georgina. She could surely have been charged as part of the conspiracy.

Relative values: The estates worth £29,000 and the annual income worth £1,208 in 1850 would be worth £3,395,375 and £141,434 respectively in 2026.

Chapter 21

The Trial of Roman Weinzoeptlein for Rape, a Roman Catholic Priest

1844

'No person will commit a crime without an adequate motive. The motive? The lust of the priest lurked beneath his questions (in the confessional) *and finally led him to the deed of darkness'*

In the absence of the regular clergyman who was on a tour of Europe, a temporary French priest, Father Roman Weinzoeptlein, officiated at the Catholic church in Evansville, Indiana. Aged in his late twenties, he was described as retiring and reclusive in nature.

Anna Maria Schmoll, aged 20, was a native of Bavaria. Her family had emigrated to America in 1840. She lived with her husband, Martin Schmoll, just 350ft from the rear of the neighbourhood Catholic church. Martin was a Lutheran Protestant whilst Anna was a Roman Catholic. They had married on New Year's Eve 1841. She later accused him of enticing her from her father's home to marry him after only three to four weeks' acquaintanceship. They had eloped and married against her family's wishes. Their marriage was performed by a civil magistrate instead of by a priest, which had led the Catholic church to deny her the holy sacrament.

For five months following their marriage she did not attend church. She consulted the Right Reverend Dr De La Hailendieve, Bishop of Vincennes, and on her executing a marriage contract on 1 May 1842, pledging that all her children would be brought up in the Catholic faith and placing that in the hands of Father Weinzoeptlein, the Bishop declared her civil marriage to be lawful, and she was allowed to return to worship and receive communion.

On the eve of Ascension 1842, a few days after delivering the marriage contract and in preparation for receiving communion the next day, Anna went to confession in the late afternoon. Witnesses later said that she had waited for others to enter the confessional, making her the last person when the church was getting dark. The marriage had been consummated, and she was about three months' pregnant.

Anna confessed all her sins to Father Weinzoeptlein in the small confessional box. It measured 8ft by 3ft and was divided into two compartments separated by a small lattice window. To her surprise, the priest asked her how many times her husband had 'used her' in a month. She was understandably embarrassed and replied that she couldn't and wouldn't say. He told her that she must answer him and tell him how many times in a week they had intercourse. She said that she didn't know exactly. He insisted that she tell him, as near as she could recollect. She answered two or three times each week. He said that there wasn't much happiness with a Lutheran, forgave her sins and gave her a penance. Still in the confessional, she commenced the customary prayer after the giving of the penance.

Anna claimed that Father Weinzoeptlein came out of his part of the confessional, took hold of her right arm, pulled her round and then took hold of her left arm and pulled her out from where she had been kneeling, threw her onto her back on the floor, and penetrated her. She told how she was too frightened to speak out or resist, and at that point she lost consciousness. When she came to, her clothes were pulled up and she cried out, 'Oh God, what have you done to me?' He lifted her up, sat her on a bench, wet her face with water, and asked her if she had remembered her penance. When she said that she hadn't, he gave her a new penance. Her straw bonnet was broken. She left for home.

It was later than expected when Anna returned home. She told how Martin asked her what had delayed her, but she just replied that she had to wait her turn for confession. Later, she was obviously agitated and distressed and before daylight was sighing and crying. Towards the morning, she told him something had happened in the church that had never happened before: Father Weinzoeptlein had asked her about Martin's intercourse with her. She told Martin that she would explain further when she returned from communion. She went to the church with her young sister and they both received the holy Eucharist from the Father.

Martin Schmoll reported how in the afternoon, when he and Anna were alone, 'She told me about the horrid outrage. She told me that she didn't know whether the Father had put his seed in her or not.' Martin cried when she told him and wanted to take a pistol and execute Father Weinzoeptlein.

She persuaded him not to be violent as Martin would be hanged for it. The next morning, she told Martin to go to the church and talk to the Father. He went to the church, woke the priest, and demanded the return of the pledge. As the priest searched for the paper, Martin told him that he knew what had happened. The priest appeared scared, gave the paper to him, and admitted that he'd kept Anna a long time at confession but that to be guilty of ravishing her he'd have to be the worst person in the world. He said that Anna was 'out of her head but would come to'.

Martin brought Father Weinzoeptlein back to their house, where Anna was in bed crying. Anna told Martin to tell the Father what he'd done as she was too agitated to say. Martin told the priest what she alleged, and she confirmed that it was true. Martin questioned the priest about what right he had to ask Anna about his intercourse with her. Father Weinzoeptlein replied that it was his right as she had said in confession that she considered her marriage unlawful and therefore he had the right to ask the questions to impose the proper penance. Martin reminded Father Weinzoeptlein that he'd said in Anna's presence only two or three days before that the Bishop had confirmed the marriage to be lawful.

With Martin's permission, Anna's father came to see her and in front of him Martin asked Anna if what she was saying was true. She said it was, and Martin said that he'd take revenge. Father Weinzoeptlein had told the couple to make a complaint to the Bishop, but Anna's father told her to resort to the law instead. On 6 May 1842, a warrant was issued for Father Weinzoeptlein's arrest. Two officers located him at Fitzwilliam, 7 or 8 miles from Evansville. He told them that he was on his way to see the Bishop at Vincennes.

The Committal Hearing

The committal hearing should have taken place on 12 May, but it was adjourned because the defence complained that the magistrate was also a protestant minister and would be biased against Father Weinzoeptlein. The next morning, before a different magistrate, Anna wept, was tremulous and agitated and finally fainted during her evidence. She was carried from the courtroom. A fight took place outside, between Irish supporters of the Father and German supporters of Anna. The priest made a speedy exit in a waggon that had been standing by. The press reported that 'the jury committed the ravisher'.

The First Trial

The trial was held in 1843. Anna was asked if she believed in a marriage ceremony performed by a civil magistrate. She answered that she did. The defence called witnesses to impeach her character, and the prosecution called witnesses to rebut them – cancelling each other out. The jury couldn't reach a unanimous verdict as one juror insisted that Father Weinzoeptlein was not guilty. A retrial was ordered. The defence claimed that due to all the bad publicity about Father Weinzoeptlein, justice could not be done by trying him within his community.

The Second Trial

A retrial took place in Gibson County in 1844. The indictment named Anna and stated that he 'did make an assault, and in a rude, insolent, and angry manner, did unlawfully touch, strike, beat, wound and ill-treat with intent and then feloniously did ravish and carnally know by force and against her will'. Anna was now separated from Martin, who had treated her and their child very badly. About two weeks before the previous trial, eleven or twelve months after the rape and after their child was born, he had driven her and the child out of his house, when they were both extremely ill. As a consequence, their child had died, and Martin was now her greatest enemy.

The prosecution claimed that Father Weinzoeptlein had mistakenly tried to claim 'benefit of clergy', to escape the jurisdiction of the civil court when he was caught on his way to see the Bishop at Vincennes. The Bishop now called Anna a 'notorious, lying, shameless girl'. An officer told the jury that on arrest the priest had sworn 'woman, Schmoll, traitor'. His fellow officer said that the priest had accused Anna of betraying him and was a traitor to him.

A witness described how he and another man had re-enacted the pulling her out of the confessional and that it was easy to do. The prosecution explained that Anna had delayed telling Martin about such an important attack on her so that he would not stop her from receiving Holy Communion after such a long absence, and that she was so desperate for the sacrament that she was prepared to receive it from Father Weinzoeptlein. They described the priest's questions to Anna about intercourse as demonstrations of his lust for her and reminded the jury that the priest had not resolutely denied her accusation of rape.

The defence claimed that receiving the Eucharist from a man whom she had reported had raped her the day before and allowing her young sister to do the same was evidence that she was lying about the rape. Father Weinzoeptlein did not give evidence at the trial because in those days the defendant was not a competent witness on his own behalf. The defence maintained that Father Weinzoeptlein did not accept the validity of her marriage and regarded her intercourse with Martin as sinful and needed to give her absolution and fix her penance.

The surprising number of five advocates, three for the prosecution and two for the defence (it would have been six, but a defence advocate was too busy to prepare his speech), made closing speeches to the jury. First, Mr Blythe for the prosecution spoke of the priest's questioning her about the marriage bed. He described her manner when testifying as 'simple, honest, and earnest', with no indication of depravity. He told the jury that Anna believed that if she didn't partake of the Eucharist the next day, she would be 'lost' as that was how she would 'consummate' her return to the Catholic church; and that it didn't change the efficacy of the sacrament if it was dispensed to her by Father Weinzoeptlein, an impure person. He said that she had no motive for making such a serious false allegation.

Mr Blythe quoted from Starkie, first volume of his *Treatise of the Law of Evidence*, 'A perjured witness ... will be sparing of his detail of circumstances which are false and capable of contradiction'. Whereas Anna had been detailed in her evidence about her conduct before she went to the church, whilst she was there and after she came away.

Mr Jones followed, for the defence. He asked the jury: why did she not give the alarm as soon as she became conscious? Her first impulse would surely be to shriek out and call for help. Families lived on both sides of the church. Why did she not rush from his presence instead of walking calmly home? Why did she try to avoid her husband on returning home, instead of immediately looking to him for sympathy and protection? Mr Jones claimed that her obviously upset manner was not because of the priest, but because of her guilt at the sins she had committed during her five months' lapse from the church: 'violating the precepts of her religion and incurring the displeasure of God'.

Mr Jones, in a roundabout way, tried to convince the jury that the motive for Anna falsely accusing Father Weinzoeptlein of rape was to stop her husband believing that she was committing adultery with the priest. Mr Jones, having said that he would confine himself to the facts, constructed and put forward the proposals, without any proof, that Father Weinzoeptlein had not forgiven Anna her sins in the confessional as Anna had sinned publicly by cohabiting with Martin; she had failed to engage in public worship and absented herself from the church; and that her civil marriage was sinful, unlawful and contrary to her religion. The priest believed that it was too soon for him to absolve her and permit her publicly to take Holy Communion. She needed to prove her devotion. So, Mr Jones continued, she went home upset and in disgrace with no intention of taking Holy Communion the next day, except what changed her mind was her realisation that Martin would be suspicious of her if she didn't.

Next, Mr Jones proposed that Martin, a jealous man and suspicious of Father Weinzoeptlein, believed that her signs of mental suffering and the fact that she had waited until last for the confessional, returning home late, all meant that that she and the priest had embraced with her consent. When they went to bed, Martin believed that she was keeping something from him. He asked her what had happened. She said that she couldn't tell him because of the secrecy of the confessional. This made it worse, and Martin complained that 'a woman can go alone to the church whenever she pleases, and her husband is not permitted to know anything that took place'.

Martin appeared driven almost mad with jealousy, Mr Jones reasoned, and Anna knew that unless she could satisfy him that she was innocent, all her hope of future happiness was forever lost. Anna had to devise a means to extricate herself and restore Martin's confidence in her. So, she suddenly commenced crying and when he asked if she was sick, she said that she had something to tell him: the priest had asked her obscene questions. Martin was even more concerned. Not only had she heard such questions, but she had answered them. He became absolutely convinced of her adultery. He asked if that was all that the priest had done, saying that he knew there was something more and he wanted to know. She realised by this time, Mr Jones claimed, that she was digging a deeper and deeper hole for herself. Not knowing what to do, she said that she would tell him more the next day.

Martin knew, Mr Jones said, that the sole reason for her confession was so that she could take the sacrament the following day. Mr Jones reasoned that if Anna hadn't taken it, the jealous Martin would be confirmed in his suspicions that she was guilty of infidelity: a crime of which the neighbours' wives who took the sacrament were not. Anna had realised this and that the priest could not refuse her the sacrament in public. That is why she attended church with her sister the next morning. When she returned home, Martin's mind was made up about her behaviour with the priest and so, Mr Jones concluded, she had to say that the priest did more than just ask her nasty questions: he had forced himself on her.

Mr Jones even suggested that as Anna had been to confession with Father Weinzoeptlein, nine months before her child was born, and since the priest and Martin both had black hair, it was not possible to be certain who was the real father of Anna's child.

Mr Chandler replied for the prosecution. He explained to the jury that a churchgoer who does not take Holy Communion once a year at Easter will be excommunicated: so, Anna had no choice. In Mr Chandler's opinion, 'This young, full blooded Catholic priest was honestly trying the difficult experiment of chastity and was overcome by the frenzy of the moment.'

He claimed that Father Weinzoeptlein's motive for going to Vincennes was to claim the benefit of clergy and secure the intervention of the Bishop so that he was exempt from the civil jurisdiction of the court and would be dealt with by the Ecclesiastical Court instead. He read from *Blackstone's Commentaries* that the Catholic Church claimed immunity and exemption from municipal jurisdiction for offences by clergy who faced capital or corporal punishment. He accepted that this punishment no longer applied to rape in Indiana, but the defendant was a young man who had recently come to the country and may not have known that.

Mr Pitcher replied for the defence. He quoted Lord Hale, 'the accusation's easily made but hard to prove'. He then quoted from *The Elements of Medical Jurisprudence 6th edition by Beck*, 'in the opinion of the writers, it is preposterous to suppose a rape can be committed without resistance; and the perpetration of rape is impossible without the infliction of great bodily injury, unless resistance is overcome by the fear of death or the power of drugs.' Mr Pitcher continued, 'nature has given to woman the power of defending herself in such emergencies ... the blood rushes to the face ... and the weakest sex becomes as strong and fierce as a tigress. The priest did not have superhuman powers to paralyse her. Chastity is a gem which a woman defends with her life. We can safely assure Mr Chandler that if he expects to attain the highest favour of the fair in no other way than by a scuffle for it, he will in all probability die with his seed in his loins, for his virtuous wrestler will resist till death, and so long as she has consciousness prove the better man of the two.'

If Father Weinzoeptlein had intended to flee, he added, he could have stepped into a boat in Evansville and in two minutes he'd be in the state of Kentucky and out of the reach of the officers. He also referred to the 'appalling' situation of a Catholic priest being tried by a Protestant jury 'on a charge involving the character of his church'.

Mr Lockhart spoke last, for the prosecution. He followed on Mr Chandler's quote from Thomas Starkie's *Treatise of the Law of Evidence*: 'No person will commit a crime without an adequate motive'. The motive? 'The lust of the priest lurked beneath his questions and finally led him to the deed of darkness.'

The jury were told that the sentence range for rape was five to twenty-one years' imprisonment. The jury was out for only half an hour and declared Father Weinzoeptlein guilty. He was sentenced to five years' hard labour.

COMMENT

The report of the trial (eighty pages) headlined the shocking words 'A Roman Catholic Priest ... for Rape ... Whilst at Confessional.' It was written by Mr W.H. Chandler, who deposited it with the Clerk's Office, District of Indiana. He wrote that the case 'excited such intense interest throughout the County': the enormity of the offence; and the novelty of the circumstances.

When his trials took place, in America in 1843 and 1844, the law did not permit a defendant to give evidence on oath on his own behalf. It followed that the defendant could not be cross-examined. The reasoning was that the court could not trust the testimony of the accused because of their interest in the outcome of the case. Their evidence would be biased and their fear of punishment, whether innocent or guilty, would cause them to perjure themselves. To protect the criminal process from perjury it was necessary to keep the accused silent. In 1863 Sir James Stephenson dismissed the arguments for change, 'It is a mockery to swear a man to speak the truth who is certain to disregard it.' The vacuum left by the absence of the accused's account was sometimes filled by his advocates. Mr Jones promised to confine himself to the facts, but went ahead and did just the opposite, constructing hypotheses to explain Roman's thoughts and actions as if they were real facts.

But change was on the way. Chief Justice John Appleton of the Supreme Court of Maine became the leading voice for reform. The principle of impartial neutrality, blind justice holding in her hands the even-balanced scales without prejudice for or against the accused, required that each be heard. He argued that the defendant's testimony was crucial in order to ascertain the whole truth and would increase the efficiency with which the guilty were convicted. He believed that the law aided the criminal. Maine, in 1864, was the first American state to deem the accused a competent witness in his defence. Other states followed and by the end of the century only Georgia still disqualified the defendant.

Father Weinzoeptlein's first trial was not conclusive, because the jury verdict was eleven to one. In America, Louisiana and Oregon were the only states to accept majority verdicts. The US Supreme Court confirmed their right to do this in 1972, but the same court then rejected its previous decision as bad law in 2020 and required all states to accept that the sixth amendment required juries to be unanimous.

American criminal law started to deviate from British law in the late eighteenth and early nineteenth centuries. American courts began to interpret and apply English common law in ways that reflected American principles and gradually developed their own precedents and legal doctrines. The court referred to several English legal reference books such as *Archbold's Pleadings* and *Blackstone's Commentaries*. John Frederick Archbold was an English barrister who in 1824 published his *Summary of the Law relative to Pleading and Evidence in Criminal Cases.* William Blackstone was an eighteenth-century jurist who wrote a four-volume work on English law known as *Blackstone's Commentaries*. Thomas Starkie was an English barrister who wrote the *Treatise of the Law of Evidence* (1824).

The prosecution suggested, without evidence, that Father Weinzoeptlein believed he was allowed to choose trial by an ecclesiastical court under canon law, rather than a secular court, and may have been racing to the Bishop's Palace to seek the jurisdiction of the ecclesiastical court, where he was likely to be treated more leniently in procedure and sentence. The Benefit of Clergy Act 1496 restricted this privilege in England and Wales to certain crimes only. By the end of the sixteenth century, rape was included in the list of unclergyable offences, and the benefit was abolished by the Criminal Law Act 1827. In America, it was abolished in federal courts by the Crimes Act 1790, but some states continued to use it in their own judicial systems. Rhode Island was the last state to abolish it in 2013.

Father Weinzoeptlein was tried and sentenced in Indiana, where the mandatory sentence for rape is currently between three and sixteen years. In many states, first degree rape is sentenced to life imprisonment and in Louisiana, if the victim is aged under 13, it is punishable by death. In

England, rape ceased to be a capital offence by the 1841 Punishment of Death Act.

In this trial, the defence claimed that a victim would always fight back, usually successfully, and always resulting in their being injured. It is still a myth, in 2026, that if a victim wasn't hurt or didn't fight off the attacker, it could not have been rape. This myth seeks to blame the victim instead of the perpetrator.

Chapter 22

Crawford v Crawford

Divorce, Co-respondent Sir Charles Dilke

1886

'The act of seduction took only a half hour. But they had heard how busy Sir Charles was'

Sir Charles Wentworth Dilke's wife died in 1874 and in the early 1880s he was yet to marry his second wife. Donald Crawford married Virginia Smith in 1881, when he was aged 44 and she was aged only 18. Virginia's elder sister, Margaret Eustace Smith, was married to Sir Charles's younger brother, Ashton Dilke. Sir Charles Dilke, the Liberal Party MP for Chelsea, did not deny having been the lover of Ellen Smith, who was Virginia's mother.

After Donald and Virginia were married, they stayed at Bailey's Hotel, then spent the autumn in Scotland, returning to London on 20 February 1882 to live at 35 Sydney Place, South Kensington. In March or April 1882, Donald received an anonymous letter at the Home Office. The letter ended cryptically, 'Beware of the member for Chelsea'. Donald said that Virginia went very pale when he showed it to her. With her encouragement, he burnt the letter. Virginia said that she believed her mother Ellen, from whom she was estranged, had sent it.

Donald reported that around that time he had a strange conversation with Virginia as they lay in bed. She asked him if he would forgive her if she was unfaithful. He replied that he didn't think that he could. On another occasion, soon after, she asked him whether if they divorced, she could keep her own money. He told her that he wouldn't touch it. Donald felt that Virginia was less affectionate towards him after their return from Scotland to London. They had quarrelled and he said to her, 'My dear, I believe the time may come when it will not be possible for us to live together.' She replied, 'I shall never leave you unless you send me away. If you send me away, I suppose I can always drown myself.'

In February 1883, Donald and Virginia moved to 27 Young Street, Kensington Square. In 1884, Donald was suspicious about Virginia's fidelity, in particular regarding a Captain Forster, who Donald believed she had first met at a ball in February 1884. In June 1884, a Miss Townsend, who worked helping the poor with Virginia at St Jude's Whitechapel, was handed a letter to pass to Virginia. Miss Townsend looked at it and handed it to the vicar, saying it was 'A silly foolish letter written by some officer in barracks.' The vicar also opened it and told Donald about the contents. Donald had serious words with the captain about it.

In autumn 1884, Donald and Virginia moved to lodgings in 61 Sloane Street, near Dilke's house. In March 1885, Donald received an anonymous letter at the Home Office: 'The first person who ruined your wife was Sir Charles Dilke. She has passed nights in his house and is well known to the servants.' Donald showed the letter to Virginia, who said, 'That's my mother, she's a fiend.' Another anonymous letter reached Donald on 10 June, 'Your wife was seen at the Metropole with Captain Forster. Are you a fool?' and a fourth letter arrived on 17 July: 'Fool, looking for the cuckoo when he has flown, having defiled your nest. You have been foully deceived but dare not touch the real traitor.' Captain Forster had left London with his army detachment. Sir Charles Wentworth Dilke was the Liberal Party MP for Chelsea in 1868–86. From 1880 to 1882 he was Under Secretary of State for Foreign Affairs in Gladstone's government. Donald Crawford was the MP for a seat in Lanarkshire and Secretary to the Lord Advocate in the Home Office. Sir Charles's influence could have helped Donald to obtain a more senior position in Scottish governance.

When Donald confronted Virginia about the allegation, she told him, 'Yes, it's true. It's time you should know the truth. You have always been on the wrong track, suspecting people who are innocent, and you have never suspected the person who is guilty.' Donald said, 'I never suspected anybody except Captain Forster.' Virginia replied, 'It was not Captain Forster. The man who ruined me was Sir Charles Dilke. He seduced me six months after our marriage, three and a half years ago and I was his mistress after that. He called on me at the Bailey's Hotel when we were there after our wedding trip. He made love to me there, and kissed me, but nothing more. He called at Sydney Place two or three days after we came to London. I met him at a house off Tottenham Court Road (65 Warren Street) the same day, where he seduced me.'

'I shall horsewhip Dilke.' Donald said. Virginia replied, 'You will have revenge on him. I can give you the means of proving it … the footmen used to let me in, and they must know me ... Sarah (Gray) used to dress me ... she is a servant who has been in his service, but perhaps she won't say anything, she has been his mistress ... Ann (the parlour maid) could tell you things too ... if she likes ... Sir Charles Dilke's coachman could give evidence also ... He made me go to bed with Fanny, a woman he had as a mistress. I did not like it at first, but I did it because he wished it ... he used to come to bed by the side of us ... he taught me every French vice. He taught me all I knew. He used to say that I knew more than most women of thirty. He said that he liked me because I was so like my mother.'

Virginia admitted spending two nights in Dilke's house in 1883. She said that they had twice gone to the house off Tottenham Court Road; would also meet at his house, where he would take her to his bedroom; and he would come to her house. She told Donald that the 'intrigue' with Dilke had finished at the end of 1884. They had always used 'French letters'.

Virginia denied being 'guilty' with Captain Forster. On 18 July 1885 she told Donald that Captain Forster had always treated her like a lady. 'He is not my lover. No, never.' She had only met with him, lunched with him, and gone to a picture gallery with him.

Anne Jamieson had been a parlour maid with Virginia since January 1882. She recalled how Virginia had stayed out all night in 1883, shortly after she and Virginia had arrived back from Scotland, but whilst Donald was still away. Virginia had gone out for a second night then, arriving home at an unknown hour after Anne had gone to bed. In 1883, Dilke also came to the Crawfords' house, 27 Young Street, about five times, fortnightly, arriving at 12 or 12.30. He'd stay for about half an hour.

The Divorce Trial

After five years of marriage, Donald sued for divorce on the ground of Virginia's adultery, naming Sir Charles Dilke as the co-respondent. The hearing was on 12 February 1886 before Mr Justice Butt in the Probate, Divorce and Admiralty Division. Virginia was not in court and Donald relied upon the full confession that she had made to him, and the evidence of their parlour maid Anne. Dilke declined to give evidence.

The Attorney General represented Dilke. He addressed Mr Justice Butt, 'I wish to make the ground clear to your Lordship. The statement which he [Mr Crawford)] has made is evidence against the lady [Mrs Crawford] but not evidence perhaps [Mr Crawford telling the court what Mrs Crawford had told him the year before about her adultery with Dilke] except in a very remote degree indeed and certainly in no material degree, against Sir Charles Dilke.'

Mr Justice Butt went even further in Dilke's favour. 'I do not recollect at this moment, Mr Attorney, that there is any bit of evidence against Sir Charles Dilke. I cannot say that there is any case against the co-respondent on the evidence … there can't be any doubt that by English law and common sense a statement made by a lady such as Mrs Crawford is said to have made cannot be evidence against a co-respondent.' He said he was satisfied against Mrs Crawford, that she would not lie about her actions in having committed adultery with Sir Charles Dilke and granted Mr Crawford a divorce decree nisi. But against Sir Charles, the evidence was not reliable enough to blame him. He concluded, 'I cannot see any case whatsoever against Sir Charles Dilke,' and dismissed him from the suit with costs.

The Queen's Proctor's Intervention

On 10 April 1886, following an attack in the press on Dilke's character and reputation, he sought to reopen the case and clear his name completely by writing to the Queen's Proctor, asking him to intervene. Dilke would not be a party to the proceedings, which would be brought by the Queen's Proctor, but he offered to pay the legal costs incurred. Evidentially, the difference with this hearing and the divorce trial was that now Virginia and Sir Charles would both give their accounts to the jury about what had been going on between them, which proved the undoing of Sir Charles.

The Queen's Proctor proceeded with the intervention and the hearing in the Divorce Division of the High Court of Justice opened on 14 July 1886 before Sir James Hannen and a special jury.

Judge Hannen made it clear to the jury that the purpose of the intervention was to prevent the decree nisi from being made absolute, it being alleged that the decree was obtained, 'Contrary to the justice of the case in consequence of material facts not being before the court.' At the divorce hearing, it had been for Mr Crawford to prove that his wife had committed adultery with Sir Charles Dilke, and he had done that to the satisfaction of Mr Justice Butt. Sir Charles had been discharged from the case 'on a formal and technical ground … the judge acted as he was bound to by the rules of the court when he said that there was no evidence against Sir Charles Dilke.'

'It is suggested,' said Sir Walter Phillimore representing the Queen's Proctor, 'that the decree was obtained by "jugglery", she was an adulteress, and he deserved a divorce. There was … no jugglery.' Mr Justice Butt did not find that Mrs Crawford had committed adultery with a person or persons unknown, but that she had committed adultery with Sir Charles Dilke. The Queen's Proctor would attempt to reverse Mr Justice Butt's finding and prove to the jury that Mrs Crawford had not committed adultery with Sir Charles and as a consequence, Mr Crawford was not entitled to the decree nisi he had obtained. If the jury was in any doubt, they must find for Mr Crawford and against the Queen's Proctor, on whom the burden of proof lay.

The evidence given to the judge at the divorce trial was read to the jury. The Queen's Proctor then called his main witness, Sir Charles Dilke. He denied ever having 'made love' or paid court to Mrs Crawford; or being intimate with Fanny Gray. He declined to say whether he had been Virginia's mother's lover.

He was asked about certain dates and denied meeting Virginia then: 23 February 1882; 6 May 1882; 7 December 1882; 13 and 14 February 1883. He had a detailed account ready of where he was at those times, including fencing; the Foreign Office; Foreign Office party; Queen's Speech Dinner; the House of Commons; Cabinet meetings; receptions; constituent meetings; dining at home; dining with friends; tennis.

He said that he went to 65 Warren Street once or twice a year to visit Madame Anna Dessouslary, who had been in his family's service for many years. He had never taken any woman there and he had never taken Mrs Crawford to any address. Instead, Mrs Crawford had visited him at his home, maybe two or three times when he was at breakfast. She was anxious about her husband obtaining a permanent place in any Scottish home rule system and talked about her charitable work in Whitechapel. He would call on her two or three times each year, more frequently since she and her husband moved to live a few doors away from him in 1884. He produced his diary, which suspiciously had entries cut out and removed. He explained that if an appointment fell through, he would cut it out with scissors and keep it on his desk to remind him that the appointment had not taken place.

Sarah Gray was in Dilke's service from 1872, until his second marriage in autumn 1885. She was not aware of any coming together between him and Mrs Crawford. Fanny Gray was her sister and was in his service for a short time aged 13, until seven or eight years previously. Fanny had disappeared before the divorce trial but had turned up shortly after the trial and given a statement to Dilke's solicitor. Fanny had complained about being harassed by detectives for Mr Crawford who had showed her a picture of Mrs Crawford, and she had told them that she didn't recognise her. It was arranged by Dilke's solicitor that Fanny would go and live with Mrs Ruffle, in Essex, and work as a servant for her. Dilke denied that this was to keep her out of the way, so that she could not give evidence against him.

Dilke was asked why he had not given evidence at the divorce trial, to challenge being named the co-respondent. He said that he had expected to go into the witness box until the last moment, when counsel advised him not to. He never thought that Mrs Crawford would be believed.

Sir Walter Phillimore QC, referred to Mr Justice Butt's ruling that Mrs Crawford's statement could not amount to evidence against Sir Charles Dilke as the reason why Dilke had been advised against giving evidence himself. It was risky, because he would have to admit to his relationship with Mrs Crawford's mother, and in the light of the judge's ruling it was also unnecessary.

Ernest Humbert, Dilke's solicitor, told how he had taken a statement from Fanny Stock (nee Gray), who had married one of Mr Ruffle's servants. Before the divorce trial she was an unwilling witness and wouldn't give a statement. Mrs Ruffle gave evidence that in July 1885, Mr Humbert had asked her to take Fanny as a servant. He said that she was mixed up in some way with the Crawford-Dilke case and he had wanted to keep an eye on her. She stayed with Mrs Ruffle for four months. Humbert paid her travel expenses.

Anna Dessouslary said that she had lived at 65 Warren Street since 1881. Sir Charles came to visit her once each year and had never brought a lady there. Fanny came to her in 1884 and stayed for one year, working as a companion and help and in return she fed her. She was later contradicted by three members of the Hillier family, who gave evidence about when they lived in 65 Warren Street. Sir Charles would come to the house fairly frequently with a tall lady, who was not Mrs Crawford. They would use Madame Dessouslary's bedroom whilst Madame stayed in the small front room or on the stairs.

Mrs Rogerson told how Virginia had confessed to her in August 1884 that from shortly after her marriage she had frequently committed adultery with Sir Charles Dilke, in her house and his. He was always in a rush and was never in her house for more than ten minutes at a time. She told

Virginia to break off her intimacy with Sir Charles and promise never to see him again.

Virginia had also confessed to Mrs Rogerson that she had committed adultery with Captain Forster. She said that she loved Captain Forster very much indeed and was his lover and met him frequently in 1885 until he left with the army. She was asked if she believed Virginia, about her adultery with Sir Charles. She replied that she was doubtful and 'went up and down' about it. On the one hand, she couldn't believe that anybody would say such a thing unless it was true. On the other, she didn't believe it because it was something so impossible, to her mind.

Several witnesses gave evidence that, based on the handwriting, Mrs Rogerson was the author of the anonymous letters to Donald Crawford. A handwriting expert gave evidence that the handwriting was similar to Mrs Crawford's.

Virginia said that she'd known Sir Charles Dilke since she was a child, when she used to see him a great deal. He used to call her Nia. She wouldn't say what she meant by his 'making love' to her at Bailey's Hotel, 'I can't go into details, it's not respectable.'

She did go into detail about how she had located the house in Warren Street: 'He told me the address but wouldn't let me write it down. He made me repeat it and described the house to me. He said it was on the North side of Warren Street with two tall houses beside it. I was to get out of the cab on the corner of Warren Street, go to the house with three bells and press one of them at 11.30am. A woman would let me in. I should go straight upstairs to the back room on the first floor. He'd be waiting for me there. He said he was going to seduce me.' She explained that the room was a bedroom and the curtains were drawn. She stayed for about one hour. He left first. She went there again at 11.30am on 6 May when Mr Crawford had gone to Oxford ahead of her by the morning train. She went to the room and Sir Charles arrived shortly afterwards. She left first, went home, got her luggage and caught the 2.15pm train to Oxford to join her husband.

She went to Sir Charles's house five or six times, at the end of July and beginning of August 1882 after her husband had left home for work. Mr Crawford had to be at the Home Office by 11am but Sir Charles was not expected at the Foreign Office until noon. She'd get out of the cab on the corner of Pond Street and walk. He'd be waiting in the conservatory by the front door and let her in without her having to ring the bell. She'd arrive at 11.15 to 11.30am. She'd go up the stairs to the Blue Room on the staircase.

From there, when the coast was clear, he'd take her up to his bedroom. She'd run up the stairs as gently as she could, so as not to make a noise. The staircase had thick carpets, which helped. They would have only fifteen to thirty minutes together. She was able to describe his bedroom. He'd leave first and Sarah, the housemaid, would help Virginia to dress. Sarah would watch the stairs and fetch her when it was safe to leave.

She met Sir Charles on 7 December 1882. Mr Crawford had left for Edinburgh. She spent the night with Sir Charles in his bedroom, leaving at 3am or 4am. Sarah helped her to dress and let her out. She joined her husband in Edinburgh, returning to London on 13 February 1883 on her own. Mr Crawford was still in Edinburgh. Sarah let her into Sir Charles's house at 9pm and took her up to his bedroom. She went to bed and was asleep when Sir Charles arrived at around 11pm. In the morning, Sarah brought her breakfast, helped her dress, and let her out at 7.30am.

They met frequently during 1883. She had gone to his house eight or ten times, and he had called on her about six or so times, around 11.30am. Adultery had taken place on those occasions. He had talked about Virginia's mother, saying that he had been her lover and how Virginia was very much like her mother, that's why he had taken a fancy to her. He had spoken about Fanny, saying she was a girl who used to sleep with him, spending the night at his house. She was nice, and young – about Virginia's age or younger. Sarah, Fanny's, sister, would let her in at 9pm, when the servants were at supper, and let her out in the morning. She first saw Fanny in August 1883 when she came into the bedroom from an adjoining room. Virginia had burst out crying and asked Sir Charles to send her away. He brought Fanny into the bedroom once more in spring 1884. Again, Virginia asked him to send her away and he did. About a week or two later, Virginia let Fanny stay longer, to please Sir Charles. Fanny told Virginia that she was 19 and was living in lodgings near Sloane Street. That's the time when Virginia's affection for Sir Charles diminished.

In March 1885, the anonymous letter naming Sir Charle Dilke arrived. Then in June, the anonymous letter saying that she had been seen in the Hotel Metropole with Captain Forster the day before. Then a third anonymous letter came in July. Because of the receipt of those letters, her husband was very suspicious of her, and she was very miserable, knowing that if she denied what the letters said he wouldn't believe her. She said that she had never been happy with Mr Crawford and had never been in love with him. She had married him because she was miserable at home, and her people wanted her to marry him. She thought that her husband should know the truth. She told Mrs Rogerson that she couldn't go on living with her husband much longer because they were so miserable together. So, she confessed to Mr Crawford about her affair with Sir Charles Dilke and left their home the next morning to go and stay with her sister, Mrs Ashton Dilke, as her husband wished.

Sir Charles came to visit her at her sister's house. He said that if she persisted in claiming that he had committed adultery with her, it would ruin her and all her family. He said that he'd do his worst and make damaging statements about her and other men. He pressed her not to attend court, said that she must retract her statement and sign a document confirming the retraction, explaining that she'd made the statement whilst hysterical and he could get doctors to confirm that. She told him, 'Do your worst.'

She admitted that she had committed adultery with Captain Forster since 1884 and she was attached to him. But he had told her in September 1884 that he was engaged to Miss Smith Barry. The engagement was called off between January and June 1885, because of a dispute about Miss Smith Barry's settlement. The captain and Miss Smith Barry finally married in September 1885. She told her husband that nothing had happened between her and Captain Forster and asked him not to name Captain Forster as a co-respondent, because Sir Charles was the man who had 'ruined' her and she didn't want to cause trouble for the recently married captain. She understood that Sarah Gray and Mrs Rogerson had both been Sir Charles's mistresses.

Mrs Ashton Dilke said that Sir Charles had visited her house on 20 July 1885. He had told her that all her sister Virginia needed was a quiet separation from her husband, without a trial. If there was any difficulty about income, he could always find money.

Captain Forster told how he used to meet with Virginia at 9 Hill Street, Knightsbridge, a house of ill repute.

Mrs Ann Gray, a housemaid to Sir Charles between March 1883 and March 1885, said that in the beginning of 1884 she had seen a woman in Sir Charles's bedroom at about 11.30am after Sir Charles had left. One afternoon she saw the lady go upstairs with Sir Charles. She wasn't able to recognise Mrs Crawford as she had only caught a glimpse of the lady.

Mr Mathew made his closing speech for Donald, describing Dilke's affair with Virginia as a gross, brutal adultery, without feeling or affection, more becoming of a beast than a man, stolen encounters between animals, with a woman who was the daughter of a friend … treating her, an English lady, worse than any man would treat a prostitute in a French brothel.

Mr Mathew asked the jury why Sir Charles had not been called to give evidence in the earlier divorce trial, despite being at court. Why had he sat silently through Mrs Crawford's confession, whilst claiming to be the victim of a conspiracy? His advocates claimed that he wished to avoid investigations into his past, but what could be worse than imputations about Fanny, and double adultery over two generations? What dark and filthy secrets remained? He was not prepared to deny her confession and his counsel felt that they could not safely call him. He had only come forward to give evidence at this trial because the newspapers had persecuted and tortured him. That was why he had asked the Queen's Proctor to intervene. It was life and death for his reputation and life politically; his seat in Parliament; his position as a public man; his credit and reputation in the world, all were at stake.

Mrs Crawford had given her account in detail, Mr Mathew continued, with facts that could be contradicted and disproved if they were not true. The jury may think some detail improbable: such as the absence of any courtship or ordinary attention paid by Sir Charles to her. The act of seduction took only a half hour. But they had heard how busy Sir Charles was. Why would she have fabricated such a shameful story if it were not true? His offer of money to her, made to her sister, if she kept quiet about their affair, was irreconcilable with his denial of intimacy.

The Hellier family should have been the Queen's Proctor's witnesses, Mr Mathew explained, but Sir Walter Phillimore chose not to call them and had 'given' them to him to use, whilst making no attack on their characters. They contradicted Sir Charles's evidence that he had never taken a woman to 65 Warren Street. And the cut-out references in Sir Charles's diary? A busy man would have simply run a pen through a failed appointment. And Fanny if she had nothing to hide? To protect her and her husband's honour she would have come to court with the voice of thunder to clear her name. At the beck and call of her sister Sarah and Sir Charles, she was put comfortably out of the way, disappearing at the critical moment when her evidence would have been fatal to them.

Sir Walter Phillimore addressed the jury on behalf of the Queen's Proctor. He told them that Sir Charles had not given evidence at the previous trial to avoid being questioned about his guilty relationship with Mrs Crawford's mother, Mrs Ellen Smith. He reassured them that if they decided for the Queen's Proctor and found that Sir Charles Dilke had not committed adultery with Mrs Crawford, there was ample evidence on which Mr Crawford could obtain a divorce anyway, without delay, by accusing someone else.

The judge summed up for the jury. He told them that the Queen's Proctor was only able to show cause that the decree nisi should not be made absolute if he presented material facts that were not brought before or known to the judge at the previous trial. Sir Charles Dilke had remained silent at the previous trial but had since come to court and denied the truth of Mrs Crawford's confession to her husband. It was for the jury to decide which of them was telling the truth.

The judge explained that the law required a man who accused his wife of adultery to say with whom it happened and make them a party. The need for the co-respondent to defend himself would ensure a proper investigation of the facts. On the one hand they should consider that Mrs Crawford didn't tell the truth when she denied to her husband having committed adultery with Captain Forster. Her motive in accusing Sir Charles was to protect the captain. And there were some inconsistencies between her confession and her evidence in court. On the other hand, if Sir Charles did say that he wished for a quiet separation between the Crawfords and offer money if there were any difficulties, that was worth a grave consideration by the jury.

The jury retired for fifteen minutes and when they returned found for Mr Crawford and the making of the decree nisi. The judge dismissed the Queen's Proctor's intervention. Sir Charles responded by issuing an address to his electors. He complained that he was not a party to the intervention and had to cross-examine Mrs Crawford through the Queen's Proctor's advocate, Sir Walter Phillimore. He stated that he was innocent of the charges and protested the injustice of the verdict.

A pamphlet published by Caxton House, Fleet Street, in 1886, appealed to *men of the world* to side with Sir Charles and told Mrs Crawford that having made her bed, she must lie in it.

'In the first place, as men of the world, we must look at the fact that the time given in the woman's evidence for the act of adultery is ridiculous. Had she been a practised harlot, without the slightest incentive save her fee, we doubt if the consummation could have possibly been achieved during the few minutes alleged.'

'We can pity the young girl flying from her unhappy paternal home to the ills she knew not of in the home of an unsympathetic husband, but we can go no further. Having made her choice between the two evils she should have abided by it and not besmirched the nest where she had found a shelter, even though it might have been cold and comfortless.

'At her house, where she artfully drew down the blinds while the coachman drove the carriage up and down, is it probable that a man with a reputation at stake would commit a compromising act in a room liable to be entered at any moment? Sir Charles is a cool, metaphysical politician ... there is no female in the world who would submit under the circumstances.

'We think that the world, in condemning Sir Charles, has been guilty of an error of judgement.'

COMMENT

There were three reports published about the trial. One contains *Evidence Taken on the Hearing With Notes* (336 pages). A second, *Containing Important Facts Disclosed Since the Trial* (158 pages), pleads the case for Sir Charles Dilke. The author, F.W.J.H. 11 Red Lion Court, Fleet Street, London EC, writes: 'Now that public excitement has cooled down, and people enabled to look dispassionately on this most interesting, extraordinary case, there is a feeling gradually spread abroad that a gross injustice has been done. If the public will only read the unabridged evidence contained in this volume, by the aid of the light which this preface has thrown upon it, I feel sure that a great number would hold with me that Sir Charles is an injured and innocent man.'

The third report (282 pages) claims that: 'There are few cases in modern times which have excited such widespread and intense interest as that of Crawford v Crawford.' The writer lists the reasons that it is 'a cause celebre and one of the most noteworthy on record: the social position of the parties concerned; the extraordinary nature of the disclosures; and the pertinacity of accusation and denial.' The author excuses himself with: 'In setting before the public a verbatim report of the proceedings it has not been our intention to pander to the prurient taste of the multitude, but merely to place the whole of the transactions before the discriminating tribunal of the community at large.'

The usual course for obtaining a divorce in 1820 was to go to the Ecclesiastical Court for a legal separation and then the Civil Court for a verdict of 'criminal conversation' (adultery). A divorce *a mensa et thoro* (from table and bed) was a legal separation (abolished in 1857). Although the couple were still married, they could live apart but not remarry. A party approaching the Ecclesiastical Court would need to have 'clean hands' and not have committed adultery themselves. In addition, the court would not assist a couple who had already separated by agreement. The only other option was to have the divorce declared by an Act of Parliament, as George IV attempted with Queen Caroline. This was exclusively available to the wealthy and influential members of society.

Under the Matrimonial Causes Act 1857, the husband could divorce the wife for adultery, but the wife could not divorce the husband unless she could also establish incest, bigamy, cruelty, or two years' desertion in addition. Between 1700 and the change in the law introduced by the Matrimonial Causes Act 1895, allowing a secular divorce, only 344 divorces were granted and only four were as a result of the wife's petition.

The Hellier family were originally the Queen's Proctor's witnesses, the Queen's Proctor having taken statements from them. When Sir Walter Phillimore chose not to call them as his witnesses, he was required by the rules of disclosure to make them available to Mr Mathew to call as witnesses instead.

Sir Charles lost his parliamentary seat. He had been touted as a future prime minister until he was cited in Virginia Crawford's divorce case.

Virginia had a successful writing career, with articles and books on art, literature, women's rights and social issues. She founded a Catholic Women's Suffrage Society to secure voting rights for women, which later became an international movement.

It is thought that the term 'French letters' was slang for condoms because they were packaged in what looked like envelopes and anything to do with sex had to have French connotations. The French used the term *capote Anglaise* (English overcoat) for condoms.

How did Mr Justice Butt decide that Mrs Crawford committed adultery with Sir Charles Dilke but that there was no evidence that *he* committed adultery with *her*? It sounds like a contradiction and 'jugglery', to use Sir Walter Phillimore's phrase. Or was it illogical but legally sound? At the divorce trial, the only evidence of Mrs Crawford's confession to her husband that she had committed adultery with Sir Charles came from Mr Crawford. Donald's evidence of her statement was hearsay, as he had testified about an out of court statement made by his wife. The judge had a discretion to admit the hearsay evidence, depending on the circumstances, and could decide what weight to attach to it. He decided to admit the statement.

The judge must have reasoned that Mrs Crawford would only confess to committing adultery if it was true, as the statement was adverse to her, although she may have named Sir Charles to protect Captain Forster. Having admitted adultery and deceit, the judge may have decided that she could not be relied upon to tell the truth about Sir Charles Dilke's involvement, and so the judge attached no weight to that part of her statement.

Although it wasn't a requirement that the petitioner name the co-respondent, the petitioner still had to prove the adultery with someone. But there was insufficient evidence at the divorce trial of Mrs Crawford having committed adultery with anybody else. Mr Crawford heard about a 'foolish' letter to her from Captain Forster; he had received an anonymous letter saying that she had been seen with him at the Hotel Metropole; and suspected that Captain Forster was her lover. She denied that he was and only admitted to keeping his company.

The judge may have wished to protect Sir Charles's reputation if possible; taken the view that Mr Crawford deserved a divorce; and that Mrs Crawford, immoral and brazen in her relations with men, was committing adultery with someone else, possibly Captain Forster. That would be the 'jugglery'.

The burden of proof in a civil case is on the balance of probabilities: 'is it more likely than not?'

Chapter 23

William Taylor v Madame Chester

An Action to Recover Money from a Brothel Keeper

1868

The judge remarked that he'd never come across a bankrupt brothel keeper before

William Taylor was a Birmingham wool merchant. He spent a Saturday night in August 1865 in Manchester with Henry Thorpe, a clothier whom he had just done business with. They went to the London Music Hall, where Henry gave William half of a £50 note, on account of goods that William had supplied to him. William said that he left the other half with Henry for safety, 'I never carry a whole note.' At the 'London' there was a supper room and a singing room with girls. At about 1.30am, William arrived by cab at Madame Chester's house, 3 Boundary Road, Chorlton-on-Medlock, Manchester. He knew about the house by its reputation. Henry had not joined him, saying that as a married man he had felt bound to go home instead. William claimed that he paid the cabman. Madame Chester said that the cabman rang the doorbell and asked for payment of his fare, but William refused to speak to him.

In the house were Madame Chester, Miss Royle, three other 'girls' and five men, all drinking wine and singing. William told how he took out his pocketbook to show the 'girls' some photographs. The note was amongst the photographs and William claimed that the Madam asked to see it, one of the 'girls' handed it to her and the Madam cooly folded it up, put it in her bosom and said that she'd take care of it. William later claimed that when he went to leave, he asked for a statement of what he owed and for the return of his note but didn't get either.

Madame Chester's recollection of events was different. When William arrived, Miss Royle asked, 'Aren't we going to have wine?' Mr Taylor said he had no money, but took out his pocketbook and said, 'Here's half of a

£50 note, and I'll give it to you if you'll give me what I want on it, while I remain in the house.' He handed the Madam the note. A bottle of spiced claret wine was brought in and the servant asked William for a sovereign to pay for it. William ignored the servant's request and complained that he'd never paid more than fifteen shillings for a bottle.

Miss Royle claimed that about one hour after William's arrival, Madame confided in her that he had asked Madame to lend him £10. She assumed it was to pay for the pleasures of the house as he only had the note. Miss Royle told her it would be all right to lend the money to him. Madame fetched ten gold sovereigns from upstairs and handed them to William.

William got what he wanted: drinking and singing followed by time in bed with Miss Royle. According to Madame Chester, as many as fifteen bottles of claret and champagne were ordered by William and shared with everyone else as his treat. He stayed in bed with Miss Royle until he requested breakfast at noon. Miss Royle asked William to pay her. He said that he needed to keep what money he had, because he was going to see some friends, but he would be back and pay her. She asked him to pay for the drinks. He refused and she didn't ask him again. He left without paying for anything.

William retrieved the other half of the note from Henry and had his bank write to the Bank of England that he had half of a £50 note, the other half having been lost or stolen. His bank requested the Bank of England to refund him the value of the whole note, as it no longer existed. Unfortunately, Madame also wrote to the bank of England with a similar tale, and the Bank declined to pay out to either of them.

In October, William went the police office in Cavendish Street, Manchester. He complained that Mary Chester had 'improperly obtained possession' of the half note, without going as far as charging her with stealing it. He said that he did owe her, but she wasn't entitled to more than £3. He'd give her £5 and be done with it. The Superintendent told Inspector Partington to go with William to Madame Chester's to sort it out. There, Madame Chester challenged him, 'I suppose you've come to pay me the £20 you owe me.' He replied, 'I don't owe you that much.' She said, 'Didn't I lend you ten golden sovereigns?' She said that he owed her £10 for the sovereigns and £10 for the wine 'and other things', and if he paid her, she'd return the note.

The Inspector told how William said that he wouldn't pay a farthing until he got the note back and refused to pay the £20. The officer then pressed William on whether Madame Chester had stolen the note from him and William agreed that he had given it to her. The Inspector advised William to offer Mary £15. He offered her £13 but she wanted more. The Inspector said that he couldn't interfere in their dispute as there was no criminal charge and he left.

The Trial

William sued Madame Chester for the return of his half note and there was a trial at Manchester Assizes before Mr Justice Mellor and a jury. At its conclusion, the judge complained that 'The trial of this action in a superior court – in a court of Assize – at Manchester, before one of Her Majesty's judges – is a gross and scandalous abuse of a court of justice' (some jurymen called out 'hear hear').

The issue for the jury was whether William had given the note to the Madam as security for a debt he was about to run up in the brothel and, if so, whether this was an immoral and illegal agreement. Mr Pope represented William and Mr Holker QC, with Mr Adison representing Madame Chester. Mr Holker QC examined Miss Royle:

Holker: 'And the plaintiff went to bed and slept with you?'
The witness did not reply, just hung her head.

Holker: 'Did he pay you?'

Royle: 'Not a penny.'

William told how only three bottles of wine were brought, which he expected to pay for. He drank about three glasses of champagne and went to bed long before the others, at 3am. He insisted that Madame Chester's claim of lending him ten gold sovereigns was absurd, and it never happened.

Madame Chester petitioned for bankruptcy on the day that she received the writ, which Mr Holker thought was very suspicious. He pointed out that the half note was missing in the bankruptcy petition schedule, as if she didn't possess it, and that the schedule didn't show William in debt to her for £20. The judge remarked that he'd never come across a bankrupt brothel keeper before.

Mr Holker and Mr Addison both made speeches, before and after the defence witnesses had been called, telling the jurors that they were men of the world, and they would likely know a man like William who would boast about having gone to a brothel to amuse himself and then left without paying; proud of it, not humiliated by his shameful and sinful act. He had played a mean and shabby trick on Madame Chester, giving her the note as security for his bill, knowing that it would be useless to her and so that he could get a supply of wine. The note was 'in pawn' and he hadn't redeemed it because he hadn't paid what he owed. He went away without paying the 'girl' for her time and her infamy. An honest man would have paid the 'girl'. He didn't even pay one shilling.

Mr Pope, for William, said that he left without paying because Madame Chester would not return the note to him. He put forward a simple and effective argument: if the £10 was lent to William by Mary for him to spend it in the brothel, then the debt he incurred was for an immoral purpose: drunkenness and debauchery. The law did not recognise a claim for anything which was illegal or an offence against morality and she could not ask the court to enforce it or the debt for the wine and 'other services'.

The judge summed up for the jury. He said that he couldn't distinguish between the parties as William's reputation was little better than Madame Chester's and each was as likely not to tell the truth as the other. She had a claim on the note as he didn't deny owing her money. She didn't steal the note as if she had he'd have gone straight to the police and preferred a charge against her. She was a 'goose' for not accepting the £13 offered by him. He was a 'goose' for not paying her the £20 she asked for.

The pleadings, the judge explained, were originally to recover the half of a £50 note given to Madame Chester for safe custody and which she hadn't returned when requested. But the judge had allowed William to amend his pleadings to state that the goods were supplied in a brothel for immoral purposes, for prostitution and debauchery, so that the defendant had no right to recover a debt for them. By the amendment, the judge added, William had admitted that he was *pari delicto* – a party to it. By his own plea, they were both sinners against the law.

The judge had two questions for the jury. Firstly, were they satisfied that the £50 half note was handed over to the defendant as security for the loan of money and goods supplied? If so, they should find for the defendant. Secondly, was the money advanced to be spent on debauchery in a brothel with prostitutes? If so, they should find for the plaintiff.

The jury returned answers of 'yes' to both questions. The judge found for the defendant: the outcome being that she could keep the £50 half note and he did not owe her any money as both debts were illegal, immoral, and unenforceable. But the judge requested Mary to return the note to William to restore the parties to the status quo ante, the situation before he went to the brothel.

COMMENT

The Special Report (thirty-two pages) describes the 'celebrated "Madame Chester" a peculiar lady, well known in Manchester.' It claims that the trial 'drew together a court crowded with gentlemen anxious to hear the revelations which it was expected to bring forth, in relation to gay life in this city during matutinal (*in the early hours of the morning*) orgies.' Cashing in on her fame, Madame Chester wrote an autobiography: *Memoirs of Madam Chester by Herself – A High-Class Courtesan in eighteenth century Manchester.*

A half of a £50 Bank of England note did have value because the Bank of England had a long-standing policy of reimbursing the full-face value of a mutilated banknote, providing that the serial number (there was one on each side of the note) was identifiable and the bank could check that a note with the same serial number had not been redeemed already. Large-denomination notes were often cut in half and sent separately by post to prevent fraud. The second half would be posted once the first half was received. The two halves could be exchanged for the value of the note, or a new note.

The principle of *in pari delicto, potior est condito possidentis*, means that when both parties are at fault, the courts will neither assist a person to enforce a debt nor recover money handed over in pursuance of an immoral or illegal agreement. Such an agreement is said to be against public policy. A person in possession of contested property may keep it.

Pleadings are formal documents containing written statements that set out the plaintiff's claim and the defence to that claim. They define the issues in dispute between the parties so that they know the arguments they will face at trial.

The judge in William's case concluded by saying that if Madame Chester didn't restore the note to William, then William could return and move the court to enter a verdict for him. But that just sounded like an empty threat with no legal force.

This case is reported (1869) LR 4 QB 309.

The £50 banknote was first issued by the Bank of England in 1725 and in the Bank's country branches from 1826. It was printed in black on white on one side only, with the 'Fifty' sum in white on black. Endorsements were written on the back.

Relative Values: £50 in 1868 would be worth £7,225 in 2026. It is unlikely that William would be foolish enough to give half of such a valuable note to Madame Chester, a brothel keeper whom he had not met before, as security whilst he ran up a debt. The ten golden sovereigns that Madame Chester claimed she lent to William would be worth £1,445 in 2026. In 1868 one golden sovereign was a day's wage for a skilled worker. The fifteen shillings that William said was the most that he'd pay for a bottle of wine or champagne in a brothel would be equivalent to £108 in 2026. The £10 debt claimed by Mary for the drinks, breakfast, and time in bed with Miss Royle would be the equivalent of £1,445 in 2026.

Chapter 24

Divorce and Custody

Catherine Walker v Wildes P. Walker, New York

1854

'She talks not of love, but of law – breathes not sweet vows, but fierce anathemas – challenges us not at the altar of Hymen, at which she pledged her troth, but at the throne of Justice, from which she throws her javelin'

Catherine and Wildes Walker were married on 15 July 1840 in Bath, Maine. She was only 19. They lived together in Boston with their three children. Wildes moved the family's home from Boston to New Brunswick in May 1849 when he became the director of a bank. Wildes engaged in a banking transaction that left him owing merchants $40,000, which he couldn't pay. He was arrested on 29 July 1850 and sent to debtors' prison until his discharge as a bankrupt on 14 December 1853.

Wildes was first detained in New Brunswick in 1850 by Sheriff's officers Deputy Samuel Cunningham and Assistant Deputy Amasa Hager. Wildes was to remain in their custody and be delivered to the prison unless he could post bail in the sum of $40,000, to match what he owed. Wildes directed the officers to a friend's address near 4th Avenue, to try and raise the bail, but he was unsuccessful. It was midnight and too late to take him to the prison at 22 Eldridge Street, New York. They stayed overnight in a brothel, the house of Fanny White at 119 Mercer Street. You can infer that Wildes had been there before as he was known to frequent another brothel on Mercer Street. That night, Wildes drank liquor and then joined a woman in a bedroom, where Deputy Cunningham locked him in until morning. That was the first act of adultery that Catherine could have relied upon in her later action for divorce and custody of their children.

Whilst serving his sentence in the prison, Wildes paid the jailor Robert Rue, or his colleague Bill Birch, $5 each time, later reduced to $3, to take him out. Rue worked at the prison between January 1850 and February 1853. They would leave after breakfast and not return until the evening. Rue told how one afternoon in 1850, Wildes took him to a confectionary store in Division Street on the corner of Mercer Street. Upstairs was a brothel. Whilst they were on the ground floor, a woman made a passing comment to Wildes, 'We had a very pleasant time last night.' Then a door burst open, and a young woman ran over and threw her arms around Wildes. Wildes told Rue that he and some friends had been there for a game supper the night before and the friends had then retired upstairs with some women. A police officer reported that he had seen young women aged between 16 and 25 and much older men come and go at that building. A police captain said that he found seven or eight females of that age and loose character there when he visited. The assumption that Wildes had been with prostitutes there was the second act of adultery that Catherine could have relied upon.

Catherine came to the prison in December 1850 and cohabited there with Wildes for a week or ten days. Rue said that this was before their visit to the confectionary store. John Hull told how he heard a conversation between Catherine and Wildes about his bad conduct in visiting the brothels. She said that she was dissatisfied with Wildes for going to such places. Wildes denied the stories, but Catherine said that she believed them. Hull said that he met her after her stay in prison with Wildes. She told him that it was the happiest week of her life and whether the stories were true or not, they were all forgiven. Catherine's living with Wildes as husband and wife in the prison, knowing about his acts of adultery, would amount in law to her condoning his behaviour and prevent her from using them as grounds for divorce. He would need to commit a subsequent act of adultery.

Wildes' cell, which he shared with one other, was a room with an ordinary house-size barred window at the rear of the prison overlooking Walker Street. Rue told how Mrs Williams, 'a woman of improper chastity', visited Wildes there twice on her own. She stayed for a half hour or so and the door to his cell was fastened behind her. She was the keeper of a brothel and Colonel Bobo, a close friend of Wilde's who introduced him to women, was boarding with her. Anna Malcolm was introduced to Mrs Williams, who brought her to the prison to meet Wildes. On 8 November 1852, Wildes wrote a letter to Bobo saying that he was very anxious to see Anna again. In a letter to Bobo in December 1852 he gave Anna: *9 points in 10.*

A fellow prisoner from January to November 1853, Henry Sturla, told how Mary Pell and Louisa Warner lived in Walker Street, facing the back of the prison. Louisa had taught Mary sign language. Wildes also knew sign language, and he used to chat with them daily, signing from his prison window and they would sign back. Anna Malcolm, Mary, and two 'cap makers' would visit Wildes in his cell, often on their own.

When Anna visited, the cell door would be locked with a hook and eye from the inside. His cellmate Turner would complain about Wildes having his 'bitches' in there and him not being allowed in. Anna visited thirty or forty times and stayed for one hour or more each time. Bill Birch, a turnkey, said that he saw Wildes and Anna drinking brandy together and sitting on Wildes's bunk, with his arm around Anna's neck.

Henry Smith was the keeper of the prison from 1853. He allowed women to visit Wildes: Anna three or four times and Miss Liman twice. Henry's wife Susan was a turnkey and would let them in. Wildes wrote to Bobo on 26 April 1853 that Anna could not bear him paying more attention to Miss Liman than to her, making her feel like a fool.

Birch told how Wildes paid him for his services, and he took Wildes out of the prison fifteen or twenty times. Wildes would say, 'Bill, let us go 'round amongst some of the girls tonight.' Wildes told him that if he had a chance, he'd make a baby for Mary. Wildes asked him to get leave so that they could go to the confectionery store and meet Louisa and Mary. Louisa visited Wildes in prison. Wildes told Birch that Louisa would let him know when her husband went out, so that she could meet him. Birch had taken Wildes out to meet Mary and Louisa in Division Street. James Britt, another turnkey, let a female in to the prison twice to visit Wildes. He saw a woman sitting on Wilde's bunk. A fellow prisoner, William McLachlan, noticed women going to visit Wildes six or seven times.

On 29 September 1853, Catherine moved with her millionaire father, mother and three daughters, the eldest aged 13, to lodgings in Brooklyn and said that she intended to remain there for some time. She then began an action for divorce, and custody of their children in the New York Court of Common Pleas.

The Divorce and Custody Trial

The trial started on 19 January 1854, before Judge Ingraham and a jury of twelve men. A 'de bene esse' deposition was given by Rue as his evidence. His fellow prisoners and turnkeys spoke about the many women who had visited him.

The defence called the women who had visited Wildes in prison as witnesses. They all swore that they were never alone with Wildes and that nothing improper happened between him and them. They said that they visited him because they felt sorry for him, locked up and lonely. The defence also tried to show that witnesses such as Charles Jackson were being paid to give false evidence:

Busteed: 'Now Charles, who told you to come here?'

Jackson: 'That gentleman (pointing at the plaintiff's solicitor's clerk).'

Busteed: 'And he told you what he wanted you for?'

Jackson: 'Yes, sir.'

Busteed: 'And he told you that he wanted you to swear that Mrs Malcolm was a bad woman, and went with men?'

Jackson: 'Yes, sir.'

Busteed: 'Did he pay you anything?'

Jackson: 'A dollar, sir.'

Busteed: 'Did he promise you more?'

Jackson: 'Oh yes sir, he said he'd pay me well.'

Mr Busteed, for Wildes, tried to paint a forgiving picture of his misdeeds, 'In an evil hour, the tornado of passion had borne us along upon its current into the vortex of sin – the storm of craving lust had hushed the calm and equal voice of duty in our soul. Our wife, our guardian angel, was far from us, when the voice of a syren war bled her fatal notes in our ears – the tempter came, and we yielded. I allowed it all true: and amid the moral ruin and devastation – amid the moaning winds that spoke our fall came a song sweeter than the voice of the false one. A woman, smiling through her pearly tears – a wife wronged, yet uncomplaining – an angel of light draped in the vesture of frail humanity, tuned her lyre to a mournful strain and sung:

Oh, what was love made for, if tis not the same,
Thro joy and thro sorrow – thro glory and shame,

I know not, I ask not, if guilt is in thy heart,
I know that I love thee, whatever thou art.

If the defence could satisfy the jury that Catherine was as guilty of adultery as Wildes, then her action against him would be dismissed: he who seeks equity must do equity.

Mr Busteed called witnesses to testify about Catherine's relationship with Dr Heartwell, whom she had known since August 1845. From 1847 until 1849, to escape the heat, she would take her children and servants several times each season to stay in the Mansion House, Harpswell, Maine, a summer ocean retreat. She had visited there since 1845 with Wildes. Dr Heartwell would visit at the same time and stay in a room opposite hers. They talked, walked, and rode together and sat next to each other at dinner, where he paid her compliments and was very attentive towards her. On one occasion, she took a 26-mile journey in a Rockaway carriage with him. Some people thought their conduct improper and Stockbridge Eaton, the hotel owner, told how he eventually refused to let her stay. His wife, Ruth, and daughter Ann Marie, claimed to have seen them walking with his arm around her waist and holding hands.

Catherine wrote an unhappy letter to her friend Mrs Waldron: 'Shall I tell you of the bright star, the star that still sheds its ray of light upon my path? Of the soothing and hold influence it sheds down into my inmost heart? Were it not for that light, the present would be as the future, a dark path upon the sullen sea.'

'Is it true that Dr Heartwell and Mrs Walker were more intimate than propriety allows?' Mr Busteed asked the jury. 'He was here during the trial. Where is he now? Why don't they call him? They dare not.' 'Her letter,' Mr Busteed remarked, 'what was she so anxious to talk about with her friend Mrs Waldron? What perturbed her conscience?'

Then the defence called evidence about goings-on between Catherine and Senator Evans, the Attorney General of Maine. Elias Pierce, Wilde's cousin, told how on the steamboat the *Charter Oak* in 1848 or 1849, travelling from Bath to Boston, he saw Catherine and Senator Evans in conversation on the deck. It was late, and he saw them enter her stateroom together and not come out. He next saw them at the Boston wharf in the early morning where the Senator helped Catherine into a carriage, got in after her and set off together.

Senator Evans told a vastly different story. He said that he was on board the steamboat *Kennebec*, travelling from Boston to Bath in 1847 or 1848.

He had met Catherine with Wildes in Boston Harbour and as she was travelling on her own, Wildes had asked him to look after her. Catherine became ill during the journey and when she was sick, he gave her his arm and took her to her stateroom, where he bade her good night.

'Why did Senator Evans not tell us about the ride home with Mrs Walker at an early hour in the morning?' Mr Busteed asked the jury.

The defence then tried to turn the jury against Catherine. 'The timid, shrinking, girlish bride, has transformed herself into the unyielding, imperious and exacting plaintiff of this action,' Mr Busteed declared. 'She talks not of love, but of law – breathes not sweet vows, but fierce anathemas – challenges us not at the altar of Hymen, at which she pledged her troth, but at the throne of Justice, from which she throws her javelin. So perishes all the hopes and loves of that hour. So is destroyed the bliss which is promised.'

Mr Busteed presented Wildes as the person the jury should feel sorry for. 'I bring you a broken-hearted man,' he declared. 'A stricken disconsolate husband – a father worse than childless. He may live on in this busy world of ours, but to him it must be a succession of cheerless days and sleepless nights.' He then quoted a poem:

> For him no more the blazing hearth shall burn,
> Or busy housewife ply her evening care,
> No children run to lisp their sire's return,
> Or climb his knee the envied kiss to share.

Mr Busteed then excused himself for attacking Catherine: 'To be the accuser of a woman is a most unwelcome office; call it gallantry if you will … our domestic gods.'

The judge summed up to the jurors, who then retired. After forty-five minutes, the jury returned and asked for copies of the notes of evidence. The advocates were unhappy about the judge's notes going to the jury, as he may have noted his comments on the evidence. Neither advocate would agree to the other's notes being used by the jury. By 7.30pm, the jury could not agree. The judge ordered that 'they be shut up for the night' and the court adjourned until Sunday morning. At 9am, the judge was told that one juror dissented on one point: whether Catherine had committed adultery with Senator Evans. The jury asked to have the Senator's evidence read to them. The jury retired again. Thirty minutes later, they returned and reported that the dissenter could not be persuaded to change his mind. The judge discharged the jury, and Catherine lost her action.

The jurors who voted for Catherine posted a notice: 'The undersigned 11 jurors would respectfully say that after a careful deliberation of the facts, there is nothing to show that she is anything but a high-minded, pure and virtuous woman; and they deeply sympathise with her in that the deep-set opposition of 1 of the jurors should deprive her of her just and lawful rights.'

The dissenting juror posted a notice *To the Public* in response: 'My attention has been called to the most extraordinary card signed by 11 of the jurors … a malicious and uncalled for attack upon the way in which I felt myself called upon to discharge a sworn duty … *The Tribune* assumes that the disagreement of the jury was the result of the stupidity or gross corruption of one man (myself) … shall a man exercising the sworn duty of a juror be thus lampooned, first by his co-associates and then by a public journal … a man whose only crime is that he dared to think and act for himself?'

COMMENT

A law reporter of the *New York Daily Press* wrote the report of the trial (143 pages).

Catherine Walker lost her action for divorce and custody of their children because a juror believed that she had also committed adultery. The eleven jurors who would have found for her posted a notice saying that the one dissenting juror was very wrong. That juror then defended himself with a counter-notice. In the United States, once a trial concludes and the jury is discharged, jurors are free to discuss their deliberations with anyone. This is vastly different from the situation in England and Wales, where after the trial, jurors must not talk to anyone about what happened in the deliberations room. There was a common law prohibition, to promote the finality of decisions by juries and to protect jurors being exposed to pressure to explain their reasoning. A statutory rule was introduced by the 1974 Juries Act that made it an offence for a person intentionally to disclose information about statements made, opinions expressed, arguments advanced, or votes cast by members of a jury in the course of their deliberations.

Relative values: the \$3 and \$5 Wildes paid to the turnkeys to take him out would be worth \$114.81 and \$191.35 in 2026. The \$1 paid to the witness Jackson would be worth \$38.27. Wildes's \$40,000 debt and bail sum would be worth \$1,530,800.

A Rockaway carriage that Catherine was said to have ridden in with Senator Evans, was a four-wheel horse-drawn carriage with a partition between the driver and the passengers and a fixed top and side curtains to shield passengers from wind and rain. It is said to be so named as it was used to carry families to the Rockaway Peninsula in Queens, New York City, known for its beaches.

The Altar of Hymen refers to the Greek god of marriage ceremonies, associated with the marriage procession, feasts, song and the wedding night.

A 'de bene esse' deposition, given by Rue, is a sworn statement taken to preserve a witness's evidence for trial when it is anticipated that the witness won't be available to testify in person.

Chapter 25

Barber v Fenton

Breach of Promise, Manchester

1862

He loves me, he loves me not

Robert Fenton first met Edith Barber at a 'Rifles' ball in Manchester in the autumn of 1861. She was aged 16 and he was about ten years older. They danced together several times. In October 1861 Robert escorted her home from a concert in Manchester. Edith's brother Charles made insinuations about her having been alone with Robert on the way home. On 13 November 1861, at another concert in Manchester, Robert proposed marriage, but Edith did not accept. The next day he unexpectedly escorted her to Bolton, where she was going to visit friends. He proposed marriage again and she accepted. He put a ring on her finger, which she considered shoddy and gave it back. He later gave her a better ring.

Robert's father was the MP for Rochdale in 1837–41 and Head of Fenton's bank. Edith lived with her family in the suburbs of Manchester.

Robert obtained Edith's father's consent to the marriage, which was planned for spring 1862. He was away for some time in different places but wrote her seventy to eighty loving letters. On 16 November 1861 he wrote: 'I am yours and you are mine … I asked (in prayer) that our love might not be a swift flame burnt out in a short time, but one that would burn stronger as we grow older and know each other better … we have bound ourselves together by a stronger tie than any earthly ceremony … I registered a solemn oath in heaven when I took your hand in the cab, that I would love and protect you all the days of my life.'

In another letter he called her *dearest Pussy* and *my own dearest little pet*. He said that he would put her likeness under his pillow so that he would dream of her.

In May 1862, Robert visited Edith and told her that he couldn't marry her and didn't love her. He said that he would write a letter of explanation. She never saw him again.

Robert wrote to Edith on 29 May 1862:

> The novelty of being engaged, the pleasant and may I say selfish thought of having someone to love me, and take an interest in all that I did, and the many other prerogatives of betrothal, kept up the delusion for some time until at last I awoke from my dream to wonder whether one could really and truly be in love. Alas, I found that I had both deceived myself and others. That I had gained another's affection without being able to reciprocate, and the only way I could make amends for my former thoughtless impetuosity was to try and make myself love you … until I found that love could not be forced … you will soon learn to forget me … you once told me that if I could not love you with my whole heart you would release me from my engagement. I now claim that promise.

Edith did not take kindly to Robert's claim that she had released him from the engagement and brought an action against him for breach of promise.

The Trial

The trial took place at the Liverpool Assizes before a judge and jury. Edith's barrister told the court that she had lost her peace of mind; was held up to scorn for the deserted love; had lost the union of a man of education, station, intellect, power; and who had it in his power to make her supremely happy. She had no protector now and what he did was dishonourable.

The defence complained about her disdainful manner and hasty temper. They referred to disagreements between them and that she had written that she was afraid that his love had worn out. It was impossible that the marriage could bring happiness to them. In law, the defence argued, Edith was entitled to something, but the jury must look at the parties and decide whether the marriage would have brought them happiness. A change had come over Robert's feelings beyond his control which absolved him from the charge of dishonourable conduct and hypocrisy.

The jury retired for a quarter of an hour. They found for Edith and awarded her £3,000 damages as compensation.

COMMENT

The report of the trial (sixteen pages), priced one penny, advertised 'Letters Read in Court' to help with sales.

Robert's grandfather established the Fenton Bank in Rochdale and built the family home, Crimble Hall, in 1810. The Fentons had owned the Crimble estate since the twelfth century. Robert's father had a half share in the bank and was MP for Rochdale in 1832–35 and 1837–41. He died in 1863, very wealthy and leaving fourteen children. The bank failed in 1878 and the Crimble Estate was sold. Crimble Hall later became a hotel, with a restaurant and night club. By 2024 it was abandoned and falling down. A couple who explored it discovered cocaine worth £74,500.

Edith was the youngest child of a Manchester cotton broker.

Relative values: £3,000 in 1862 would be worth £315,000 in 2026.

The Rifles were the Rifle Brigade and The King's Royal Rifle Corps in the British Army.

Chapter 26

Compensation for Criminal Conversation with Plaintiff's Wife

The Trial of Viscount Glerawley v Captain Burn

1820

'When poverty came to the door, love leapt out the window'

In May 1803, the Honourable William Richard Annesley, the Lord Viscount Glerawley, aged 34, married Lady Isabella St Lawrence, aged 20. They had one child, Mary Annesley, born in 1804. Isabella was said to be extravagant. In 1815, the Lord moved the family to Amiens, France, to live more frugally. Captain Burn, a young lieutenant in the 10th Hussars and eldest son of the late General Burn, was already living in Amiens where there were many Irish families. He was introduced to Isabella and became a constant visitor to her home. She once wrote in a letter to Burn: 'When poverty came to the door, love leapt out the window.'

The Lord participated in Irish politics and contested an election in Ireland. He was absent for prolonged periods in London and at his father's house in Ireland. The captain had been on close terms with Isabella since 1816, and during the Lord's absences would spend most days with her at her home.

Isabell Duigeman had been a servant in the Lord's family since the age of 9. She told how when the Lord was away, Isabella and the captain would walk together, talking and laughing, and go riding. The captain was at their house for tea, dinner, late at night and first thing in the morning.

By 1817, the family had moved to Versailles and the captain visited frequently. To Miss Duigeman's discomfort, she had seen them sitting for hours on a bed in Isabella's daughter's bedroom, which was next to the sitting room. The bedding gave the appearance of two people having laid down on it. During the Lord's absences, the captain would stay at Isabella's home. Miss Duigeman would see him in the morning in Isabella's bedroom, wearing his dressing gown without stockings. Often, at night time, she would hear the sound of someone walking softly on the stairs and Isabella's door opening. One night, when she was in Isabella's bedroom and Isabella was in bed, the captain came in and told Isabella to come and listen to the governess snoring. He pulled off Isabella's night cap and she laughed. The captain's possessions in the house were removed hastily just before the Lord's return.

Theodore Lorenza joined the family in 1817 as a butler. When the Lord was away, he frequently saw the captain at the house. After the Lord returned, the captain would come to the house at night time and meet Isabella in the garden, the stable or the kitchen, whilst the Lord was in bed. The groom and the governess left their employ because of what was going on. Theodore told the Lord what was happening between Isabella and the captain. The captain wrote to the Lord from Paris: 'The ungenerous censure thrown on Lady Glerawley by the most gross accusations of a villainous servant, is not forgiven; and I trust my Lord, your good sense will cause you despising the falsehoods of a servant.' The Lord refused to believe Theodore and sacked him without a reference. The family moved to Havre-le-Grace with Zoe, an Italian greyhound that the captain had given Isabella.

The captain wrote letters to Isabella, begging her to leave the Lord:

> 14 July 1819 … My dearest love … our scared oaths to each other … my beloved angel … you must fly with me to some retired retreat where we shall pass our days in real joy and dearest bliss … my only love … my love, let me know the exact names of the towns you slept in, and the hotels, that I may sleep in the same beds after you and Zoe … prepare to fly with me from Havre.
>
> 15 July, If you don't separate, after all I have done, I will kill you Isabella, and myself.
>
> Tues night, I am determined to possess you … I shall be with you in a few hours … I am yours and only yours until death.

Mrs Belin, who kept the school at Havre, told how Isabella 'eloped', leaving her to look after their daughter Mary. Mrs Belin went to Paris with the Lord to find Isabella. They spotted Zoe in the street and found the house in Rue Richelieu where Isabella was living with the captain. Isabella refused to return to Havre.

The Trial

The Lord Viscount Glerawley sued in the Court of King's Bench to recover damages from Captain Burn. The Lord claimed that Captain Burn had criminal conversation (sexual intercourse) with Lady Isabella, his wife. The case was tried on 30 June 1820, by the Lord Chief Justice with a jury. Mr Scarlett represented the Lord, with Mr Puller and Mr Rogers and he claimed £20,000. Mr Brougham and Mr Manning represented the captain.

Mr Brougham conceded that adultery and 'elopement' was proved and that the jury would award damages to the Lord. He asked the jury to take account of the Lord leaving his wife on the Continent for periods of six months and eighteenth months, whilst he attended to his parliamentary duties or went to the sea for the benefit of his health, leaving her exposed to all the seductions of Continental manners. He said that when Lady Glerawley was balancing on the brink of crime, the Lord should have been near her and shown her a little kindness. The Lord should feel guilty about making her an easy prize.

The Lord was fourteen years older than Lady Glerawley and she, in turn, was ten years older than her lover. Mr Brougham reasoned that it was likely, because of the age difference between her and the captain, that she, not he, had made the first advances, or they at least had met halfway. Her conduct with the captain was so notorious that servants left their employ, yet the Lord left her exposed in a foreign country to all the temptations surrounding her and abandoned his duty as a husband. He asked the jury to disregard the foolish letters from the captain because he'd already lost her affection by then. Finally, he told the jury to consider whether the captain could afford to pay the damages: a Lieutenant in the Dragoons, formerly of the Hussars, on half-pay. The jury retired and, on their return, ordered damages of £1,500 be paid to the Lord.

COMMENT

The report of the trial (sixteen pages), price fourpence (equivalent of about £1 in 2026), promised 'Crim. Con. With the Whole of the Extraordinary Letters that Passed between the Defendant and Lady Glerawley, Disclosing Many Curious Love Scenes, and was on sale at all booksellers and news venders.'

Relative values: £1,500 in 1820 would be the equivalent of £126,000 in 2026.

Acknowledgements

Oscar Wilde – Libel and gross indecency trials 1895: Christopher Millard.

The Shrigley Abduction – The Trial of Edward Gibbon Wakefield, William Wakefield and Frances Wakefield 1827: John Murray Publ.

Queen Caroline of Brunswick – A trial before the House of Lords to deprive her of her title of Queen Consort and dissolve her marriage to George IV 1820: Edward Barron; J. Nightingale; J. Robins & Co.; H. Rowe Publ.; J. Cockroft Publ.

Breach of promise trial between Maria Foote, the celebrated actress, and Joseph Hayne 1824: John Fairburn Publ.

The trial of Waterhouse v Colonel Berkeley, for criminal conversation 1821: Turner & Hadley Publ.; the Observer.

Trial of Adelaide Bartlett 1886 – The Pimlico Poisoning: Edward Beal; Stevens & Haynes Publ.

Custody – In the matter of the most noble Duke and Duchess of Marlborough 1853: Richard Bethell; Henningham & Hollis Publ.

The death of W.R.H. Carew and trial of his Wife for Murder in HBM Court for Japan 1897: Japan Gazette.

Scrope-Ferrers v Apthorp – A breach of promise of marriage case 1906: Publ. D.R. Apthorp

The Beattie case – Murdered his wife 1911: The Phoenix Publ. Company.

The trial of Henry Stanton v Louisa Stanton – For Perjury 1815: L. Stanton; Seale & Bates Publ.

The killing of Stanford White by Harry Kendall Thaw 1906: Benj. H. Atwell; Laird & Lee Publ.; William Travers Jerome and Francis P Garvan; Boehn & Rathbone Publ.

Acknowledgements

Re Fynn – Custody of Infants 1848: W. Clowdes & Sons Publ.; The Law Times.

The trial of William Sawyer for the wilful murder of Harriet Gaskell at Campo Grande, Lisbon 1814: Geo Kent Publ.; the weekly Dispatch.

Gill v Aubrey – Trial for criminal conversation at Worcester Assizes 1820: G. Morgan Publ.

The Great Trunk Mystery of New York City 1871 – The murder of the beautiful Miss Alice A Bowlsby: Barclay & Co. Publ.

The trial of Mortimer J. Smith for libel 1847: Castigator Press.

Nannie A. Dickey v John B. Tytus 1878 – Sued for bastardy and breach of promise: Independent Publ. Co.

The trial of James Greenacre and Sarah Gale for the wilful murder of Hannah Brown 1837: Dean & Munday Publ.; J. Duncombe & Son Publ.

The Queen v Thomas Jacob, Jane Jacob and John Jacob for conspiring to procure a marriage by unlawful means: P.W. Brady Publ.

The trial of Roman Weinzoeptlein, a Roman Catholic priest, for rape 1844: The Indiana District Court.

Crawford v Crawford – Divorce, co-respondent Sir Charles Dilke 1886: Caxton House Publ.; F.W.J. Henning

William Taylor v Madame Chester – An action to recover money from a brothel keeper 1868: Unknown

Divorce and Custody – Catherine Walker v Wildes P. Walker, New York 1854: C.C. Childs Publ.; New York Daily Press.

Barber v Fenton – Breach of promise, Manchester 1862: John Heywood Publ.

Compensation for criminal conversation with plaintiff's wife – The trial of Viscount Glerawley v Captain Burn 1820: G. Morgan Publ.

Relative values calculations: The inflation calculator www.bankofengland.co.uk

Index

Dear Reader,

We hope you have enjoyed this book, but why not share your views on social media? You can also follow our pages to see more about our other products: facebook.com/penandswordbooks or follow us on X @penswordbooks

You can also view our products at www.pen-and-sword.co.uk (UK and ROW) or www.penandswordbooks.com (North America).

To keep up to date with our latest releases and online catalogues, please sign up to our newsletter at: www.pen-and-sword.co.uk/newsletter

If you would like a printed catalogue with our latest books, then please email: enquiries@pen-and-sword.co.uk or telephone: 01226 734555 (UK and ROW) or email: uspen-and-sword@casematepublishers.com or telephone: (610) 853-9131 (North America).

We respect your privacy and we will only use personal information to send you information about our products.

Thank you!